Big Miracle

Big Miracle

Tom Rose

St. Martin's Griffin
New York

www.stmartins.com

Design by Kathryn Parise

ISBN 978-0-312-62519-1

*To Jack Amiel and Michael Begler, whose
two-decade commitment to developing this story into a
major motion picture proves that those who don't
give up usually get what they want.*

Contents

Big Miracle

1

The Hunt

The bitter weather came early along Alaska's North Slope in September 1988. The Siberian air that rolled in brought high winds and unseasonable cold. In one week, the average temperature went from ten degrees above to twenty degrees below zero. An unusually strong rim of ice formed along the shore, sealing off America's northernmost coastline from the fierce Arctic Ocean.

Most of the thousands of whales that feed in these waters began to migrate south a few weeks early. Three young California gray whales did not. Two adolescents and one yearling did not sense the ice closing in overhead. Had they known what was in store, they obviously would have joined the others. Instead, they continued to feed on the tasty crustaceans that lined the endless ocean bottom.

These whales were in no hurry to leave. Why should they be? Their food supply was as limitless as their appetites were voracious; they faced no dangers of which they were aware. Besides, once they left these rich feeding grounds for their winter, warmer home off Baja, California, they wouldn't eat again until they returned to Alaska the following spring—five months later. By then they would have completed a 9,000-mile round-trip, the longest migration of any mammal in the world. That's a long time for an eating machine to fast.

Migration meant confrontation. Killer whales, great white sharks, and many other predators feed on young grays because it is their youth that makes them such easy pickings. These uninitiated gray whales would soon be provided a first-rate education in the real world of Arctic survival.

The whales heedlessly rolled on their sides to suck the shrimplike amphipods from the seabed just a few hundred feet off Point Barrow, a narrow sandspit five miles long. It was the very tip of North America. Four miles to the southwest stood Barrow, the largest, oldest, and farthest northern Eskimo settlement on the globe. At any other time at any other spot on the Arctic coast of Alaska, the whales would have drowned unnoticed under the ice.

In just a few short weeks, a strong case can be made that these three creatures would become the luckiest animals in all history; the recipients of unprecedented assistance from an alien species. The first of their kind before or since to be spared—at least as far as we know—the fate that had doomed all the others. They would not drown like other stranded whales; they would not be reduced to Japanese beauty products or Russian ice cream by high-tech factory ships; nor, at least for now, would they end up as local Inuit dinners, as the Inuits took advantage of unfilled whaling quotas.

After each spring thaw, carcasses of young whales almost littered Alaska's Arctic coast. The locals who found them months after their deaths every year knew the most probable cause of death was drowning because nearly all the carcasses were of young or even infant grays. Lest a tear be shed in vain, one can rest assured that these dead did not die in vain. Nothing in nature ever does. They were an important element all the way up and down the Arctic food chain.

These three whales occasionally stopped eating to scratch their ungainly snouts on the gravelly bottom for relief from the whale lice and barnacles infesting their skin. Ironically, it was these itchy pests that would deliver them from the first of many death traps they would encounter over the next several months.

Since time immemorial, local Inuits (they used to call themselves

Eskimos—and did not take offense when others did, too) built an entire subsistence civilization around the whale upon whom they depended for survival. Over the centuries, they acquired a taste for the much tastier bowhead whale. The bowhead's clean, glossy sleek skin made far better eating than the unsightly and unappetizing California gray.

While the barnacles annoyed these three grays, the tiny pests were nothing compared to one local Eskimo hunter. Despite a five-foot-three-inch frame, his prowess as a whaling captain earned him the nickname Malik, which, in his Inupiat language, means "Little Big Man." He spent most of his sixty-odd years roaming the always oscillating ice shelf off Point Barrow in search of the bowhead. Most older Eskimos, like many other peoples only recently introduced to the Western calendar, can't tell you exactly how old they are.

Until recently, whales were the only food source plentiful enough to feed all the people who lived at the frozen and forlorn top of the world. The bounty from a typical sixty-foot bowhead whale could feed a standard-size Inuit village for an average year. Outsiders called Malik's job "subsistence whaling." But one man's subsistence whaler is another man's cowboy.

By early September 1988, Barrow's whaling captains were starting to worry about what was turning into a dismal fall hunt. No one from the area had caught a whale since spring, and winter—which comes quickly in the Arctic—was nearly upon them. And when winter comes here it doesn't come empty-handed. It brings with it six months of some of the world's coldest temperatures and sixty-seven days of absolute darkness. In Barrow, Alaska, the sun sets every November 17 and doesn't rise again until January 21 of the following year. Temperatures of fifty degrees below zero are not unusual. Factor in the howling winds that whip down from the North Pole or across the Beaufort and Chukchi seas from Siberia at speeds of up to 100 miles an hour, and the windchill reading can drop to 175 degrees below zero. Of course, Alaskans don't bother with windchills. The ambient readings are bad enough.

As any Alaskan knows, the forty-ninth state has only two seasons: winter and damned late in the fall. This gets less funny the farther north you travel in Alaska—and Barrow is as far north as you can get.

Barrowans proudly called their town "The Top of the World."[1] For all intents and purposes it was. Located 320 miles north of the Arctic Circle, it could be reached only by air except for two or three weeks in the summer when the ice receded far enough for a thick-hulled supply ship to get through.

Malik and his people have called Barrow home since their forbearers first paddled, walked or skated across the Bering Sea from Siberia as long as 25,000 years ago. These intrepid seafarers came in nimble open boats made of dried walrus or sealskin called umiaks. These were certainly among the first people to have permanently settled in North America. Whether they displaced anyone else is not known, so they call themselves the first Americans, and who can blame them?

By 1988, there were a little more than 3,000 people living in Barrow, around 2,700 of whom claimed to descend in some degree from those original explorers. On the night of September 16, 1988, Malik assembled his six-man whaling crew outside Sam & Lee's on Nachick Street, advertised as the world's northernmost Chinese restaurant, to arrange their gear. When the gear was sorted, assembled, and packed, the men were ready to hunt the open waters of the Arctic Ocean in search of migrating bowhead whales.

In one of nature's most daring matches, these seven men sought battle with an immensely powerful, agile and resilient forty-ton whale. These men hunted not from an umiak, but from a much sturdier but still small aluminum dinghy powered interchangeably by oars and a modern outboard motor. A kicking whale's tail or slapping whale fins could easily capsize the boat. Together, the whale's tail and fins, called flukes, propel and guide the massive mammal with both precision and stealth, equally able to challenge or simply evade anything or anyone foolish enough to confront it.

If cast out of their boat and into the frigid waters—for any reason, be it man caused, ocean caused, or whale caused—the jettisoned men would not have long to enjoy the refreshing chill of the eight-degree Arctic Ocean

---

1 The current town of Barrow derived its modern name from Point Barrow, America's northern-most point, named by English explorer Frederick Beechey in 1825 to honor British admiral Sir John Barrow. The Inupiat name for Barrow is *Ukpeagvik,* or "place where snowy owls are hunted." Maybe that's why the name Barrow is now used by all.

water before dying. But the prospect of a bitter winter without locally hunted whale blubber—more appetizingly called muktuk, the primary but long since essential food choice for natives—provided these whalers with the chance to simultaneously ply their trade and win local plaudits.

In one of modernity's most predictable phenomenon, the prosperity delivered by Alaska's oil wealth did not cut Barrowans off from their past; it helped them recreate it. Before the oil boon of the mid-1970s, Eskimos hunted whales only in springtime. Prior to widespread adoption of the outboard motor and two-way radio, hunting whales anytime other than in the spring was pointless. The only way premodern whalers could effectively hunt was by waiting out on the sea ice in pitched tents for days, sometimes even weeks at a time, for whales to pass them by.

While their cultural betters down in the Lower 48 lamented the "lost innocence" of Inuits and other newly modern peoples, Barrowans were as eager to improve their own lives as anyone else. Why they should continue living as fossilized museum pieces so that members of the faraway commentariat in the Lower 48 could congratulate themselves for preserving was a question few people on the North Slope had the time to waste asking.

Now that they had outboard motors, Malik didn't have to wait for whales or the approval of their distant and unknowing superiors. They could go get the whales themselves. Once they found and harpooned one, they could use their two-way radios to get help towing it in. But make no mistake: while whaling was much easier than it had ever been, it was still challenging and dangerous.

Malik's father and grandfather earned the title of Great Whaler. Even though this title usually followed a family's line, Malik had to prove he, too, was worthy of it. He listened to his elders. He learned their lessons. With over seventy harvested whales to his credit, Malik was well known in every whaling village up and down Alaska's Arctic coast. The adventures of whalers like Malik were the popular subject for elaborate epic poems celebrating the hunt. These poems were taught in schools, preached in churches, and retold on local radio and television.

On the morning of September 12, 1988, the strong gusts that had prevailed over previous days calmed. But even so, the thickened clouds trapped the unseasonably cold air keeping temperatures near zero degrees. To keep warm, Malik and his six-man crew wore two layers of department-store

quality long underwear under handmade sealskin pants and rawhide parkas. As they launched their boat from the beach behind the Top of the
World Hotel, the whalers wondered whether they would be able to return
there before the beach froze over.

About an hour after shoving off, the crew heard on their two-way radio
another local whaling crew report their having spotted a bowhead roughly
two miles off the tip of Point Barrow. Malik squatted in the bow. He redi-
rected his helmsman to throttle up in order to get to the site, eight miles
north–northeast as quickly as possible. The dinghy's top speed of twenty
knots should get them there in about thirty minutes. The windchill made
it feel far colder than the zero degrees it really was. The men rolled down
the fur seal linings of their hoods to protect themselves from frostbite during the ramped-up ride across the rough sea.

From more than a mile away, Malik could make out the unmistakable
mist on the horizon. The fine spray lingering thirty feet above the surface of
the water before vanishing into the atmosphere was proof the initial sighting
was accurate and that the spotted whale was still in the area. But Malik had
company. Two other whaling crews were now hovering in the same area.
Still, Malik was better positioned than his rivals and would remain so—
unless the whale decided to change course. Without dramatic changes, the
whale was Malik's for the taking. Malik signaled to slow the boat. He pulled
off his hood and exchanged his fur mitts for the baggy bloodstained cotton
work gloves he wore to kill many whales. The crew sorted the weapons they
would use to strike their prey.

Before local whalers started using the modern machines and tech-
niques developed and perfected by their more efficient commercial whaling competitors, the only way Eskimos could kill a whale was to repeatedly
stab it with their handmade animal-derived ivory harpoons until it died.
By 1988, those days were long over. Malik grabbed his four-pound graphite harpoon armed with a unique explosive device designed to detonate on
impact to produce a larger diameter, and thus more severe wound. The
helmsmen loaded the explosive cartridges into a shoulder gun, a stubby
brass rifle custom made for killing whales.

Crew preparations proceeded quietly and unobtrusively. Malik and his
men tried to remain invisible to the whale, or at the very least, distant and
nonthreatening. While not much can threaten a forty-ton whale, why add

to its already copious advantages? Malik looked at his watch: 10:30 A.M. His crew had seven hours of daylight. If they got lucky and struck the whale soon, getting the haul onto land before nightfall would still be a tall task and was by no means assured. The crew would need help. Lots of it. Everyone in town with a boat would be called upon to lend a hand. Darkness just added to list of dangers all creatures had to endure to survive in the Arctic: exposure, the cold, disorientation, and good ole Nanook, the omnipresent, rarely-seen-but-always-feared polar bear, an animal whose nondiscriminating tastes range from the tiny Arctic fox to the huge bowhead whale and a growing fondness for human dumpster delights tossed in for good measure.

For the moment, the six men and their boat lay between the beach and the site of the whale. Malik ordered his rudderman, Roy Ahmaogak, to try and position the boat north and east of the whale so that they could run with the harpooned mammal toward the shore. They didn't want to tow a huge and unstable carcass any farther than they had to. But Roy knew that his main objective was to keep the boat close enough to attack the whale. If it meant a longer haul home, so be it.

Malik waved his paddle to signal other whalers in the area to back off as his crew was preparing a strike. It appeared to Malik that the fifty-five-foot whale was still not aware of his predicament as it continued to surface and breathe normally. Its hot breath formed a spout almost directing its pursuers toward the precise spot where they could collect their biggest and tastiest gift of the year.

Observing the whale's trajectory, the depth of its dives, its rate of respiration, and the distance between surfacings, Malik directed his crew to the site where he calculated the whale would next appear. Trailing the bowhead by about a hundred feet, Roy skillfully piloted the boat to intersect the whale's path. Malik held his breath, hoping the whale would not decide to surface under his boat. All the modern technology at his disposal could still not guarantee he wouldn't position himself and his crew directly on top of the moving whale rather than astride it.

Whalers aim their harpoons at a spot behind the two perpendicular breathing holes located at the base of the whale's skull. It is the animal's most vulnerable part, exposing a narrow cavity leading to the heart. If properly executed, the harpoon pierces through the blubber, through the cavity, and into the unprotected heart. A lacerated whale heart pounds with such force that those few whalers expert or lucky enough to have landed the "perfect strike" compare notes on how long they were able to maintain a hold on the harpoon before its wild pulsations knocked them off their feet.

Had this whale sensed the shadowy forms on the crew hovering ominously above it? Malik did not know. All he could do was prepare his harpoon. But for the puttering idle of the Johnson outboard, the crew was silent, consumed by their anticipation of the instant when the silence and stillness would be shattered.

Anxiety mounted as the whale submerged longer and deeper than at any point since it was first spotted. Before its last dive, Malik and his crew were close enough to actually see that the whale's blowholes did not open wide enough to signal a longer or deeper dive, yet longer and deeper it was. But it couldn't go on. The whale would have to surface. And when it did, Malik would be sure to be ready.

He grasped the harpoon firmly in his left hand, undulating comfortably to the rhythms of the churning sea. No one needed to be told where to look for the whale to next emerge. These were whalers, born of and for this moment. Nor did Roy, the rudderman, need to be told where or how to shuttle his craft into Malik's desired position. The two men did not need to communicate. They worked as integral parts of a whole.

At that instant the whale's shimmering black skin effortlessly glided upward through the surface of the roiling waters of Chukchi Sea at the precise point where every eye on Malik's crew was trained. Malik cocked his arms behind his round, thinly thatched head. His triceps tightened as he raised his hollow graphite harpoon. He knew the whale was at its most vulnerable immediately before starting its exhale. Harpoon in hand, a strong impulse ran through Malik's wiry frame lunging him forward toward his target. Carefully but forcefully shifting his weight from his back foot forward, Malik's throwing mechanics generated enough linear momentum to pull his shoulders around to create the rotational momentum needed to properly launch the harpoon. The force of such an explosion would have tossed nearly anyone else into the swirling waters below. But Malik emerged from his harpoon release as firmly planted in the bow of his boat as any baseball pitcher's feet would be at the base of the mound.

The razor-sharp tip pierced the lustrous black skin of the graceful giant. A primer charge planted at the end of the harpoon detonated as it lodged inside the whale. Recoiling from the shock of a bomb literally exploding inside it, the whale roared in confusion and terror as it plunged below the waterline in a hopeless attempt to escape its fate. The next blast came seconds later. This bomb, on a five-second fuse, detonated even deeper inside the whale and tore apart its pulmonary cavity.

Roy waited patiently for the sound of that second blast, which was his signal to raise his forty-pound brass shoulder gun to land still more exploding shells at or near the whale's head, a target so huge he could hardly miss. The whale surfaced, exhaling a geyser of blood, at which point Roy jerked the trigger of the lumbering weapon back toward him. The charge misfired. Instead of detonating only after it had lodged inside the whale, it instead exploded on contact. Chunks of charred blubber spewed in all directions. The whale fell back into the sea, leaving a storm of crimson hail in its wake.

Roy reloaded and fired twice more. The whale violently writhed in a frantic but powerful attempt to unshackle the inflated sealskin floats tied to the harpoon securely lodged inside it. The whale spun circles as the red water foamed in its wake.

After Roy scored his third shot securely in the whale's arched back, Malik motioned the helmsman to steer him still closer to the crippled and disoriented whale. As wounded as it was, the whale was still capable of escaping the crew, if not its fate, by plunging deep beneath the surface. If Malik could hit the whale with another wire-guided harpoon, the harpoon's floats might slow down the whale just enough to kill it. Malik readied and fired again. The sudden bloat of the whale's shiny black skin signaled another hit. The whale's huge tail caught one side of the boat, slamming it violently forward into its diamond-shaped shoulder blade.

Drenched in the whale's blood, the men grabbed hold of the gunwales to steady themselves inside their rocking dinghy. When Malik regained enough balance to look up, he saw a sluggish whale too gravely injured to carry on much longer. Concerned that the bowhead might make one last attempt to dive beneath a patch of ice before it died, Malik reached for another harpoon. Just because the beast was mortally wounded did not mean it had yet been subdued. The whale's size and its will to live could still push it onward for many miles, prolonging the endurance test between whale and Eskimo.

Malik need not have worried. Before he could fire again, the whale suddenly and quietly succumbed. Now the challenge was to secure their prize before it sank and the men did not have much time. Three other whaling crews out that morning watched and cheered the strike through binoculars from their respective vantage points stretched across the Chukchi horizon. Once the whale was dead, neighborly cooperation replaced friendly competition. Upon confirmation that the whale had succumbed, the sidelined crews went from passive spectators to active participants. They rushed to help Malik's crew keep the dead whale on the surface so it could be towed to shore for butchering.

As in ancient times, the modern way of "sharing the whale wealth" was to distribute the tasty proceeds in accordance to the contribution of the recipient. The more a crew participated, the more meat it got. The crews now rushing to Malik's assistance would be compensated with the butchered whales' choicest cuts.

People have always been the most important resource in a subsistence whaling community. The act of hunting, catching, securing, towing, butchering, distributing, and disposing of a creature as large as a bowhead whale required as many people as possible to help. Dragging a giant dead whale onto the beach for butchering—particularly one this size and during such an unusual time of year—is no small task. As word spread that Malik's crew had a whale in tow, Barrowans readied themselves to help.

Within minutes, regular programming on KBRW-AM, the only commercial radio station on Alaska's North Slope (serving an area bigger than the state of California) was interrupted to broadcast news of the kill, particularly Malik's current sea location so that designated town volunteers with boats could meet Malik at sea and help his crew ballast the whale and bring it safely to shore. Within an hour, more than eighty people in twenty-two boats had arrived on the scene. Even with such help, it still took four hours to haul the mammoth carcass across six miles of choppy seas and back to the beach.

By the time Malik and his six-man crew did get back to shore, it was too dark for them to see the hundreds of people who had assembled to greet and assist them. This was the moment every whaler dreamed of as a child and cherishes as he ages.

Before Christianity made its way to the Arctic coast in the early nineteenth century, Inuits, like nearly every pagan subsistence culture ever studied, revered—even worshipped—the source of their sustenance. That this seems somehow remarkable to us shows how the most revolutionary conceptual discoveries are quickly assumed to have been obvious to all. But this was not the case and native peoples were there to prove it. Before the notion that our world was created by a God that transcends time and space, it was only natural for people to worship a visible product of creation than an unseen, unknown creator. The religious revolution was to see God not in nature, but above and in control of nature.

Combining the ancient pagan practices of their ancestors with their own late twentieth-century American Protestantism, Malik gathered everyone on the beach to hear him offer thanks to the whale and to the God who created it. Then Malik's wife emptied a plastic bucket filled with fresh water into the dead whale's open mouth and then into its blowhole. Somehow, this "Arctic baptism" would make the whale's spirit a permanent part of the village. While no doubt thankful for the honor, the whale would probably have preferred to have restored to him what was once rightfully his.

If Barrowans wanted their whale meat raw—which they did—the butchering had to start straight away. If left unbutchered, even for a short time, and even in freezing temperatures, the process of decomposition would quickly convert the dead whale's massive energy supply into heat, roasting the carcass at temperatures near 300 degrees. Malik assigned several men to start carving up the whale.

Like Lilliputians tying down Gulliver, a half-dozen Eskimos mounted and climbed ladders against the side of the dead whale, carrying sharp fan-shaped knives mounted on traditional long wooden handles, called ulus. They stood on top of the two-story-high carcass, carving the blubber into a checkerboard pattern. Hot putrid air hit them in the face as they ripped two-foot-thick squares of muktuk from the whale's back with large iron hooks.

Plumes (more like big puffs) of steam purged from the whale as the men peeled away the long slabs of blubber. The steam could be seen for miles around Barrow's flat, featureless plain. Lying hundreds of miles farther north than the hardiest tree could grow, it didn't take much height for something to be seen from great distances. It took less than an hour for the entire circumference of the fifty-five-foot whale to be stripped clean of its muktuk, leaving something that looked more like a pink airplane fuselage than the skinless remains of a fifty-five-foot whale. The slabs of muktuk were quickly spirited into twenty-two neat piles reserved for each crew involved in the hunt. While the property of the each crew's chief, the piles were payment to be dispensed at the chief's discretion.

Once the muktuk had been stripped, the butchers went back to work removing the whale's meat by repeating the same process of cutting giant rectangular slaps and then peeling them off. By dawn the next morning, the entire operation, employing over a thousand people, was all but done. With a few more tasks, the forty-ton whale, the carefree master of the sea just hours before, had been hunted, ruthlessly killed, towed to the beach, and carved into thousands of pieces.

By 1988, whale was more of a luxury than anything approaching a necessity. The Inuits could get through a winter without whale meat the same way you could get through your winters without whale meat. While the cookie-cutter politically correct (that is, false) portrayals of native Inuit life emphasized the price that modernization was extracting from their traditions and culture, it was a price everyone, including Malik, was more than happy to pay. Survival beats starvation, and a modern heated home trumps exposure. Nonetheless, Malik's catch assured that this winter would be both modern and traditional.

Until their once impenetrable isolation was broken, subsistence whaling villages like Barrow killed only as many whales as they needed to survive—although for reasons having everything to do with what was practical (hunting, killing. and securing giants whales was far from easy) and almost nothing to do with what was "environmentally responsible." As World War II ended, the modern industrialized nations with commercial whaling industries suddenly realized the only way to save their dying industry was to save the few whales they had not yet killed. The first global effort at whale conservation came in 1946, with the establishment of the International Whaling Commission (IWC).

Ostensibly, the IWC was created to allow whale populations to recover by limiting the number of whales legally permitted to be killed each year and by regulating what kind of whales could be killed and by what nations. Exemptions became the rule. Nations like Japan and the Soviet Union successfully argued with some truth that their whaling industries were needed to help their economies recover from the war. Norway and Iceland made the same argument but with no truth. Although invaded by the Nazis in early 1940, Norway was overrun so quickly it suffered almost no war damage, while Iceland emerged from the war in far better shape than it entered it as a result of its role as the primary Allied staging area for the vital war of the Atlantic.

The United States and Canada argued that their own Eskimo populations, barely removed from subsistence status, deserved the right to continue subsistence whaling. These "subsistence quotas" were based on the size of each village and the projected number of whales in their areas. As the number of whales increased, so too would the quotas.

As with most well-intentioned government interventions, the IWC mandates delivered the opposite of what they were intended to produce. Rather than limit subsistence whaling, the IWC quota system created a range of new incentives that markedly increased whaling.

Now, rather than just hunt for what was needed, Eskimo communities had a valuable new resource; the tradable commodity of whale quotas.

Each year, Eskimo settlements from Russia to Norway to the United States would eagerly await news of the IWC's quota announcements to learn how many whales their communities were permitted to take. In 1988, the International Whaling Commission gave the people of Barrow, Alaska, a quota of eight whales it could hunt; many more than they needed to insure that everyone in Barrow had plenty of whale meat. Malik's strike marked Barrow's fifth IWC-approved whale. While all five were bowheads, there was no rule that said they had to be.

Another unintended consequence of IWC action was to create markets for whales that otherwise would never have been hunted. According to the IWC, Barrow whalers were free to fill their eight whale quota with any eight whales they could get their hands on.

Remember the three California gray whales we left aimlessly frolicking off the Barrow coast? Well, this is both where and how they enter our story. Until the IWC's quota system, no one in Barrow would have given the gray whales a second thought, let alone invited them home for dinner. But the IWC's quotas created artificial demand for any kind of whale, tasty or otherwise. The organization established to save whales created new reasons to kill them.

Thus the three California grays could be legally hunted and killed just as if they were bowhead whales, but only if certified native Alaskan blood— whatever in the world that was—coursed through the hunter's veins. Even though gray whales were inedible due to their barnacled skin and tough acrid meat, Barrowans still had three more whales they could legally kill before the end of the year—which was rapidly approaching. The IWC's counter- productive interventions didn't stop there. Not only were subsistence whal- ing towns allowed to kill any kind of whales they could catch, they were also allowed to "trade" their quota—that is, sell their excess whales to other vil- lages. Towns could contract whale hunts for other towns, even if they had reached their own annual limits. Call it cap and trade for whales.

Barrow was not only the oldest continuously settled Eskimo village in the world, but by 1988 it had become the biggest. It was home (adopted or otherwise) to the greatest whaling legends, and some of the greatest whalers, like Malik. Not surprisingly, it also became the home port to a new and valuable little industry—professional subsistence whaling.

On Thursday, October 6, 1988, Roy Ahmaogak, a member of Malik's crew, got a phone call from someone in the village of Nuiqsut, a tiny in- land Eskimo settlement eighty miles south of Barrow. The Eskimos of Nuiqsut survived by roaming the frozen tundra in search of land animals. Nobody from Nuiqsut would have had a clue what to do with a whale had one managed to flop its way across eighty miles of tundra to their front door. Whaling was as alien to Nuiqsut as tarpon fishing was to Barrowans. At least it was before the IWC.

The Nuiqsut caller asked Roy if he could help hunt for any of the three whales allotted to the village's quota. If Roy got lucky, he and his crew could make a tidy profit partnering with Nuiqsut to sell those whales on the international market. One whale could fetch $50,000 in 1988, if not more. That was plenty enough to interest Roy Ahmaogak.

Over the next few days the weather took a nasty turn toward winter. Temperatures plummeted to twenty degrees below zero. Strong winds pushed the massive polar ice pack south on its annual surge toward the Barrow coast. Each day saw new ice that was forming around the shore expand farther out to sea. In the next few weeks, the new ice would stretch for miles covering the surface of the Chukchi Sea, eventually the constantly expanding and contracting polar ice pack. When the two met, the new shoreside ice would be consumed by and subsumed into the floating pack, perhaps never again to melt.

As large as Australia in winter, the polar ice pack is thought to be the biggest single piece of ice in our solar system. For millions of years, the polar ice pack has floated frozen across the top of the world thousands of feet thick. For nine months of the year, it stretches across 3,000 miles of sea from Alaska to Norway. In summer, the circumference of the pack shrinks as its outer edges melt away. Every year, gigantic icebergs the size of Rhode Island break off and float freely in the icy Arctic Ocean until reconnected to the encroaching pack during the next change of season. During July and early August, the last of the snow and ice melt away from Barrow's beaches. By the beginning of October, summer in the Arctic is only a memory.

Winter was back.

Roy told the caller from Nuiqsut he would look, but was not optimistic. It was too late in the year, he said. Surely, by now, all the whales would have left the area on their way south for winter breeding and birthing. Nonetheless, Roy Ahmaogak spent a good part of Friday, October 7, 1988, riding his ski machine up and down the coast around Point Barrow on the lookout for any signs of straggler whales. Daylight hours and temperatures were both fading fast. By the time he ended his search, the temperature had dropped to twenty-five degrees below zero. Roy turned his ski machine around and started back to Barrow across the eighteen miles of glassy-smooth Arctic Ocean ice, convinced there were no whales to be found.

But as he passed the long sandbar north of Point Barrow on his ride back to town, he drove right past the stranded whales just after they had surfaced for air. Roy excitedly jumped off his ski machine, hoping to find bowheads. Instead, when they popped back up he saw they were California grays. They weren't flocking anymore. Now, trapped under a growing ice patch, they appeared in full panic. Since the thin ice around the whales was too weak to support his weight Roy could not get any closer to them.

Still, he was plenty close enough to clearly make them out. It appeared as if the whales were clinging to an air hole barely big enough to fit their heads through.

It looked like their game was up. As soon as that hole froze over, which wouldn't be long, the whales would drown. As much as Roy might have wanted to help, he knew there was nothing anybody could, or perhaps even should do, to help these now helpless giants. This was nature. Who knew how many whales died every year after failing to escape the icy Arctic waters in time? The carcasses of decayed whales that washed up on shore every spring proved the answer was "plenty."

When he got back to Barrow, Roy unloaded his bear rifle and assorted standard-issue Arctic survival gear from the ski machine, and went inside to warm up. After snatching a bite to eat, Roy called two biologist friends, Craig George and Geoff Carroll, who ran the local wildlife management office. He told them what he had just seen on the ice. To ask who could have predicted that a routine report of a routine whale stranding literally at the top of the world would end up becoming the biggest animal rescue ever attempted is the wrong question. A better question might be, Why would anyone have made such a prediction? Sure, small isolated events can trigger greater global events—think World War I—but whales stranded at the top of world, not by man but nature?

Within just three weeks, at least twenty-six television networks from all over the world would converge upon one of the world's most isolated and hard-to-get-to towns, just to broadcast live, up-to-the-minute reports about three California gray whales popping their heads in and out of small holes in the Arctic ice. The images would captivate the world—or at least captivate those drawn to television news. The most widely covered media nonevent in the history of electronic news was now officially underway. Suddenly the nonevent had very much transformed itself into something very real.

Of course, for Eskimos the only news was that the whale stranding itself was news. Noah Webster defined news as "new information about things previously unknown." Everyone in Barrow knew that gray whales died under Arctic ice. So what was newsworthy about this? Apparently plenty. The rapidly unfolding rescue of the three whales would cost tens of millions of dollars, involve the president of the United States, the general secretary of the Soviet Union, push a democratic government to the brink of collapse, and capture the attention, if not the imagination, of millions around the world before two of the three whales would eventually be freed. Journalists from competing networks would trample each other in pursuit of new angles of a nonstory while becoming far bigger stories in and of themselves.

The whale rescue would unite environmentalists and oilmen, Inuits and whites, Alaska and the Lower 48 states, the United States and the Soviet Union, and two people seven thousand miles apart who would meet and marry.

Lucky whales.

2

From the Edge of the World to the Center of the Media Universe

On Saturday morning, October 8, the day after Roy Ahmaogak found the three whales, he and Malik drove their ski machines along the Point Barrow sandbar to the spot where Roy had seen them. As they got closer, Malik's windswept face lit up. He had an intimate kinship with whales that environmentalist do-gooders had a hard time understanding. From miles away, Malik knew enough about whales and their environment to see that the three whale spouts were hanging unusually close to each other.

Malik grew excited as they approached. Roy grew relieved to see the whales had made it through the night. The two Eskimos parked their five-hundred-pound ski machines on the snow-covered sand at the edge of the spit. The ocean ice was too weak to hold the machines. In fact, the area around the whales wasn't really ice at all. It was still just a thick slush, but hardening by the minute.

The closer Malik got to the whales, the more he wondered why they didn't just swim away. Were they too afraid to swim out to open waters? Maybe they were afraid to leave the breathing hole to explore the unfamiliar water farther out toward the open channel? In the Arctic, the autumn's weather was always the most unpredictable. Did the whales know that, too? It was impossible for man to predict ice conditions for more than a few hours. Perhaps the whales' internal weathermen were no better?

Malik feared that if the whales did not make a move soon, the ice would harden enough around to really strand them. To complicate matters, he also knew what the whales knew: that if they left this hole, they might not find another. What would happen if they ran out of air before they got back? What if they became disoriented under the ice? The answer to these questions was obvious: They would drown. The gray whales were unlike their cousins, the bowhead whales, who would have had no problem breaking their snouts through the thick slush to breathe. Malik lost count of the number of bowheads he missed over the years as they dove under large ice patches to dodge his harpoons. He was surprised to see how different these gray whales seemed.

Malik and Roy stood on the beach (or maybe on sea ice near the beach—they couldn't be sure), waiting for the whales to surface. Sure enough, each one surfaced in its turn every few minutes to breathe. It was their constant surfacing in the same place that kept the ten-by-twenty-foot hole from freezing over. In all his years whaling, Malik never saw anything like this.

He would have loved to get closer, but this was as far as they could get. The ice was too thick for his boat to get through but not strong enough to support a man's weight. Unable to do more than watch, the two Eskimos climbed on their ski machines and headed back to Barrow.

Inuit whalers from the tiny inland village of Nuiqsut, eighty miles southwest of Barrow, learned about the three whales from radio reports broadcast across the region. Several of them gathered at the hamlet's single telephone (remember, there were no cell phones yet) to call their colleagues up in Barrow. Malik was nonplussed to learn how quickly folks down in Nuiqsut were to harvest the stranded whales. Why shouldn't they be? The whales were there for the taking. And since the whales were fated to die, why was the ocean bottom more entitled to reap their bounty than the Inuits of Nuiqsut? The "old school" that valued whales not for glory or profit but only for survival was in fact, no school at all. It was myth: the pseudocosmopolitan product of modern environmentalism that aimed to delegitimize the modern by glorifying the past—even if it meant falsifying it.

When the twentieth century finally got to Barrow, the century was already half over. But the Barrowans quickly made up for lost time. Everything changed ... and fast. Most of the change was welcomed, but not all of it. Subsistence whaling was formalized at the very moment whales ceased being a subsistence source. Whales would never again mean the difference between life and death, but instead took on the same meaning the modern world had placed on them since the eighteenth century: commerce. The whales, so central for so long, became a luxury almost overnight. Many Eskimos were apprehensive about how modernization would affect them, but not enough to turn back the clock. The uncertainty of present-day times sure beat the certainty of death by starvation every winter.

Modernity meant it was now possible to put the soon-to-die whales to good use. Rather than letting them drown, harvesting the whales would inject tens of thousands of dollars into the local economy by providing several hundred people with work for a day or two.

As Malik and Roy watched the whales gasping for each breath, they knew these whales weren't trapped where they were found by accident. The very geography that threatened to entomb the whales allowed them to be discovered and, in the end, rescued. The whales were caught among the sand shoals at the very tip of a narrow five-mile-long sandbar marking the northernmost tip of Alaska stretching north–northeast until it slipped into the sea. At its widest point, the Barrow sandspit was a hundred feet across. The far end lay nine miles north of modern Barrow. The fragile earth barrier was all that separated the calmer waters of the Beaufort Sea from the raging tempests of the Chukchi Sea.

The whales gravitated to the sandspit, which served as a natural windbreak, allowing them to feed more comfortably in its shelter. But when the calm Beaufort Sea water started to freeze, the whales did not realize that the waters just across the spit—which were much rougher—were still ice-free. If the whales had been any farther from shore they would never have been discovered because they wouldn't have been stranded.

That night, over beers, some of Malik's whaling friends asked him what he thought about harvesting the three gray whales. Malik shrugged with disinterest. He didn't see the point of killing them so long as there was a chance they could swim free. If they couldn't escape, then all bets were off. He took no pleasure in seeing animals suffer, but then again, he took even less pleasure seeing his fellow human beings suffer. Why should Barrowans be deprived of benefiting from the whales if there really was no way to help them?

Malik thought there must be some way to help the whales overcome their fear enough to get them to start swimming. Because they were young, they had probably never seen slush before and simply assumed it was ice. While the whales acted like they were trapped, as of Saturday afternoon, October 8, they were not. Later that night, reports of the stranded whales started to trickle through town. The newer, younger whaling crews clamored for permission to harvest the whales.

However, they weren't allowed to do anything until Craig George and Geoff Carroll had the chance to study them, but the two biologists were hunting caribou in the tundra, and weren't scheduled to return until Monday. Craig and Geoff helped start the local government's Department of Wildlife Management in the early 1970s. The job offered these two adventurers a chance to study whales in a way other biologists could only dream of. Their management responsibilities were not just to protect local wildlife, but also to help locals hunt and kill it. In particular, the most important part of their job was to help the Eskimos hunt and kill bowhead whales.

The two conducted an annual census of the bowhead whale population for the North Slope Borough (NSB), Alaska's equivalent of a county. What they found would be the basis for negotiating next year's quota with the International Whaling Commission. Geoff and Craig exemplified a remarkable fact of modern Eskimo life. The Inupiat Eskimo lived primitive lives by conventional American standards, but they were smart enough to hire the best modern expertise their money and influence could buy. The Eskimos had no shortage of help to manage their stormy entrance with the modern world—which is what made so much of it so stormy.

Herein lay another hard to break media myth about native peoples in the United States, Alaska in particular—that their hard-bitten plight was the consequence of government disregard. In fact, on a per capita basis no other group of Americans received even close to the level of federal and state assistance annually disbursed to native peoples. By the 1980s, federal and state aid to these peoples was massive enough to transform entire communities into little more than state wards. The government micromanaged the land they lived on and the houses they lived in. The government not only paid for, but directly delivered, their health care, which goes a long toward explaining why it was the worst in the country. Dozens of federal departments and agencies had their own designated "native American" programs, nearly all of which were available to Alaskans. And that's just the feds. By 1988, the state of Alaska had its own fully developed but largely redundant assistance bureaucracy.

The consequences for native peoples in places like Barrow were somewhat incongruous. What but government could produce poverty in people with relatively high per capita incomes? What entity but government could shorten the life spans, deepen the chronic health problems, and increase the rates of social and family dislocations as they increased involvement? Naturally, the worse government assistance made things, the more activists would clamor for more government assistance. By 1988, the federal trusteeship imposed upon native-Americans as supposed to compensation for federal crimes committed against them was proving more calamitous than the crimes themselves.[2]

The greedy talk of slaughtering the gray whales appalled Malik. He knew it would reflect badly on his people. The young whalers sounded like the prospectors who were looking to stake another claim. It pained him to imagine all the careless whaling crews in a mad dash to kill three useless whales. At best, they would be used for dog food.

Before leaving on their weekend hunting trip, Geoff and Craig reported Roy's discovery back to their boss, Dr. Tom Albert, 1,200 miles to the south in Anchorage. Albert wanted them to check on the whales before they left, and to report back to him on whether they believed the animals would survive the weekend. In his brief dispatch back to Albert, Geoff offered his prediction that the whales would be gone by Monday—not dead, but en route on their 7,000-mile journey to winter breeding grounds.

Geoff and Craig were required to investigate each reported stranding of any animal on the government's endangered species list. Protected from the rusty harpoons of commercial whaling fleets since 1947, while

---

2 Per-capita income for American Indians living on reservations remained low through the end of the century. The 1999 U.S. census found Indians living on reservations earned $7,846 per capita compared to $14,267 for Indians living off reservations and to $21,587 for all U.S. citizens. Terry Anderson—Property and Environmental Research Center http://www.perc.org/articles/article1355.php

still on the endangered list, gray whales were flourishing. By 1988, biologists estimated there were 22,000 gray whales, an all-time species high. As the old joke goes, the nearest thing to eternal life on this earth for people is work at a government bureau—and for animals, placement on the endangered species list.

While whale strandings were common, the confluence of events regarding this whale stranding would be a cascading series of "firsts." Geoff and Craig would be the first biologists to actually observe gray whales naturally trapped in ice. Gray whales may well have been familiar to nature lovers and whale watchers along the Pacific Coast of the Lower 48, but precious little was then known about them in their Arctic environment. The closer the two could get to the whales, the more they could learn about the animals' behavior under extraordinary stress. Locals long knew whales died under the ice, but until now, scientists could only theorize as to how and why it happened. On Tuesday morning, October 11, 1988, four days after the whales were first discovered, Geoff and Craig would get to see them firsthand.

The bearded biologists loaded sleeping bags, flares, and emergency survival rations onto wooden dogsleds hitched to the backs of their ski machines and were ready to go. But they didn't know where exactly they were supposed to go. They needed a guide to help them find the exact spot of the stranding on the featureless and endless horizon of frozen sea. Since Roy was not available, they asked Billy Adams, a skillful hunter who, having seen the whales on Sunday, knew where they were. Besides, Billy would be good company. He had his own ski machine and a great sense of humor. The three men encased themselves in a hybrid mixture of modern and traditional cold-weather gear needed to keep them, if not warm, then at least able to function in the mind-numbing temperatures that would consume them as they sped out across the frozen sea.

As the sun rose just above the southern horizon, the trio traveled along Barrow's only road until it abruptly ended along with Alaska's northernmost coast seven miles north of town. From there, it was still another five miles to the whales. When they got as far as they could on the ski machines, Billy led them on foot the rest of the way toward the very tip of the soft-surfaced sandbar. Craig stopped to marvel at the surroundings. He squinted to view the sandbar. Remarkably, the Arctic Ocean's frozen glare can be blinding even under heavy overcast skies, which made this tiny sliver of what remained of North America hard to see.

As it tapered off into the sea, the total and uniform solitude over-whelmed him. Not a trace of life: no vegetation, no variation in scene, no visible image of anything. A void without end. Stark. Disconsolate. White. "Magnificent desolation" were the words first spoken by Apollo 11 astro-naut Edwin Buzz Aldrin nineteen years before to describe the surface of the moon. It came to Geoff's mind, but he knew the desolation that seemed so omnipresent on top of the ice was in fact a bountiful habitat teeming with an extraordinary cacophony of life on the underside of ice. Walrus, seals, polar bears, and of course whales thrived on a copious abundance of sea life almost impossible to quantify.

The three men stood on the frozen sandspit, gathered their bearings, and waited for spouts. They would know one way or another in a matter of minutes. If the whales were alive and still using these holes to breathe, it wouldn't be long before they came up for air. If the men saw no sign of the whales within five or six minutes, that would have been the end of this story. The whales would either have made it to open seas or they would be dead by drowning. As much as Geoff and Craig hoped the whales were free, they still wanted to see them. They had already begun to construct the scientific line of inquiry they would try to compile if they could collect enough data.

As two minutes became three, Geoff and Craig had a sinking feeling. Three minutes became four. The banter trailed off, overtaken by silence. At four minutes, resignation crept into acceptance that the whales were gone. Then, at the moment Geoff started to collect his things for the return trip to Barrow, Billy heard a low rumble gain momentum and traction. Sure enough, the mammoth head of a barnacled and slightly bloodied gray whale poked through the ice. The whales (one at least) had made it through the weekend but were fading fast. Craig, George, and Billy cheered with joy. They punched their fists through the cold air, shaking hands in con-gratulations for the vicarious achievement they rejoiced in.

Like a locomotive letting off steam, the whale exhaled. Only a warm-blooded mammal could make that deep gargle. "FFWWWSSSSHHH," the whale belched. As soon as it filled its giant lungs, the whale slipped its head back into the hole and disappeared into the black sea. The displaced water rippled through the weak ice surrounding the hole, freezing as it moved. Then, a second rumbling. Another huge head, this one bigger than the last, fit into the hole with barely any room to spare. Looking through binoculars, Geoff could distinguish one whale from another by the pattern of barnacles on its snout. This second whale swallowed its portion of air and vanished as quickly as the first.

From what Geoff and Craig could observe, the whales stayed under as long as they could. They seemed to be protecting, even guiding each other. It sure looked as if the whales had worked together to develop a breathing system designed to allow them to share the hole. They pulled their heads back under and away from the hole to give each other a turn to breath. Remarkable. This behavior was new to Geoff and Craig. Nothing quite like this had ever been seen by anyone before. Neither biologists recalled learning or hearing anything about whales acting so cooperatively in any similar life-threatening predicament.

After the second whale surfaced there was a long pause. What happened to the third whale? Roy Ahmaogak reported seeing three. They didn't have to wait long to have that question answered. The third whale emerged; much smaller and much more timidly than the first two. It looked battered and tired. Nearly all the skin on this whale's snout appeared to have been rubbed off; probably from having scraped up against the sharp edges of the air hole. It swam with much less authority than the other two whales.

It seemed like the larger and older whales stayed under longer in order to give the smaller whale more time to breathe. How old was this third whale? Was it a baby . . . or somewhat older? Geoff and Craig could not immediately tell, but that it was a young one they had no doubt. When the two bigger whales surfaced, they rammed up through the sharp sides of the hole. Whales are many things but self-destructive is not one of them. The whales weren't purposely trying to hurt themselves; they were trying to expand their shrinking air hole. Their ramming kept slush from turning to ice. Here was more evidence that these whales possessed a keen and sharply developed social intelligence.

Billy knew a bowhead could break breathing holes in ice up to half a foot thick. These grays had trouble even with soft ice. No wonder it was grays and not their bowhead cousins that drowned under the ice. Each whale took several turns breathing and then dove for about five minutes. Craig dug into his knapsack and probed for his 35-millimeter camera. He had borrowed it from the borough to document the whales. Whatever photos he took would belong to the government. But this was a fantasy performance; he wanted copies of every shot for his photo album.

For almost an hour, the three men consumed as much sensory imagery as they could absorb. There was nothing they could do to actually help the whales yet since they still couldn't reach them. All they could do was watch and learn. None of their training and experience prepared them for this. They knew how to study whales. They were paid to help Inuits hunt and kill them. They didn't know how or even if they could help these whales.

The whales were tantalizingly close...so close that the men were lured to test the ice. The three men trod upon uncertain ground, which of course was not ground at all, but frozen ocean. Giddy at their unexpected good fortune, they carefully walked out until the ice could hold them no longer. Now they were only fifty feet or so away from the whales. From what little they could see, the hole did not appear much bigger than any of the whale's head.

Billy went to his sled to fetch the hollow aluminum pole he used to probe ice. He scampered nimbly back to where Geoff and Craig kneeled at safety's edge. Billy carefully measured a few paces beyond his companions and pushed the end of his pole deep into the hardened surface. He had to lean quite hard to get the ice to break. Once through, the pole easily probed the slush. Billy knew it would not stay slush for long.

Craig held the camera under his parka to shelter it from the cold. The brittle film nearly snapped in the sub-zero weather. (The days of digital cameras had yet to arrive.) Learning from the past when he would rip or break the film from winding the spool too roughly, this time he wound deliberately and tenderly. The sun vanished behind a low-lying bank of thick Arctic fog as he waited for the whales to begin their next breathing cycle. He popped open the back of his camera to adjust for the changing light conditions by replacing the film.

The forecast high for that Tuesday, October 11, was four degrees above zero degrees Fahrenheit, seventeen degrees colder than the average for this time of year. Since it seldom got that cold at that time of year without insulating cloud cover, the men knew they might confront "whiteout," a dangerous but common Arctic weather condition. The slightest wind can trigger it by whipping the dry, almost weightless snow into the air, blending it so uniformly with the white sky that all else is obscured. Whiteout blinds everything in its midst, but since it usually sticks very low to the ground, the Arctic's most deadly predator, the polar bear, which on its hind legs can stand up to fourteen feet high, uses the paralyzing condition to hunt defenseless prey. While aware of the danger, the three men were smart enough to be cautious but calm.

The whales resumed surfacing after a four-minute dive, right on schedule. First the two larger whales, followed by the smaller one. Craig snapped his way through an entire roll of film in one such respiration cycle. He hurriedly reloaded his camera to shoot more before the whales dove again. He was tempted to get flustered, but remembered he was an expert, not a tourist. Suddenly it dawned on him that he could take all the time he wanted; the whales weren't going anywhere. He could hang around the edge of the spit for as long as he could stand the cold. The next time the whales reached up for air, he could take even better pictures.

For nearly an hour the men said barely a word. Then, when the silence was broken, all three spoke at once. Their exhilaration was tempered by their inability to help do much for these magnificent creatures. The whales seemed stuck in what looked to be a hopeless quagmire, yet they were rational and deliberate. They avoided the panic they must have instinctively known would doom them. Their fate was intertwined and they seemed to know it. The whales had to work together to survive, which required both leadership and cooperation. One of the three whales had to be in charge, but Craig and Geoff couldn't quite figure out which one that was yet.

It was a mystery that would remain unsolved until the very last hours of what was to be a nearly three-week odyssey. What was it that enabled the whales to prioritizetze, strategize, and improvise their own survival? Was it genetic code, sheer intelligence, or a combination? These were some of the questions that would dog biologists, rescuers, reporters, and millions of people around the world for the weeks to follow.

The whales' unusual surfacing was the most obvious unanswered question Geoff and Craig could not answer. By the late 1980s, the gray whales' migratory and habitat patterns were well known; but only in its warmer, winter waters off the coast of Baja—not in the Arctic. Younger whales, especially grays, rarely wander more than a mile from shore. Shallow waters are safer waters—there was less room for killer whales and great white sharks, the gray whales' two natural predators.

In normal times, the gray whale, like all whales, breathes while swimming parallel to the surface. The whale only needs to arch its back just enough to expose its blowhole ever so slightly above the waterline. But these were no ordinary times. The only way these whales could survive was to shoot out of the small hole like a submarine-launched cruise missile.

"We have to get this on videotape," Craig shouted. "These would make great pictures." He wanted to get back to town to see if he could borrow equipment from local TV studio operated by the North Slope Borough's public access channel. The two biologists tightened their hoods, pulled down face masks, affixed goggles, and throttled up. Craig looked at his watch. Four hours had passed since they first saw the whales. Getting to town and back before it got too dark would require operating on fast forward.

Living in pre-Internet times, Craig was forced to find the studio's phone number by actually looking it up in a hard-copy seven-page Barrow phone book. He called Oran Caudle, the director of the borough's then state-of-the-art television studio and filled him in. He asked if they could take a video camera to get some footage of the stranded whales. Oran was intrigued. Originally from Texarkana, Texas, Caudle didn't know much about whales—but compared to everyone he left behind in the Lower 48, he was a veritable expert. One thing he did know, however, was that the Arctic could all too easily devastate his expensive equipment. "Sorry," he told Craig, "no can do." While disappointed, Craig was hardly surprised.

It wasn't that the thirty-one-year-old Caudle didn't want to share his equipment. He wanted it to be used as often as possible so long as it wasn't ruined or lost at sea. He knew if anything happened to his equipment, getting any of it replaced would be hard to do. After all, anything would be more exciting than his current production job on the North Slope Borough's employee benefits package. Oran was so anxious to get the hands-on television experience he knew he needed to get anywhere in the cutthroat, high-skilled, but low-paying world of TV production, that he was literally willing to move to the end of the world to get it. Ever the intrepid type,

Caudle was always on the prowl to produce interesting and valuable local programming for Channel 20, the North Slope's local public access channel, and these whales sounded like a chance to do just that.

The more Oran heard the two men talk, the more he sensed this might actually be something interesting, really interesting. But rules were rules, and Caudle followed them. He told Craig there was just no way he could lend out any of the NSB's equipment to nonauthorized personnel. After all, this was government property they were talking about. Sure, he could assign a camera crew and would just as soon as he could, but there was no way he could get any of his people out there until tomorrow at the earliest. As the light on his phone went off, the light in his head lit up: Caudle determined he would go out to the whales himself.

Oran Caudle was a big bear of a man. His ready smile radiated genuine warmth. He endeared himself to almost everyone in Barrow, even Eskimos, many of whom resented a non-Inuit presence, let alone a successful one. But this was a decidedly minority view. Tales of racial tension between Eskimos and non-natives were greatly exaggerated, particularly by those seeking to profit from their grievance peddling. The worse the problem, the greater the need for more publicly funded "intervention" and "mitigation programs."

Locals joked that the intermarriage rate was over 100 percent—when you factored in multiple marriages. Barrow's divorce rate was the highest in the state—75 percent. Caudle's own marriage recently ended in divorce. He was trying to rebuild his life, but Barrow was not the easiest place to do it.

Despite a generation of being conditioned to view themselves as victims, self-reliance died hard in Barrow. In addition to being at the highest latitude on the continent, the small town at the top of the world was bigger, richer, and safer than ever before. Statistics that looked appalling when compared with other American towns—high rates of murder, rape, suicide, alcoholism, and domestic violence—did not look nearly as bleak when measured against the only metric that mattered to them: their lives were measurably improved over that of their fathers and grandfathers. It was a bridge too far for many to even pretend otherwise.

Still, the obstacles were formidable. Aside from the isolation, the desolation, and the cold, there was the darkness—three months of insufferable, inconsolable, and complete darkness. Oran had to create his own support system that many locals simply inherited. He joined the Barrow Calvary Baptist Church. Its geographically tailored message that "only in darkness can small lights shine bright" had special resonance three hundred miles north of the Arctic Circle. After church on Sunday, October 9, he talked with some of his fellow worshippers about the whales Roy Ahmaogak found two days earlier. Almost everyone in town seemed to have heard about the stranded whales.

Caudle knew about gray whales not from books or Sunday-night nature specials on PBS, but from seeing them near the shore. Even when he didn't see them, proof of their presence was all around him, from the slimy barnacles that were always washing up on shore when not iced over, to the bounty of whale meat enjoyed during the long winters. If he could get close enough and the video proved interesting enough, Oran thought he might produce a twenty-minute evergreen segment for Channel 20. If there was anything that interested the people of Barrow more than whales, Caudle sure didn't know what it was. Aside from government, Barrow had only one industry and that was whaling.

Wednesday morning, October 12, 1988, came early for Oran. All mornings came early for Caudle; a self-described night owl. The division between day and night, taken for granted in more southernly climes, took on a completely different meaning in the Arctic; a meaning very hard for a tunik (white) like Oran Caudle to adjust to. In Barrow, a midnight in summer means broad daylight, while a winter "high noon" is marooned in pitch-dark blackness. The time of day just didn't mean the same thing. Humans react like other animals in the Arctic. During the long season they sleep more; during short season, they sleep less. Psychologists call it "seasonal affective disorder"; everyone else called it "the winter blues."

It was all Oran Caudle could do just to sit up in bed to grab the remote control. He clicked on CNN, which at the time was the only cable news channel. It was his (and everyone else's) link to the outside world. He showered, shaved, and downed his daily breakfast: a granola bar and a can of apple juice. Hearing the first bars of the music jingle for the show *Sonya Live* signaled it was 8:00 A.M., Alaska Standard Time and his cue to be out the door—which was just as well for Caudle, who couldn't stand the high-pitched Sonya Friedman and her lowbrow show. He slipped on his new felt-lined boots his mother had bought for him. Caudle thought they looked ridiculously large, but since they managed to keep his feet warm in temperatures down to eighty degrees below zero and everyone else in town wore them, he made his peace with them. He wasn't sure how long he would be out on the ice, but at least his feet wouldn't freeze.

Craig had warned Oran that unless the ice grew stronger overnight, fifty feet was as close as they could get to the whales. Maybe Oran could use the expensive zoom lens he persuaded the North Slope Borough into buying. This was the first time he took it out of the box since it arrived air-freight from Seattle three months before.

He packed a sensitive directional microphone that he stored along with batteries, assorted cables, and plenty of blank videotapes in specially lined cold-weather bags. He loaded it all into the back of the TV studio's white Chevy Suburban. Oran and two technicians picked up Billy Adams and together they drove to Craig and Geoff's office located out at the old Naval Arctic Research Laboratory, known to everyone as NARL. NARL was a sprawling complex that combined old World War II Quonset huts with more modern prefabricated buildings on wooden stilts at the northern edge of town. NARL used to be the center of town and a key component of U.S. national defense. Before the rise of satellite technology, NARL was the site of a massive radar station designed to warn against a transpolar nuclear attack from the Soviet Union. It looked a bit like NASA(National Aeronautics and Space Administration) drawings of futuristic Mars or moon colonies set against the backdrop of strange and hostile surroundings; and in truth that is very much what NARL really was. There was not another permanent man made structure between NARL and the North Pole.

When Oran, Billy, and the technicians arrived at NARL at 8:30 A.M. Wednesday morning, they found the biologists looking worried. Craig and Geoff thought that time was running out for the whales. The National Weather Service said temperatures could fall to forty degrees below zero out on the ice. With such cold, the whales' only hope was for wind to keep the sea from freezing, but the forecast predicted no wind. Without wind, the holes would freeze and the whales would drown before the day was out.

The ride out to the whales took longer than Oran expected. When the six of them brought their ski machines to a halt ten yards from the snow-covered beach, Geoff and Craig were amazed at how much new ice had formed overnight. The whales were right where the biologists left them. They continued their grim dance. The baby seemed steadier, taking more regular breaths. Billy Adams crept out to see how much farther he could walk. He was able to get much further beyond his earlier footprints. Remarkably, his tracks from yesterday looked as if they were just made—proof of the Arctic's low humidity and quiet winds. At this rate, the whales did not have long to survive.

Too excited to lament their fate, Caudle was spellbound just by the sight of the whales and almost dropped his camera. Craig told him to calm down. "Just relax, these whales aren't going anywhere," he assured him. "Take your time. Do what you have to do to get ready. The whales don't have much choice; they have to wait for you."

This was new. Here were three animals in their natural habitat that could be treated as though they were props back in his production studio. Normally in the wild, photographers are lucky to get any pictures. Oran calmed himself down and set up his camera. Equipment failure was still his main worry. At forty degrees below, any failure was not only possible, it was likely. Still, even if his gear worked, Oran wasn't sure how long he could keep it working. It was more than cold; it was dangerous, both for him and his gear. When he breathed the bitter air too deeply, it singed his lungs. In weather this cold, bones become brittle and easily break.

When Oran looked into the viewfinder, he saw only fog. He knew not to rip the camera apart to get at the droplets of water causing the condensation. There was only one thing to do. He put the camera on the tripod and waited for the inside of his camera to get as cold as the outside so that the condensation would vanish. Geoff and Craig noticed the whales were still not comfortable with all the commotion on the top of ice. The animals most likely feared the men's footsteps were those of a prowling polar bear. Breathing holes are favorite stalking grounds for polar bears. Like fish in a barrel.

The trapped whales were extremely vulnerable and they knew it. Every time they rose to the surface, they were dangerously exposed. A polar bear could kill a giant whale with one devastating swipe of its paw. The whales tried to stay underwater as long as they could. But sooner or later they had to face whatever was stomping around above them. They had to breathe.

While Oran fiddled with the expensive equipment, Geoff and Craig tallied the effects of the whales' predicament. They tried to think of ways to nudge the whales toward open water. The ultimate question was whether they could influence gray whales even if they could come up with a plan to do so. Oran asked Craig to sit down so he could take his first pictures of the whales surfacing in the background. He lifted his heavy twenty-five-pound video camera onto his shoulder, focused the zoom lens, and squeezed his thumb against the soft rubber record button. Caudle lumbered about trying to record every aspect of the whales. He put the camera on a tripod and filmed Billy Adams testing the ice in the foreground with the whales bobbing their gigantic heads against the stark white background.

Since the water was rapidly freezing, Caudle wanted to know how far the solid ice now extended. Would it be safe to walk right out to the edge of the breathing holes by the next morning? Billy Adams thought it might. In a guttural Eskimo accent, he said, "If the holes aren't froze over, we could probably get close enough to pet 'em."

Oran had an idea. "Let's do some interviews," he suggested. "We can edit them to go with the pictures of the whales for local TV. Which one of you guys wants to be interviewed?" Caudle inquired of his captive audience. Since the film would be shown on the local channel, Oran had to get some local flavor. That meant Billy or his assistant Marie.

Of the six people now on the ice, Marie seemed best suited to conduct the interviews. She was director of public information for the North Slope Borough. She was also Geoff Carroll's wife. In spite of her title, she didn't agree at first; Oran had to coax her. Geoff and Craig pretended to be completely absorbed in their various tasks. They were collecting lots of new data they would need to analyze, but they were also camera shy.

Oran assured Marie she looked great. Besides, if she didn't, who would ever know? After more playful prodding, she agreed to question her husband and then Craig. Oran thrust the microphone into her hand and pushed the Record button. "Go ahead," he said with one eye squinted shut and the other buried in the viewfinder. "Ask him what he is doing out here and what he thinks of the whales."

Marie was quick to pose coherent questions. She asked Geoff how the whales were discovered and what he thought their chances that they would either be able to escape or be harvested. Geoff said he didn't know for sure on either count; all he knew was what he could see in front of him. The whales were not in great shape.

She then interviewed Craig, who sounded professional, factual, and concise, if a little stiff. His stark face matched the terrain. With the whales active in the background, Oran knew he was finally recording some good stuff. (If he only knew how good!) Craig told Marie that the Wildlife Management office had a rare chance to study a natural phenomenon he was not sure anyone had been able to see before. "Unfortunately, there just isn't enough data yet to comment with any authority as to how these whales got stuck or what their chances might be to swim free," said Craig. Little did he know what good practice these quick sound-bites would be for the gathering storm looming on their personal horizons.

Oran wanted Billy in front of the camera to lend authority to the story's locality. Billy was an Inupiat whom everyone in town knew and who would make the setting more authentic, the story more compelling. And it would get critics off Oran's back. As much better paid advance men for major party presidential candidates were proving at the same time down in the Lower 48, visual backgrounds were rapidly moving into the foreground of what critics now deemed to be "good" television.

As Billy and Marie began speaking into the microphone, one of the two larger whales rose to breathe and burst brilliantly into frame. Oran stumbled in the slush as he backed up for a wider shot. He couldn't imagine a more powerful image. He couldn't describe what he naturally intuited. These creatures had a remarkable pull over the imaginations of everyone who saw them. Here the whales were fighting for each breath in front of people who went to great lengths and not insignificant personal risk just to see them. Oran's reaction didn't seem much different than anyone else's. It was more emotional than journalistic. It had to be—other than new data collected, there was nothing inherently journalistic about three whales either stranding themselves or being stranded at the very tip of North America.

What would become clear soon enough was that this story's real drama was unfolding not under the ice but on top of it: people gathering to watch captive whales becoming themselves captive to their fate.

As Billy spoke, he motioned behind him to note the stressed condition of the baby whale. At that moment, the baby rose timidly through the ice and stole the show. Bloodied and tired, the desperate animal lay motionless. The pathetic creature seemed to appeal to the camera for help, as if it somehow knew its message would soon be transmitted to creatures of an alien but caring species. The audio came across the bleak landscape perfectly, but Oran wasn't paying attention to the sound. He was spellbound by the immense power of the pictures he was shooting. Billy and Marie called and shouted his name several times before they got a response. They were trying to tell him they were finished.

"What do you mean you're done?" Oran bristled. "Just keep talking, I don't care what y'all say," he bellowed. "Just keep talking. Nobody will listen to what you say; it's the pictures they want to see and the pictures need some audio. This is just too incredible." Everyone was astonished. They never saw Oran so insistent. How could he possibly be so interested in hearing what they already said three times? Oran beseeched them to keep up the charade. Marie asked Billy the same questions over and over.

Watching these whales was like being on a drug so good it had to be illegal. As much video as Oran got, he had to have more. He had long since forgotten about the cold. Was it cold out here? When he finally ran out of tape, the others convinced him it was a good time to head back to town. By the way, yes, it was cold. In the four hours they spent out on the ice, the shelf of what appeared to be solid ice had grown an amazing twenty-five feet or so out toward the whale hole. If the cold kept up, they would be able to walk all the way out to the whales by tomorrow. But that begged the central question: just how long could the breathing holes stay open? In any case, it was time for these shivering humans to get back to town.

The return trip on the back of the snowmobiles was even colder than the ride out. But after all the excitement, enough adrenaline was circulating to keep their blood warm enough to manage the ride back without too much discomfort. After a chance to warm up and grab a bite to eat, Craig used Geoff's office to notify the Coast Guard about the trapped whales and to see if they wanted to send someone out to see if they could think of any way to help them. The closest permanently manned Coast Guard office was 1,200 miles to the south in Anchorage. He and Geoff thought the whales could easily be freed if there were a ship in the area to break a path through the soft slushy ice. Maybe the Anchorage office could authorize one of its North Slope vessels to cut a quick channel from open water into the whales, which at that point was still less than a mile. They didn't need a big ship; certainly nothing like an icebreaker. The ice was still slushy enough for any medium-size ship to do the job.

The biologists hoped their request would not be considered a big deal. Wednesday afternoon, they left a message with the Coast Guard duty officer who promised to pass it on. Later that night, a reporter named Susan Gallagher called the Coast Guard to see if anything newsworthy was going on. Gallagher was an Alaska night-beat reporter for the Associated Press. It was part of her job to phone the Coast Guard every night to find out if there were any late-breaking stories. The Coast Guard was constantly mounting search-and-rescue efforts to find lost or stranded hunters, whalers, adventurers, and who knows who else—especially late in the fall. But, a rescue effort for whales? That was a first. And within hours, the biggest rescue by humans of nonhumans in Alaska history—who knew, maybe even in all history—would be underway.

Gallagher dutifully took down the details as they were relayed to her by the Coast Guard duty officer and turned it into a nondescript, quick wire-service story. She couldn't spend that much time on it as there were other, seemingly more important news—involving people—that had to get turned into copy before deadline. When the night editor of the *Anchorage Daily News* saw Gallagher's story come across the wire, he decided to run it as a small item below the fold on the front page of Thursday morning's edition. Six days after the whales were first discovered, a small story about them made page one—and with no pictures!

Lucky whales.

Gallagher wrote: "A trio of whales trapped by ice in the Arctic Ocean used two openings for life-saving air Wednesday as biologists sought help to free the animals. The three California gray whales apparently were swimming from the Beaufort Sea to their winter grounds off Mexico when they got caught in the ice east of Point Barrow a week ago, said Geoff Carroll, a biologist from the North Slope Borough. He said the whales' movement kept open two holes in the ice, but those openings shrank as temperatures plunged and new ice formed. By Wednesday, when Barrow's minus thirteen degrees set a record low for the date, the holes were 450 feet offshore."

The chain reaction had begun. The next link in that chain was a tele-

vision reporter at KTUU-TV, the NBC affiliate in Anchorage, named
Todd Pottinger. Pottinger saw the front-page story in Thursday morning's
Anchorage Daily News as he got ready for work. Each day, work started with
a morning assignment meeting that would determine which stories everyone was to cover in anticipation of that evening's newscast. At the age of
twenty-six, Pottinger had already been in the television news business long
enough to know that whales always meant news. The minute he saw the
story, he was sold. People loved whales. Whether they were beached, mating,
or just swimming by, whales were always worth a segment—sometimes
more—on the Anchorage evening news. The news director needed no convincing. Whales were sure, safe. It was Pottinger's story to run with.

Pottinger flipped through his Rolodex for Oran Caudle's phone number.
Alaska was much too big for one local news agency to cover alone. Newspapers, wire services, and television stations relied on freelance stringers
across the state to report on the areas they couldn't cover themselves. For
TV stations looking for footage of any kind from Alaska's North Slope, Oran
Caudle was that man. He operated that region's only modern television
facility.

When Oran got to work that Thursday morning, a hand-scribbled message stating that Todd Pottinger from Anchorage had called was promi-
nently placed on top of his desk. Oran was confused. He knew the whales
would connect, but could Pottinger be calling about them already? How
would he know about them? Oran himself had only just seen them the day
before. No matter. Whenever anyone from Anchorage called, it was good
news for Oran Caudle. It meant he had a chance to interact with someone
in the state's media capital, not to mention the opportunity to connect the
North Slope Borough with the rest of the state. He watched Todd read the
Anchorage news every night on TV up in Barrow and was proud to know
him. The two were friendly and had worked together in the past. Part of
Oran's job was to assist outside television stations covering Barrow. While
he was supposed to make sure that whatever coverage he helped outsiders
collect would be favorable to the NSB, there was no real way to do that.
Journalists were journalists; they report what they want. This wasn't just a
theory for Oran; he had been burned enough to know this to be the bitter
truth. Barrow was too far for same-day delivery of the *Anchorage Daily News,*

meaning he didn't know yet that his whales were page-one news in the state's most important city. Still, the instant he saw the message, he knew Pottinger had to have heard about the whales somehow.

One of Oran's biggest frustrations running Barrow's TV studio and production facility was that whenever he thought he had a big story, he had to go begging for his downstate contacts to consider it. The Anchorage and Fairbank TV stations only seemed interested in bad news from the North Slope—making them, in fact, no different at all from TV stations anywhere else. The bad-news stories from the Arctic usually fell in one of a few predictable categories: corruption, crime, alcoholism, bear attacks, or the weather. But for North Slope weather to make news in Alaska? Well, it had to be worse than bad. It had to be awful. And those were not the kind of stories that Oran could push anyway as the seventy-five-degrees-below story was not one local tourism folks were keen to publicize.

Sure enough, when Oran returned the call, Todd wanted to know if anyone had anything new to report on the stranded whales. Whale news was always good news. Pottinger wanted to find out more and hoped Oran could help. Not only did Caudle know all about the whales, he told Pottinger, he had just spent several hours filming them.

"You mean you've got video of them?" Todd Pottinger excitedly asked.

"You betcha," Oran proudly answered, employing the ubiquitous Alaskan idiom.

"Can you wait just one second?" Pottinger asked, conveying his own excitement as he put Caudle on hold. Todd's hunch paid off. Before Oran could collect his thoughts, Pottinger came back on the line asking how soon Oran could arrange a satellite transmission of some of that footage down to Anchorage. He knew Barrow was home to one of Alaska's biggest white elephants, a highly sophisticated satellite-transmission facility that stood just south of the town's runway—the only year-round transportation link in an ambitious billion-dollar state project to use some of the proceeds from the oil-rich 1970s to connect Alaska's rural villages and settlements with the outside world. But like many other ill-conceived projects of that free-spending era, the transmission facility was rarely used. Although the giant satellite dishes constantly received transmissions, they rarely sent much.

Oran told Todd he wasn't sure the "send" mode of the expensive system even worked. Caudle couldn't recall ever having used it. To him it seemed like a fixture misplaced from a different decade in the frozen tundra. Todd urged him to get an answer back to him as quickly as possible. In the meantime, Pottinger adjusted KTUU's satellite dish in Anchorage so it could receive a transmission from Barrow, should one be sent. Todd didn't have time to wait for Oran to call back. If he wanted to try to get some footage for that night's newscast with time to edit it, Pottinger needed to book thirty minutes on the satellite immediately. He called Alascom, the telecommunications company that owned the $100-million Aurora I satellite launched in October 1982. Aurora I orbited 22,500 miles above the Earth connecting the once isolated forty-ninth state with the rest of the world by telephone, radio, and television.

Pottinger scheduled the feed for Thursday, October 13, 1988, at 1:30 P.M., Alaska Standard Time. On behalf of his Anchorage station, KTUU, Pottinger agreed to the $500 satellite time fee whether or not Caudle could figure out how to transmit by then. Meanwhile, Oran Caudle sent his only technician back to the transmission shed to see if he could tune in the video test pattern Oran sent him from his studio to the transmission complex outside the NSB building complex. On the very first try—without any tweaking—the test pattern came in perfectly. Oran called Pottinger to tell him that things seemed all set.

"Oh, by the way," Todd mentioned matter-of-factly before hanging up, "KING-TV in Seattle wants to downlink the feed for their news." The Aurora I satellite was parked in geosynchronous Earth orbit 22,500 miles above the north Pacific—making Seattle the only city in the Lower 48 that was able to "see" the Aurora I. This meant that whenever someone in Alaska wanted to transmit or receive a signal from beyond the Pacific Northwest "gateway," the signal had to be transferred—almost always in Seattle—to a different satellite. This was called "looping." Even though looping added 45,000 miles to a picture's journey, traveling at just below the 186,000 miles per second speed of light, this detour took less than half a second.

By the time all the arrangements were made, it was 11 A.M., leaving Oran Caudle only two hours to reduce the hours of whale footage shot yesterday down to a twenty-minute satellite-ready package. For a network news producer who did this kind of thing every day this would have been no big deal. But Oran Caudle was not a network news producer. He did not do this every day. To him it was a very big deal indeed.

A sudden fear seized Caudle. Could he do it? The footage he shot for local Barrow television was going not only to Anchorage, but also down to Seattle. He always wanted to work with real news professionals. Now he was getting a chance. Oran locked himself in the edit suite where he frantically fast-forwarded through two-and-a-half hours of videotape, screening it for the best shots.

The phone rang. It was Todd. He had called back to reassure Oran. When they last spoke, he had sensed Oran to be a bit on the nervous side. Todd told him to relax. No need to make every edit perfect, he said. That was a job for KTUU's editors.

The task, when completed at 12:15 P.M., did not in hindsight appear so daunting. Now, Caudle needed step-by-step instructions on what to do next. He called Todd, who told him to put the edited cassette into the tape machine. Caudle waited for a pattern of color bars to appear on his screen accompanied by the familiar sound of the test tone. When it came through, he was looking at the picture coming back to him in Barrow from the Aurora I. Everything seemed to be working.

Todd Pottinger's report that he saw the same thing at the same time on his monitor down in Anchorage confirmed that all systems were go. Patiently, Pottinger talked Oran through his first live television transmission. "Whenever you're ready," Todd said, "just hit the Play button and we're in business." Todd couldn't believe how good the video was. The instant he saw the first shots of the whales, he knew this would be a big television story. He just had no idea how big.

Minutes later, KING-TV in Seattle called to tell Oran that NBC News was rushing to arrange an immediate transmission of Oran's footage to New York. Something about Tom Brokaw wanting to run it on the *NBC Nightly News.* At their boss' suggestion, Brokaw's producers were always looking for a unique, visually appealing story to end the show. When the three trapped whales came up during Thursday morning's conference call, NBC News bureau chiefs readily agreed with the Los Angeles bureau that if the video was any good, the whales might make a good "kicker," TV slang for the story that ends each newscast.

Oran could hardly believe what he was hearing: His story on *NBC Nightly News?* He was just glad Todd didn't pass on that bit of news before they finished transmitting. He was already a nervous wreck. Now he was a speechless nervous wreck. It wasn't so long ago that Caudle was covering local beauty pageants back in Commerce, Texas.

Thursday, October 16, 1988, at 12:30 P.M. Alaska Standard Time, the three frightened whales still concerned only a handful of people in a small Eskimo town straddling the top of the world. Hours later, 15 million Americans saw them for the first time. (Back in 1988, people actually watched the *NBC Nightly News.*) They watched as the whales gasped for air. It was a sudden and unexpected diversion from the day's big news: the closing weeks of the 1988 presidential campaign between Republican Vice President George H. W. Bush and Democrat Massachusetts Governor Michael Dukakis.

The moment the first image of a stranded whale appeared on a television screen at KING-TV in Seattle, no one could have imagined that days later, America would turn its attention away from its great quadrennial event and direct it instead toward the nonevent of three California gray whales trapped in frozen waters off the continent's northernmost point.

But for those assigned to cover the story, it was even harder to prepare for the world they would soon enter, the world of Barrow, Alaska—a world like no other.

3

The Eskimos: 25,000 Years
Below Zero Degrees

In 1826, an Arctic explorer named Thomas Elson took one of history's great adventures. One day, while exploring Alaska's northern coast, Elson took a step 25,000 years back in time. He stumbled upon a string of prehistoric Eskimo hunting settlements along the edge of the world's northernmost periphery. What Elson did not know at the time was that he had discovered evidence of a people whose very existence defied human logic. These people not only managed to survive longer than any other known civilization, but they did so in the world's harshest known environment, one where life itself seemed a miracle.

Although the natives called their home Utqiagviq, Elson named it Barrow, after a British patron of Arctic expeditions. For 25,000 years, these nomadic tribes scattered throughout both Alaska's coast and interior evolved in complete isolation. Their Inupiat language and their unique culture seemed based upon a single primary influence: the whale. The whale provided not only food, but heat, shelter and spiritual moorings. The whale was more than a food source to these ancient people. It was more than a creature. It was to them a spirit, its capture a gift. What other visible source could provide the Eskimo with everything they needed to survive?

Whale meat was the perfect food source. It was so rich with vitamins and minerals that those who consumed it seemed immune to nutritional diseases that ravaged others. It provided a high concentration of vitamin D, a vital nutrient most people got from the sun, a source never strong enough to deliver amounts necessary for survival in the high Arctic. The meat from the bowhead whale had the highest fat concentration of any known natural food source, yet heart disease seemed to be unknown. The pre-Modern Inupiat Eskimos ate no fruits, vegetables, or grains, yet their diet contained as much fiber as any other.

They lived in the world's most unforgiving climate where even the most prepared often die when exposed to it. Before their introduction to non-Eskimo peoples, ways, and pathogens, local records seemed to indicate that Inupiat lived long and healthy lives. Time would prove the Eskimos to be most fragile. So long removed from contact with other peoples, the Inupiat Eskimo was defenseless against diseases carried by those now entering the Eskimo world. Like most other native peoples in North America, the Eskimos had no way to prepare for or to protect themselves against the arrival of the nineteenth century.

Thomas Elson's first visit lasted but a few days, but it would forever change the Inupiat people. Romantics, undoubtedly white and who lived far away, would mourn visits like Elson's as being unmitigated disasters—that each new outside influence would accelerate decline and leave one of the world's oldest civilizations vulnerable to the future's risks but also anxious to partake of its opportunities.

At first, visits from the outside were few and far between, but like change everywhere else, when it landed on the shores of Utqiagviq, it could not be stopped. It could, however, be managed. And it was: sometimes it was managed well, other times not so well. Local Inuit civilization didn't start its visible "decline" until several decades after Elson's first visit, but since no one from the outside really had a good sense what life was really like before the explorer's arrival, the benchmarks for measuring decline could only start from the early nineteenth century.

Whaling was America's first great global industry. The explosion of commercial whaling in the eighteenth and nineteenth centuries was no cheap trick, changing and shaping the development of the young United States like no other single industry. Whaling ships were state of the art, and played a central role in America's war of independence. Whalers provided products that profoundly improved the lives of everyday Americans, generating the huge capital required to fuel America's burgeoning Industrial Revolution.

The environmental narrative, increasingly accepted as the only narrative, accepts almost as a given that all our modern ailments derive from the changes spawned by the Industrial Revolution, namely the move from water to coal as the economy's primary source of fuel. But like most stories, this one has two sides, and in this story, equating the bad with the good is being generous to the bad. The benefits of industrialization far outweighed its costs and not just to humans but also to the environment. The Industrial Revolution's success was in no case more vivid than the story of the whale itself.

The Industrial Revolution saw both the expansion of commercial whaling and also the end of commercial whaling. In nearly destroying the species, the Industrial Revolution paved the way for whales not just to recover but to flourish as never before. When the Industrial Revolution started in the late eighteenth century whales were to humans what they had always been: an animal hunted for its food, its fuel, and the countless other products developed over the centuries. The whale's oil came from the blubber that sheathed its body, with the oil of each whale species varying in both quality and use.

The most prized of all whale oils was that found in the nose of the sperm whale used to make what experts even today contend were the finest candles and perfumes ever made. Whale parts were used to make everything from fertilizers to fishing rods and umbrellas to piano keys. But by the closing days of the Industrial Revolution, the first third of the twentieth century, the great mammals had become something entirely new to humanity—a magnificent and endangered creature to be protected and enjoyed.

While whaling was a major industry in the nineteenth century, and the United States was the preeminent whaling nation, the industry was so competitive it was never particularly profitable for those actually in it. Even as prices for whale products rose, profit margins seemed always to fall. By the middle of the 1800s, one out of ten whaling ships failed each year. But no matter how much trouble the industry had eking out its own share, they never lacked demand for their products. That demand reached such extraordinary heights that the richest New England whaling companies plowed millions of dollars into new ships that could spend years at sea looking for whales in waters stretching to the farthest corners of the globe.

By the second half of the nineteenth century, commercial whaling had become the world's first major global industry and it was dominated by the United States. From heating oil to cosmetic products, the whale was a veritable gold mine to any group of men intrepid enough to hunt and kill one. Giant fleets of whaling vessels incorporating then state-of-the-art seafaring technology plied the high seas in search of fortunes for captain and crew. They enriched the New England towns which they built, housed, and maintained these great fleets.

The whales' last great sanctuary was under attack almost as fast as the sleek new vessels could make it up Alaska's uncharted coast. Its waters were the richest yet. They proved so fertile, in fact, that some companies established whaling stations along isolated stretches of Alaska's northern coast to service their fleets with fresh food and fuel. These stations would serve as the first permanent inroad into Eskimo life. The isolated depots quickly grew in importance to natives and to whalers. For the first time, the Eskimos began to trade for goods.

The whalers introduced the Eskimos to unheard-of luxuries like wood and textiles. The white man quickly learned the Eskimos' strengths and weaknesses. Their strength was their uncanny ability to survive in the Arctic. Their weakness could be summed up in one word: alcohol. The damage was both instant and catastrophic. The white man was destroying not only the great whales, but the people who depended on them.

Almost immediately after the whalers arrived, Eskimos contracted alien diseases and died from them. Early on, it was not unusual for hundreds to die of disease every year. Scores of Eskimos went to work for the whaling crews anxious to exploit their skills. Countless others were murdered by competing whalers—not because they were Inuit but because they helped competitors.

We have to feel guilty about something if we are going to count ourselves among the modern sophisticates, don't we? Surely, we must atone for one tragedy or another at all times—be it colonialism, trans fats, slavery, or secondhand smoke. So why not whales? Public confessions of guilt are well and good but guilt about the past without worry for the future makes the guilt offering incomplete. Thus public-issue worrying is tantamount to flaunting moral virtue. Besides, worrying works; it edifies and ennobles the worrier. Not to mention that worrying is both easier and cheaper than actually doing something.

Even though more whales were now being hunted due to surging global demand, because the Eskimos were catching fewer themselves, more started dying from starvation, although no one has real or reliable numbers. Too many of their able-bodied hunters were too drunk to hunt. To make matters worse, the town's anxious elders, unsure how to make their way in this new and unfamiliar world of enterprise and barter, offered to give American whalers the servitude of their best whalers in exchange for molasses to make liquor.

In less than a generation, the long self-sustaining Eskimo community Thomas Elson discovered had been devastated. The changes came too fast for too many to adjust to. In less than two decades, both the Eskimos and the whales had been nearly wiped out. But one thing that had not yet changed was the Eskimos' dependence upon the whale.

The discovery and commercialization of crude oil that ended large-scale commercial whaling did not arrive until the first third of the twentieth century; too late to prevent much of the dislocation that devastated Alaska's native populations. Barrow plunged into abject poverty—or so the narrative went. "Facts are stubborn things," famously said John Adams, and there were just not enough facts about Barrow before time arrived to sustain any of the before-and-after poverty statistics. After all, the portrait of nineteenth-century Britain drawn by Charles Dickens is one of overcrowding, squalor, and grinding poverty. But where is the image of what came before Dickens?

Why was London so crowded? Did the untold hordes flock to such a crowded, poor, and filthy place in order to make their lives still more miserable? Or did they come because they thought conditions we now think of as appalling, would be in fact better than those they left? So, probably, it went with Barrow. No matter how you slice it, Barrow's population tripled in a century and a half after its discovery. The invisible living conditions before Elson were likely much worse than the poor but visible conditions seen after him.

To survive, the Eskimos tried to resume their subsistence hunting ways. But the whales and the skills to capture them had atrophied. Barrow listed, even though its population continued to climb. It remained un-known to all but a handful of missionaries and white traders until shortly after World War II. The cold war gave Barrow and its location a sudden burst of strategic importance. By the early 1950s, Barrow's northern pe-riphery was the perfect site for the U.S. Air Force to build its Distant Early Warning Line (DEW Line) radar station to alert against Soviet bombers flying overhead on their way to drop nuclear bombs on the United States or Canadian mainland.

At its peak in the mid to late 1950s, DEW Line employed hundreds of locals before being made obsolete in the 1960s by the intercontinental bal-listic missile that flew too high and too fast to stop. The rest of the town continued their age-old hunt for bowhead whales, whose population was recovering from the days of unrestricted commercial whaling.

On February 18, 1968, Barrow's fortunes changed again. After $125 million of fruitless drilling on the tundra 270 miles east of Barrow at a desolate place called Prudhoe Bay, the Atlantic Richfield Company (ARCO) finally struck what was the then the single largest single oil and natural gas field ever found. Geologists in the late 1960s' estimated there might be 15 billion barrels of oil and up to 26 trillion cubic feet of natural gas just two miles beneath the surface. To see just how far the science of oil and gas drilling has advanced since then, projections published by the U.S. Geological Survey (USGS) in 2009 estimates that the Barrow/North Slope coast contains 83 billion barrels of oil and 1,600 trillion cubic feet of natural gas in recoverable untapped reserves.

The Eskimo always thought that the black liquid they called Uqsruq that oozed from the surface of their frozen land was a poison of an angry spirit, not that different to what medieval Arabs thought oozed from their lands. They watched as Uqsruq killed people, strong birds, and mighty animals. But the white man seemed to find great value in it. Soon the Inuit would see the benefits and want his share of them. So anxious were outsid-ers to use this plentiful and powerful resource, they would commit the largest private capital investment up to its time—$20 billion—to designing and building the massive infrastructure needed to safely and efficiently get the oil out of the ground and through 825 miles of pipeline stretched across some of the world's most treacherous terrain and onto super mas-sive supertankers at the Southeastern Alaskan port city of Valdez waiting to transport it around the world to be refined into gasoline to power our cars, trucks, and airplanes we rely on to get us where we need to go.

The fields at Prudhoe Bay would provide, at their peak in the mid-1980s, nearly a quarter of all the oil consumed in the United States, or nearly 2.2 million barrels of oil per day. Alaska's three-dollars-per-barrel tax on state-produced crude generated enough revenue to fund 90 percent of Alaska's state government. Alaskans of all kinds seemed only too delighted. Good thing for Alaskans that the oil companies were as greedy as they were. The state taxes paid on their profits were so great, that Alaskans themselves paid no state sales, property, or income taxes. By the late 1980s, Alaska was not only America's least taxed state, it was also its fastest growing state. A coincidence?

By 2011, just two North Slope oil fields, Prudhoe Bay and Kuparuk, had delivered more than 16 billion barrels of high quality American produced oil to the Lower 48. But by 2011, production had declined by nearly two-thirds, causing the oil pushed through the pipeline to travel much more slowly and at lower pressures, dramatically increasing the problems of clogging and rapid freezing, threatening the long-term viability of the multibillion dollar pipeline—precisely as environmentalists had been hoping for all along. If the pipeline is forced to close, Alaska laws require that it be dismantled.

As productive as Prudhoe Bay and Kuparuk have been, the potential of these fields is dwarfed by untapped resources lying below federal land nearby. To the west sits the 23-million-acre Alaska National Petroleum Reserve, established back in the 1920s by President Warren G. Harding, where recent surveys estimate 15 billion barrels of easily recoverable oil. Just east, on only two thousand of the 19-million-acre Arctic National Wildlife Refuge (ANWR), lies another 16 billion barrels of recoverable oil. Look north out to the vast sea and there are another 30 billion barrels of oil equivalent—twice as much oil as forty years worth of oil produced at Prudhoe Bay.

Yet there the oil sits. Keeping ANWR off limits has been an environmental cause célèbre for decades. While filing suit against every attempt to open up new federal or state lands is the newer tactic, it took almost twenty years until additional lease sales in the Chukchi Sea could even get provisional approval in 2008. But even then, once the rights to nearly three million new acres were auctioned off, environmental groups filed suit to prevent the deal, which a judge halted in July 2010.

By 2010, it took more than thirty separate permits from various federal and state agencies before one could even start exploratory drilling in Alaska. This caused companies like Shell Oil, that had spent years running the regulatory gauntlet, to close up shop in Alaska altogether. Even President Barack Obama's approval of new lease sales in Alaska's National Petroleum Reserve in 2011—proposed in response to record high gas prices—has fallen on deaf ears inside his own Army Corps of Engineers, which denied ConocoPhillips's request to drill in an area it already owns inside the Petroleum Reserve.

Few people in the Lower 48 knew much about their fellow countrymen settling America's last, harshest, and potentially richest frontier. America's forty-ninth state was a giant paradox: a land of contrasts, contradictions, and immeasurable beauty. Unlike other Americans, late-twentieth-century Alaskans continued to think of themselves and their great land as a separate, distinct place—almost its own country. Alaskans called people who lived elsewhere "outsiders." Any place outside the expansive borders of America's biggest state was referred to as "The Outside." Separated from the Lower 48 by thousands of miles, Alaskans were also separated by an ethic long lost down south: the ethic of nation building.

What a place it was. At more than half a million square miles, Alaska was one-fifth the size of the continental United States; nearly as big as Western Europe. Alaska spanned two continents and three distinct climatic zones. Reaching deep into Asia, Alaska held the distinction of being both America's eastern- and westernmost state. Seventeen of North America's twenty highest mountains were in Alaska, as were more than 100,000 glaciers. Alaska encompassed an island chain—the Aleutians—that was longer than the continental United States was wide. Despite being America's least settled territory, Alaska, by virtue of being the first stop off the primordial Asian land-bridge, was also America's first settled territory.

By 1988, less than thirty years after its admission as America's forty-ninth state, Alaska was America's least densely populated state: less than one person per square mile, one of the world's lowest man-to-land ratios. In the late 1980s, Alaskan caribou outnumbered Alaskan humans ten to one. By 2010, the ratio jumped to twelve to one.

While Alaska had the highest per capita income of any state, Alaskans could hardly have been called the richest Americans because Alaska also had the highest cost of living. And then there was the weather. Always the weather. Outsiders weren't the only ones who considered life in Alaska brutal, backward, and harsh. So, too, did Alaskans; which is why many of them loved it. Nearly as many Alaskans had private pilot licenses as they did driving licenses. Still more lived quite happily—so they said—without plumbing or electricity. It was the rugged spirit of adventure that drew many to the Last Frontier; economic opportunity drew more.

But of all the adjectives used over the centuries to describe America's "last frontier," the one that has kept most of its relevance over that time is remote." The state had only one major road, the two-lane George Parks Highway connecting Anchorage and Fairbanks, which was regularly closed in winter, a nine-month season in Alaska. Half the state's population lived outside those two cities, meaning the only way they could get around was by air, sea, or dogsled. In an age of space shuttles and instant satellite communications, Alaska still remained remarkably uncharted. In 1988, less than one-twentieth of 1 percent of Alaska's magnificent terrain had ever even been visited.

For the rest of the country, Alaska meant cold and ice, and for good reason. Outsiders knew Alaska was big, but few had any idea of how big or how remote it really was. Outsiders knew that Alaska was home to exotic creatures like polar bears and moose, but few understood both the fragility and resiliency of its magnificent ecosystem until the infamous March 1989 spill of the *Exxon Valdez* that devastated southeastern Alaska's Prince William Sound. Fortunately, the dire predictions of the most alarmist of environmentalists did not come to pass. The most studied environmental disaster of all time revealed that species were not wiped out; that the biologically diverse Prince William Sound did not become a dead zone. The region, thought to be so fragile, in fact revealed itself to be remarkably resilient. It recovered far faster and much more vibrantly than anyone thought possible—not that disgorging half a million gallons of tar-thick crude oil in a sensitive and isolated marine rich environment is ever recommended.

But in a very real sense, it was environmental activism that caused the *Exxon Valdez* disaster. If it were up to the oil industry, there never would have been a ship called the *Exxon Valdez* in the first place. The oil industry wants to transport their crude by pipeline where and whenever possible because pipelines are cheaper, safer, and much easier to control. A consortium of Alaska drillers wanted to extend the Trans-Alaska Pipeline across Canada and down into the Lower 48. They were prevented from doing so by opponents who said that a pipeline would be too environmentally destructive. But as everyone found out in 1989 (and forgot quickly thereafter), supertankers are much more environmentally dangerous and disruptive than overland pipelines. Oil spills on land are infinitely easier to stop, contain, and clean up than those at sea.

Similar points were made following the 2010 deadly blowout of BP's Deepwater Horizon rig in the Gulf of Mexico. Why are companies like BP risking billions of dollars to drill so far out to sea and in waters so deep? Because environmentalists have succeeded in locking up available and accessible oil resources closer to shore not to mention dry land. Surely the oil companies would prefer to spend fifteen dollars to extract a barrel for oil in shallow waters, not to mention five dollars per barrel it costs on land, rather than the seventy dollars or more it costs to extract each barrel from deepwater wells.

If the BP disaster was caused by America's increasing reliance on foreign oil, then why have we locked up our domestic oil resources on land and in shallow waters in the Lower 48 and Alaska? The world's largest known oil shale deposit, the Green River Formation, lies under huge swaths of Colorado, Utah, and Wyoming. It is estimated to hold an astonishing 1.8 trillion barrels of recoverable oil; every drop of which is off limits.

Even the most alarmist projections about the BP disaster creating massive "aquatic dead zones"—which thankfully did not come to pass—paled next to supermassive aquatic dead zones that really do exist in the Gulf, created not by oil companies but by environmentalist and agribusiness demands that government mandate huge biofuel and ethanol production, which has dramatically accelerated corn farming, the colossal agricultural runoff of which is conveyed to the Gulf by the Mississippi River system.

Will the Gulf be cleaner after American oil companies are banned from drilling there? We can't ban Russia, China, Venezuela, or even Cuba from drilling in international waters—after all, we don't "own" the Gulf—which all four nations are now busy doing, less than one hundred miles from

Florida. Will Chinese oil companies drill as safely as the American oil companies they would replace? Will Russian firms hire American workers? If so, will they pay their workers U.S. wages and protect them according to U.S. standards? Will Cuban oil rigs lessen America's dependence upon foreign oil?

One of the great ironies of the modern energy universe is that while governments around the world have dumped hundreds of billions of dollars into developing new "green" energies like wind, solar, and biofuel, nearly all the significant technology and production breakthroughs have occurred in the old-fashioned oil and gas industries. Everything from hydraulic fracturing that opens up huge new resources in shale to horizontal drilling that gets more oil from existing wells to new seismic technologies—they all mean we can open up literally oceans of untapped oil and gas.

If Outsiders knew anything about the Alaskan Arctic, most of it had to do with its native Inuit inhabitants—known commonly as Eskimos. For even the best educated, the history of the Inupiat Eskimo was a blank page. It wasn't much more than that to the Inupiats themselves. Most of what Outsiders thought they knew about the native Arctic people's way of life was incomplete, or even wrong.

Alaska's Eskimos never lived in igloos; they kiss just like everybody else, and they liked the accoutrements of the modern world. Few Americans were that familiar with Eskimo culture or history. They can hardly be blamed; there wasn't much recorded history to know. Few knew then or now that on a cash basis, Alaska's North Slope people were the richest in America. Nor did they know the reason why: oil. Before they realized its far-reaching potential to dramatically improve the quality and comfort of their lives, Inupiats were naturally uncertain about the impact oil development would have on their lives.

Inupiats wondered what impact it would have on their hard scrabble subsistence way of life. They found out with the passage of the 1971 Alaska Native Claims Settlement Act (ANCSA). The act was the first and last settlement between the United States government and the native peoples of Alaska for all the land and rights "usurped" or otherwise acquired by the federal or state government since the U.S. acquired Alaska from Russia in 1867 for $7.2 million—less than three cents an acre. The Alaska Native Claims Settlement Act awarded the natives a billion dollars and 45 million acres of Alaska's choicest land. The act gave Alaska's North Slope Eskimos power to tax their land, which just happened to sit atop trillions of dollars worth of oil and gas. Suddenly, Barrow was awash in cash.

For a village that had spent the previous few decades developing itself using whale meat as its primary means of exchange, Barrow's sudden petroleum based wealth brought enormous and mostly positive change. Not only were Barrow's elders not yet wise to the ways of managing money, most of them rarely used it. Illiterate subsistence whalers who didn't speak English were suddenly charged with figuring out how to manage multibillion-dollar portfolios. Inupiat culture faced a new but welcome challenge: progress.

Suddenly Barrow was not a forlorn frozen wasteland. It was the newest open gate to American opportunity on the Last Frontier. The newcomers descended on Barrow and reconstructed it in their own image. They came to build, manage, and profit from the remarkable societal transformation taking place. When the snow settled, Barrow had a new lifeline, a 7,000-foot jumbo-jet-ready commercial runway that connected the town with an Outside anxious to get in. Modern Barrow sprang up around the runway's southern edge.

The Arctic had a new and thriving bird: the construction crane. Modern prefab houses flown in from the Outside were assembled next to tiny driftwood hovels. Pathways were widened, sprinkled with gravel, and called streets. Several of them were laid out on tundra near the airport. For eleven months of the year they were frozen, snow-covered, and navigable. But in the short weeks of summer, when the top few inches of the 1,200-foot-thick permafrost melted with nowhere for the standing waters to go, Barrow's five miles of roadway were long thought impassable rivers of mud. Then a clever Eskimo mounted an old abandoned set of DC-3 aircraft tires on his pickup truck. The vehicle created a terrible mess, but the Eskimo got where he was going.

Barrow grew more in the twenty years since the oil discovery than it ever had. Its population increased about threefold to around three thousand. Although it was always the Alaskan Arctic's largest town, Barrow's sudden wealth put it on the fast track to veritable cosmopolitanism. It brought get-rich-quick schemers, wonderlust start-agains, real entrepreneurs, and plenty of Inuits from surrounding (a 1,000-square-mile radius) smaller Arctic villages anxious to experience life in the big city.

But having said all that, even with its Arctic-inflated two-billion-dollars' worth of oil-financed growth, Barrow in 1988 was still not a whole lot more than a tiny outpost at the top of the world. On foot, depending on the weather, the village was around five minutes wide by nine minutes long. The colder the temperature, the smaller the town got. People walk faster in the cold. But with all their newfound wealth, Barrowans proved themselves to be very much like the rest of us—they grew more sedentary. As a result, industries not thought needed in town emerged. In a town as small as Barrow, taxis did a booming business. There were at least three companies that each charged about twenty-five dollars for the five-hundred-yard ride from the bottom of the town to its top: the Top of the World Hotel. Eighty hotel rooms sprang up to accommodate an increasing number of business travelers looking to hawk their wares to nouveau riche Eskimos.

Barrowans didn't blanch at spending $200 million to build an all-glass, three-story office building, reputedly the most expensive per square foot building in the world. Nor did they balk at buying their children the world's most expensive school, but the $80 million price tag attached to Barrow High School included a modern basketball arena and the Arctic's only swimming pool—indoor, of course.

Not only was Barrow on the fast track, it could eat fast food on the way. Arctic Pizza delivered for just fifty dollars a pie. A cheap breakfast at Pepe's North of the Border Mexican restaurant could be had for as little as twenty bucks, and one even had a choice of Chinese. Good and bad. On Wednesday nights, Sam & Lee's offered egg roll specials for just eleven dollars. An extensive gas main network pumped the heating oil into dwellings of all kinds; rickety shacks to well-groomed homes. Women no longer needed to risk their lives collecting driftwood for heating from the frozen ocean shore. Virtually every home had telephones and electricity.

Even indoor plumbing was available, albeit at a nominal charge of $400,000 per hookup. Nimble ski machines whined past unemployed sled dogs. Barrow's high-tech television studio and satellite transmission and reception facility piped the world into the most modest Eskimo abode. Sonny Crockett and his fellow vice-fighting cops were as popular in snowbound Barrow as he was in his pastel-colored Miami.

Caribou, which migrated through Barrow backyards by the hundreds of thousands, could now be killed during commercial TV breaks just by sticking a rifle out the kitchen window. Their carcasses, dressed and hung frozen outside in the winter, could be quickly defrosted in Barrow's ubiquitous modern appliance: the microwave oven. In a place where the summer's highest temperature rarely rose above freezing, instant defrosting became a sudden necessity.

In less than a decade, Barrow went from being one of the poorest towns in North America to one of its richest. In fact, by 1988, measured in real dollars, Barrow had the highest per capita income of any city on Earth. Royalty payments from the North Slope oil amounted to more than $90,000 per person per year. But so inimical was this region to even the most basic elements of modern life that it took the world's highest per capita income to support a lifestyle the U.S. government still classified as impoverished.

Barrow was not only the world's richest poor town, it was also its most expensive. The one grocery store was as well stocked as any grocery in Alaska, but every item on the shelves was flown in from Anchorage or Fairbanks, where prices were high to begin with. By the time groceries reached Barrow, the prices were high enough for families with six-figure incomes in 1988 dollars to easily qualify for food stamps. Fresh milk was six dollars a gallon, corn flakes were seven dollars a box. As long as the price of hamburger hovered near five dollars a pound, subsistence hunting for many remained a necessity. Besides, most Eskimos, at least the older ones, preferred muktuk and caribou steaks to "white man's food," which they considered bland and unwholesome.

Barrow's rapid-fire modernization gave the Eskimos the one commodity they never before had: leisure time. Since the beginning of time, whaling had been the backbone of Eskimo life. Whalers were once society's most important members; now that skill was no longer critical. Seventy percent of Barrow's working age populace depended upon government work programs for their livelihood. The only difference between them and the Soviet laborers who joke, "They pretend to pay us, we pretend to work," was that the minimum wage was eighteen dollars an hour and the workers didn't even have to pretend.

Contact with Western society remained limited until the discovery of oil in the Alaskan Arctic. Suddenly, in the late 1960s, the Eskimos confronted wrenching change as they were forced to become part of American society. Barrow's sudden material wealth resulted in a monumental cultural meltdown.

The Eskimos were collapsing under the weight of their own riches. The elders, who embodied Eskimo culture, were shunted aside by Barrow's new masters. Their talents no longer necessary for their people's survival, many of the Eskimo elite fell into despair.

Alcohol, already a severe problem, now impacted everyone, from the third of the town that were directly alcohol dependent, to the two-thirds who lived with them. The problems related to this scourge were Barrow's cross to carry into the twenty-first century. The primary difference between the late twentieth century and the period following the decline of commercial whaling was that Barrow's survival was no longer physical—it was spiritual and social.

Barrow voters overwhelmingly adopted a 1986 referendum outlawing the sale, consumption, and even possession of alcoholic beverages. The very people consumed with alcohol voted to ban it. It instantly became the most widely evaded law in town. Consumption actually went up, not down. Enforcement was impossible because everyone continued to drink. Bootleggers thrived. They were so confident they would not get caught, they had listed phone numbers and plastered advertisements across town. Before the media arrived to jack up the price, a case of beer or a fifth of cheap whiskey could be had for as little as one hundred dollars.

The local Eskimos of Barrow didn't have many positive local models to draw upon in the 1980s. Their town was so ravaged by alcohol and drugs it seemed unfazed by the regular drunken rages of its then mayor, George Ahmaogak. Just months after the whale rescue in January 1989, he was arrested on an Anchorage street for allegedly assaulting his wife with a metal briefcase after she reportedly refused to accompany him to another bar. News of his arrest ran on the front page of the *Anchorage Daily News*. No charges were ever filed.

But news of this kind was sadly neither new nor news to the people of Barrow. The problem was that there was so much bad local news. Barrow was no longer just an isolated Eskimo hamlet on Alaska's northern rim. Its sudden wealth made it a household name across the state, a name synonymous with fantastic and sudden wealth, corruption, and crime. But outside Alaska, Barrow remained on the periphery of America's geography and consciousness.

4

Here Come the Media

Oran Caudle wasted no time spreading the news. Immediately after KING-TV told him they were editing footage for the Thursday, October 13 edition of *NBC Nightly News*, he phoned home. He was so excited he dialed the wrong number twice before finally getting through to his parents back in Texarkana. He could hardly contain himself.

"Hello Mama, you're not going to believe this. I am producing a piece on tonight's *NBC News*. We are going nationwide!" he exclaimed in his North Texas drawl.

Half an hour later, Todd Pottinger called to ask for another favor. "Can you meet our crew at the airport?" Todd asked.

Oran was confused. He didn't understand what Todd meant. "Airport? What airport?"

Todd told Oran that in the last few minutes, NBC News and KTUU decided they wanted their own news crew in Barrow. They booked three seats on the day's last flight to Barrow on MarkAir, a state wide commercial and cargo carrier that served the town. It was scheduled to leave Anchorage at 3:30 P.M.

While Anchorage TV stations occasionally sent television crews to Barrow, plans were usually farther in advance. KTUU had twelve months to prepare for the year's biggest story, the first sunrise on January 21, which ended Barrows' sixty-seven days of darkness. Now, KTUU told Oran that they would be in town in less than three hours and wanted a package ready for that night.

Oran could not understand why Anchorage wanted more footage of the three whales. Oran had just sent them a half an hour of video on the satellite, with hours more yet unscreened. As remarkable as the whales were, Oran couldn't imagine why KTUU had decided to send its own crew so quickly. What could they do that he couldn't? For NBC, the answer was easy. For Oran, it was an unpleasant reminder of where he stood in the network pecking order. While his footage was good, it was not "original," whatever that meant. Of course the problem was not Oran's fault at all. When he was out, the ice was not strong enough to let him get close. The real problem was that they did not know Oran or his facilities well enough to trust that he had the "stuff" to get the job done. NBC was so desperate for someone they thought they could trust, they offered to pay all Anchorage affiliate's KTUU's expenses until the network could get its own crew to Barrow.

KTUU picked Russ Weston, an experienced cameraman who had worked in Barrow before. But as the MarkAir 737 lifted off the Fairbanks runway after a brief stopover, he, like everyone else on the flight still felt an undiminished sense of wonder at the scenery passing beneath. Nothing but virgin magnificent wilderness, endless wilderness. For as far as he could see, forests of spruce and pine sprawled in every direction. There was the gaping winding Yukon River basin, lit by the dimming light of the northland's setting sun. The Yukon was America's longest and greatest river, half again the length of the Mississippi. All this greatness, he thought, untouched by the hand of man.

The farther Weston flew, the terrain below grew sparser and more hostile. The heavily wooded wilderness thinned. As if a line was actually drawn in the earth, the vegetation vanished after crossing the imaginary Arctic Circle at sixty-seven degrees north latitude. Such extreme latitudes were more than even the hardiest trees could bear. Then, out of the white void emerged the stark pristine magnificence of the Brooks Mountain Range that formed the Arctic's impregnable southern boundary. Only a small part of the 10,000-foot peaks that constituted the world's northernmost and least explored mountain range was visible. Its tranquil countenance seemed to belie its creator's desire to keep its uncharted peaks...well, uncharted. Many of those who had explored the dangerous peaks to unlock its hidden treasures never returned.

As the plane began its descent, the wonder of where it would land outweighed Russ's own experience of descending onto a sea of Arctic desolation. No matter how many times he had done so, Weston still thought they might be making an emergency landing on a frozen lake bed in the middle of the tundra. Then, there it was. A 7,000-foot runway built at the edge of the universe.

Looking south as the aircraft taxied to the hangar, Russ saw the same expanse of white he saw from the air. Only the bizarre Buck Rogers look of the North Slope Borough television transmission site interrupted the bleak vision. It was the presence of this site that brought him back to reality. Stepping off the plane, Weston could not believe he had just traveled 1,200 miles without seeing a trace of man. It was sixty degrees colder in Barrow than in Anchorage. He awoke that morning prepared for just another day as an Anchorage television cameraman. The day ended as one of the most remarkable of his life.

Biologists Craig George and Geoff Carroll were driving back to the Wildlife Department after sliding down their quota of greasy thirteen-dollar quarter-pounders at the local Burger Barn when they saw Oran descending the wrought-iron steps of Barrow's city center, the airport hangar. Geoff and Craig were struck by the sight of the two strangers who accompanied him. Their bright ski clothes stood in marked contrast to the drab but warm look of the locals.

Unaware of his own conspicuousness, Geoff stepped on the brakes, bringing his Dodge Caravan to a stop right in the middle of Ahkovak Street, one of Barrow's busiest roadways. Ahkovak Street was crowded not with cars, of which there were few in Barrow, but with ski machines, and even these were infrequent so early in the season.

A car in the Arctic often proved not worth the bother. It needed special heaters to keep the engine from freezing *even as it ran.* The brutal cold destroyed transmissions within weeks, not years. And if the owner ever wanted his car to start in the winter, he had to keep the engine running—sometimes for six straight months.

The fact that Barrow sat atop the world's largest oil field did not mean fuel came cheap. To the contrary, gas cost more in Barrow than anywhere else in America. Once drilled, the oil had to go all the way to Southern California for refinement into gasoline only to be tankered back to Alaska and then flown to Barrow aboard special aircraft. At three dollars a gallon in 1988 (the national average for unleaded was then ninety-five cents), it cost two hundred dollars a week just to keep a car running. Stealing a car wasn't a problem. There was nowhere for a thief to take a stolen car as the town had no roads out of it.

Whereas Geoff was curious to find out who was carrying the television camera, Craig was more interested in the reporter. When they pulled up alongside them, Oran introduced Russ Weston and Julie Hasquet, the KTUU correspondent. After sizing up Russ, they focused on his attractive but obviously uncomfortable companion. She looked as if she had fallen off a spaceship and landed on the wrong planet.

As strange as Barrow looked to her, her designer jeans, bright red ski parka, and blow-dried hair looked every bit as strange to Barrowans. She asked Russ to let her get back on the plane before it left her stranded in Barrow. If she missed it, she would be stuck there for the night. She wondered whether she could handle much more than fifteen minutes in Barrow. She ran to the check-in counter to see if she could still board the plane. She hurriedly climbed the stairs to the plane, thrilled that her short visit to Barrow would not turn into something worse.

When Oran told Geoff and Craig that Russ had come to town because of the whales, Geoff looked knowingly at Craig. Could they both be thinking the same thing? If the whales were news in Anchorage, then the Coast Guard might be more receptive to their request for a ship to break them out. Fifty feet from where they said good-bye, Geoff and Craig's truck vanished in the thick ice fog as it pulled away. The only proof of its proximity could be heard, not seen. Against a blank-white backdrop, the clear sound of the tires crunched crisply upon the snow-packed road. Oran realized he forgot to tell them that the whales were becoming a national news story, but he was reluctant to reveal too much of his excitement to Weston. Caudle tried to pretend as though the arrival of an outside TV crew under direct network auspices was not nearly the big deal he knew it to be.

It was Oran's job to escort outside media. The reason Barrow built the state-of-the-art television production and broadcast center was not only to ensure local's access to the same television programming seen elsewhere but also to improve the town's somewhat grimy image. Barrowans used their broadcast center to paint a portrait that relayed two images: a prospering Arctic community working hard to better itself while taming its hostile surroundings as well as a town with profound social scars that necessitated massive infusions of state aid to keep that model alive.

Helping outside news agencies report on stories from Barrow was one of the NSB television studio's most important functions. Was there anywhere else in the world where a news crew fly in and find a state-of-the-art studio and transmission facility ready for their use—absolutely free. As Oran drove the half mile up Momegana Street past the already frozen and litter strewn cemetery, Russ marveled at Barrow's hard scrabble existence. He followed Oran into the broadcast center. A familiar but incongruous sight took him by surprise.

"Oh, this," Oran remarked. "Welcome aboard the Arctic's only elevator." Before leaving to fetch a cup of coffee, Oran told Russ to feel free to walk around but not to touch any of the equipment—realizing only after he had said it that Russ probably knew the equipment much better than Oran did. It was a habit. Weston seemed not the least fazed.

When Oran returned, Russ asked him where he should stay. With a comforting wave of his left hand, Caudle motioned all would be well as he used his right hand to dial the number of the Top of the World Hotel.

"No problem," said the Colombian woman at the switchboard in her Spanish accent when asked by Caudle if there were any rooms and what they might cost. "A hundred dollars cash per night and that includes running water." When Russ asked Caudle if he could pay with his American Express card, Caudle repeated the question. From the grimace it was clear to Weston he had been rebuked. Barrow was a cash-only town.

In a place where some things, like construction, can cost up to a hundred times more than in the Lower 48, Oran realized the Top of the World was an outright bargain with rates only three times more expensive than those charged for a similar one-and-a-half star roadside motel in the Lower 48. In part, the motel kept costs down because it stood on stilts above the frozen ground. Instead of digging an entire foundation, the construction crew saved millions of dollars by drilling holes just large enough for the stilts. The newly refurbished thirty-five-room Top of the World Hotel was by far the biggest of the three motels in town. North Slope lodging at its finest.

The Top of the World was one of the first businesses to hook up to the $300 million Utilidor municipal water system started in the early 1980s. Because of the arduousness and expense of the project, only about half of Barrow's homes were able to take part in the Arctic miracle of indoor plumbing. It was by far the most expensive and sophisticated water system ever built. Never before had such an ambitious construction project been undertaken in the Arctic. Special graphite pipes carried waste and drinking water thirty feet below the ground in tunnels that could not simply be dug into the ground. They had to be dynamited through the permafrost.

The tunnels were so deep to prevent the permafrost from thawing and the pipes from freezing. If the permafrost did melt, the buildings above it would collapse into a morass of sinking earth. Oran asked Russ if he wanted to join him after the news for some tacos next door at Pepe's North of the Border. Mexican food 320 miles north of the Arctic Circle? Preferring indigestion to starvation, Russ agreed to go along. After Caudle checked Russ in at the hotel, it was nearly time for *NBC Nightly News*. Caudle wasn't about to miss his debut on national television. There was a big television set in the small but tidy lobby of the Top of the World.

It was already a little past six. KTUU tape-delayed the newscast so that it aired at 6:30 P.M. throughout the state. The Aurora I satellite beamed the Anchorage stations to all Alaskan villages as part of the statewide Rural Alaska Television Network, known as RATNET.

Oran went next door to Pepe's to excitedly announce to folks milling about the lobby that Barrow "was going nationwide." As the newscast progressed, more and more people gathered around the set. The program's first and second blocks reported on the presidential campaign. The third segment was devoted to the Middle East, and the strategic arms talks between the U.S. and USSR in Geneva, but nothing yet on the whales. Oran was starting to worry. He sure would be mighty embarrassed if, after all his boasting, the whales didn't make the news.

With Tom Brokaw's words "And finally tonight," Oran Caudle exhaled a giant sigh of relief. Brokaw introduced the video by reading a sentence from the teleprompter. "In Northern Alaska, winter comes early. And for three California gray whales it may have come too early this year." With the words "gray whales," the NBC technical director ordered the technician to "roll tape." Oran's first pictures flashed onto the screen of millions of television sets throughout the country. The audio engineer in the control room of NBC's New York studio turned up the sound of the first whale struggling to breathe in the middle of the frozen Arctic Ocean.

In the few seconds it took for the zoomed-in lens to capture the whale's head coming out of the water and exhaling a lungful of air and water, the three trapped whales were no longer alone in the remote frozen waters off Barrow. They were now national news. Because of the four-hour time difference between the East Coast and Alaska, the stranding was already old news in the Lower 48. Stung by NBC's first blow, every other news agency in the country immediately put reporters on the story. The Top of the World Hotel was immediately deluged with calls from news agencies trying to book rooms for the following night.

Todd Pottinger called Russ to tell him that NBC News had assigned Don Oliver, a veteran correspondent, to come to Barrow to cover the whales. Oliver was regarded by his peers as one of the industry's best reporters. He covered the 1975 fall of Saigon where his furious outbursts earned him the nickname "El Diablo." Oliver's risibility was complemented by the more mild-mannered approach of his sidekick, producer Jerry Hansen. After flying all night and most of the next day from Los Angeles, Oliver, Hansen, and their technical staff of four arrived in Barrow around midday Friday, October 14.

A week to the day after the whales were discovered, an American television crew was walking down the sturdy but loud aluminum steps that would allow them to descend from the elevated airport hanger to plant their feet squarely on the frozen tundra. When the first blast of cold air hit them, they knew they would be in for a rough ride. It wasn't that they left behind what they should have brought, it was that they didn't own what they should have had, nor did they even know how to get it.

When their NBC producers in New York and Los Angeles sent them to Barrow, Hansen and Oliver had no idea how long they would be there or under what conditions they would be forced to operate. There was nothing unusual about that. Such was life for the vagabond television news fraternity. Their job required them to be ready to go anywhere, anytime. More often than not, the "anywhere" was someplace strange, often violent and frequently remote, and the "anytime" was now.

After more than twenty-five years in the business, Oliver kept learning that just when he thought he had covered about all the kinds of stories there were to cover, another one would come his way to prove him wrong. As he gazed out at his surreal surroundings, Oliver instantly knew he was in for another unprecedented adventure.

Unlike Russ who had worked in Barrow before, the NBC crew assumed that there would be no broadcast facilities on site. So they brought virtually an entire TV station of their own packed tightly into twelve large and heavy metal cases. The cases were filled with cameras, waveform monitors, vectorscopes, batteries, cables, editing equipment, and camera heating pads.

But buried in the safest catacomb was the Los Angeles bureau's newest piece of equipment. They had been waiting for it for years. Only when both protagonists in the eight-year-long slaughter known as the Iran-Iraq War started attacking unarmed oil tankers in the Persian Gulf in late 1988 did the NBC Bahrain bureau agree to transfer their portable $17,000 gyrostabilizer back to the states.

Attached to the outside of a camera, it allowed steady pictures to be taken from a flying helicopter. When Oran Caudle casually pulled out his own gyrostabilizer the next day, Don Oliver nearly fell out of the open-doored chopper. Barrow's gyrostabilizer was even more sophisticated than the one Oliver liked to brag about.

Before leaving Los Angeles, the producer Jerry Hansen checked to see that someone at the assignment desk would take care to assure accommodations and ground support were arranged once they arrived in Barrow. Hansen had one request. He wanted his own room. Don Oliver may have been a great reporter, but his snoring was too much to bear. Luckily they were the first to Barrow; had they arrived any later, Hansen would have been forced to use the snoreproof earplugs he packed just in case. The town's eighty hotel rooms were going quickly. To allow for late-arriving competitors and the rising value of a warm bed, the hotel started renting beds, as opposed to rooms.

This wasn't the first time NBC News reported from the Arctic. But they had never before done it with so little preparation. As he was walking out the door of his Burbank, California, office Jerry glanced up at the map on his wall. Just where was this place Barrow? As he squinted to better familiarize himself with the little speck on his map it finally started to sink in. Barrow really was at the top of the world. When he stepped off the plane, a blast of Arctic air hit him square in the face with the force of unexpected exhilaration. Barrow was the top of the world and he was here.

Even though there were only four miles of total road in the town, Jerry, Don, and the rest of the crew still needed a way to get themselves and their heavy gear around Barrow. To Hansen, the answer was obvious enough: rent a car. He thumbed through the seven-page Barrow telephone directory several times before he finally realized that there were no rental cars. The hotel manager suggested Hansen call the folks over at the North Slope Borough, the local government. The NSB owned most of the town's vehicles. If anybody had extras, it would be the NSB.

When word spread through the new all glass NSB building that NBC News was in town, everyone just assumed they were in town to cover the North Slope Mayor's Conference, then taking place in Barrow. But that seemed odd. Who cared about that? Locals were even more taken aback when Hansen told them that, in fact, he and his crew were in town to cover the stranding of the three whales.

"The whales?" one astonished Eskimo asked, "What whales? What is so newsworthy about whales?" "I don't know," Hansen answered. "People just love them." The man at the NSB gave Hansen a list of names of people who might have cars to rent. Not many people in Barrow may have heard the word "chutzpah" before, but they sure seemed to have it.

The first local he talked to wanted a thousand dollars a day for a 1975 Chevy Suburban. Hansen burst out laughing...but the last laugh was on him. The best deal he could find was with a hooded character who wore sunglasses at the NSB, who agreed to rent him three old pickups for just six hundred dollars a day each. The ruddy-faced owner said he couldn't remember when he came to Barrow or exactly why, but after meeting the likes of Jerry Hansen who was willing to pay six hundred dollars a day in cash for a broken-down heap, he didn't regret his decision.

No one anywhere else would have paid half that amount to buy them. In between his grimy exhalations of cigarette smoke, the man gave Hansen the keys and told him never to drive on the ocean—as if that occurred to Hansen—and never ever to turn the car off.

"Never turn the car off?" asked Hansen. "When is this dream going to end," he inquired in a failed attempt at shock himself back to reality. That's when the white-haired Hansen remembered the surreal sight of a line of empty parked pickup trucks, all with their motors running as he walked out of the airport terminal.

The NBC Burbank desk asked Russ Weston to stay an extra day to produce the Friday story for *NBC Nightly News*. Weston jumped at the chance. Producing a story for the network news was an opportunity he wasn't about to pass up. But to get the story, Weston had to see the whales. He saw everyone in town transporting themselves on the back of whining ski machines. Surely this was the best way there. But when he tried to rent one, he ran into the same problem Hansen had. The first man Weston found willing to rent a ski machine asked the same thousand dollars that Hansen was quoted for a car just hours earlier—except the thousand dollars wouldn't give him access to the ski machine for the day; it would buy him one round-trip out to the whales.

Weston turned to Oran in disbelief. Could Caudle find him a ride to the whales? Oran suggested getting in touch with the North Slope Borough's Search and Rescue (SAR) department that operated a fleet of helicopters and small fixed-wing aircraft. Perhaps they could arrange to take him up in one of their helicopters for some aerial shots.

Russ's face lit up. He begged Oran to help him get one of those helicopters. He didn't care what it cost; NBC told him to spare no expense. Oran was as anxious to see Russ succeed as Russ was himself. Oran was filled with excitement. Of course he would help. He dialed his friend Randy Crosby, the director and chief pilot of the department, and asked if they could get a lift out to the whales. Crosby said that barring any rescue emergencies, he would meet Caudle and Weston at the SAR airport hangar the next morning and fly them out for free.

After waiting in the large hangar for first light, Geoff, Craig, Russ, Oran, and Randy took off in a Bell 214 helicopter around 9 A.M., for a comfortable, heated twelve-minute ride to the languishing whales. For the first time, biologists Geoff and Craig would be able to survey the whales' condition from above. Neither mentioned the possibility that the whales might have died since the last time anyone saw them. The dark orange light of this early Arctic morning revealed the magnificence of a rare cloudless day.

From the climate-controlled cabin of the helicopter, the rising sun looked deceptively warm. But it was above the horizon for such a short time and, at such a low angle, its feeble rays were powerless to lessen the bitter cold.

The helicopter flew due west from its pad at the airport and headed straight out to the ice covered Chukchi Sea and flew parallel to the long Point Barrow sandbar. The chopper followed the sandbar north until the two holes in the ice came faintly into view. Their aerial reconnaissance gave Geoff and Craig an idea of what a ship might encounter in the unlikely event the Coast Guard dispatched one to break the ice. They could see that more than a mile of solid new ice stood between the whales and open water. An icebreaker seemed the perfect solution to freeing the three whales.

But Geoff and Craig knew the present circumstances made the use of such a ship impossible. The state of America's icebreaking capacity was a hot issue in Alaska at that very moment. In fact, the Coast Guard's complaints against President Ronald Reagan's administration for its refusal to authorize the construction of more icebreakers was on the same *Anchorage Daily News* front page as the first story about the Barrow whales.

Randy lowered the helicopter onto what looked like the last firm patch of sand on the spit before it drifted below the frozen blanket of ocean. Once on the ground, he had to keep the helicopter at half power so it wouldn't sink into the shifting sand. Russ, Geoff, and Craig jumped out the flimsy door and hopped more than they ran across the sand onto the ice. The ice had grown strong enough to support the weight of three men and their gear and was rough hewn enough to pose no serious risk of slipping or falling down. Billy Adams's prediction of a few days earlier was right on the money.

The ice was now firm enough for them to walk right up to the edge of the hole itself. When they got there, the whales were waiting for them at the surface. The change in their behavior was obvious to Craig and Geoff. When they left them a day earlier, the whales did not yet seem reconciled to the visits of these strange new characters. It was a week since Roy Ahmaogak first discovered the whales swimming in slush on his way back from scouting for the Nuiqsut whalers. Now, they were genuinely trapped. The slush had turned to solid ice half a foot thick. The ice was so deceptively firm, it lulled the men into believing they were walking on terra firma.

Russ set his camera on the ice at the edge of the hole. He opted to shoot parallel to the sea's open and visible waters rather than mounting the camera on a tripod. Russ knew that would make for a more dramatic shot. By rising squarely into the middle of the picture, the whale's head would fill the center of the frame much faster. Russ focused on the churning water in the middle of the hole, turned on the camera and stepped back. Then he waited for the whales to surface. When the first whale came up for air, Russ exhaled a sigh of satisfied relief. His plan for the shot was right on the mark. The focus Russ captured was a spectacular moving image of the whale. It also managed to remarkably convey just how cold it was on the ice. When the whale exhaled, Russ watched through his viewfinder as the water vapor of the whale's breath froze in midair and landed as ice crystals on the lens of the camera. A video veteran of many Alaska whale strandings Russ was still awestruck.

Russ raced back to the helicopter as soon as the baby whale sank beneath the dark water, completing the sequence. He was scheduled to transmit his story to NBC via satellite in less than two hours. He needed to get back to the studio to start editing the footage. Snow whipped by the helicopter lashed Geoff and Craig, who remained behind as Randy lifted off for the trip back to Barrow.

Randy maneuvered his $1,250,000 single-blade helicopter to hover just two hundred feet above the whale's last remaining air hole. Since it was too loud inside the cabin to speak, Russ tapped Randy on the shoulder and motioned that he wanted to take some pictures with Oran's gyrozoom. The aerials would confirm once again NBC's dominance of the early stages of the stranded whale saga. They broke the story, got the first close-ups, and now the first pictures that showed how small the hole really was.

Until Jerry, Don, and Steve Shim—the NBC crew's video editor—had finished setting up shop, NBC's only option that day was to use Russ Weston's video. They weren't sure what to expect of the Anchorage videographer, but Jerry was delighted with what he saw when Russ showed him his footage. He called his assignment desk at NBC with the good news. They responded with good news of their own. The footage would run again tonight on *NBC Nightly News*, only this time for longer and earlier in the broadcast. Clutching a scotch on the rocks, Hansen warmly joked he didn't need his own crew as long as Weston was in town.

5

A Whale in Every Living Room

When Oran Caudle returned to his office following his sojourn with the whales, he found a shell-shocked look on his secretary's face. There were messages on his desk from CBS, ABC, CNN, all the other local stations in Anchorage, and at least a dozen television and radio stations across the country. The soft-spoken Texan laughed in disbelief. He did not know what to make of his instant prominence. In less than twelve hours, the story which he hoped to run on Barrow's local channel really had gone nationwide. The world's most remote television studio and the man who ran it were suddenly sought after by America's leading national broadcasters.

Oran was treated like a man of great importance when he reached the assignment desk by phone. They called him "Mr. Caudle" and even "Sir." *Sir?* Oran thought. Sir was not a word often used in Barrow. In fact, about the only people who ever used that salutation when addressing him were divorce lawyers and collection agents. But he was their only link to a story suddenly ripe with importance. NBC ran it. Now the other networks had to cover it, or provide darn good reasons why not to. If that meant resorting to flattery, so be it.

NBC's exclusive footage of the trapped whales the night before was immediately recognized as an industry "mini-scoop." Network news producers loved animal stories. They gave the network anchors a chance to display, in the spirit of the 1988 presidential campaign, and one of its candidate's emphasis on being "kinder and gentler," how kind and gentle they could be. But for a reason as sublime as it was elusive, whale stories were the best of all, and a whale story like this, was the best of the best. Tom Brokaw had touched a warm spot with even his most cynical viewers at the end of Thursday's broadcast. The struggling whales couldn't help but touch the human heart, and Brokaw could not help using that appeal to stoke his own network's competitive advantage.

If the other networks wanted in on the game, they needed to get moving. Time was wasting. If they worried about money, they could never play. By whatever means they could muster, ABC and CBS, not to mention CNN, had to figure out how to get their own video of the whales on the air to close their own Friday night newscasts. They tracked down Oran through a graphic NBC News superimposed on the footage it used the night before. It read, "Courtesy of the North Slope Borough."

At first, nobody at the networks knew what the "North Slope Borough" meant, let alone what it was, but finding out was the very thing reporters were trained to do. They called Alaska directory assistance and got the number for the North Slope Borough. When they asked for the person responsible for the video that appeared on NBC News the night earlier, the switchboard operator transferred them to Oran. The first calls Oran returned were from the networks. After talking to CBS, ABC, and CNN, he found his freelance camera services at the center of a two-way bidding war. CBS and ABC crews were on the way to Barrow. But until they got there, they needed Oran Caudle to help them get the footage they had to have for their Friday night broadcasts.

Until the other networks put their own footage on the air, this story was an NBC exclusive. People interested in finding out more about the trapped whales would tune in Brokaw and tune out Peter Jennings (ABC) and Dan Rather (CBS). NBC had the obvious advantage—Don, Jerry, and Steve were already on the ground and transmitting.

CBS and ABC wanted in on the game. They asked Oran to go back for "fresh" video of the whales. Each time they spoke to him they raised their cash offers by hundreds of dollars. As he could not serve two masters simultaneously, Caudle sold his exclusive services a day at a time. In the end, CBS won the Day Two Oran Caudle sweepstakes by agreeing to pay him two thousand dollars to arrange one trip out to the whales. That was the going rate for exclusivity.

"Wowee, I can't believe it," Oran exulted in his north Texas drawl. He would make in one morning more than he would in a week and a half with his job at the borough.

Oran knew CNN could never compete with the cash offers made by the networks. These were the halcyon days of network news; immortalized just the year prior by the Hollywood hit movie *Broadcast News,* which starred William Hurt and Holly Hunter. But Caudle personified the subtle change seeping over American TV viewers. He preferred CNN; not because it was CNN necessarily, but because it was a full-time news network. At six o'clock every morning, it ran the Barrow temperature. Oran felt that any network that acknowledged Barrow deserved to be acknowledged itself. He would give CNN free use of the footage he shot for himself the day before as long as it gave the borough credit on the air. The twenty-four-hour news network was only too glad to accept.

Oran barreled into Russ Weston as he ran out the door in his hurry to get back to the whales before dark. In his exuberance, Oran told Russ that the other networks were sending up their own crews. "Isn't that great?" he asked. Needless to say, Russ did not quite share in Caudle's enthusiasm. Russ's exclusive would soon enough be no such thing. From now on, he would have to compete with his competitors for the story that up to that point was his alone.

The transmission facility was destined to start heating up with activity. Since only one signal could be transmitted at a time, Oran knew the task of handing out the time slots would fall in his lap. Had Oran been at the Anchorage International Airport that Friday afternoon, he might have gotten a glimpse of what would soon be descending on his quiet studio over the next two weeks. The normally quiet MarkAir ticket counter hummed with unexpected activity for the afternoon flight to Barrow.

MarkAir was more than the only commercial and freight airlines serving Barrow. In a village with no land or sea routes, it was Barrow's lifeline, its only physical connection to the outside world. Without it, the town would find itself stranded. Outside of government, it was Barrow's biggest business, the source of everything from food and gasoline to transportation to all away games for the Barrow High School basketball team. The three daily flights carried much more than people. They carried the town's future, supplying virtually everything modern Barrow needed to survive its brutal environment.

MarkAir's new fleet of Boeing 737 jets had movable bulkheads. Usually, the front two-thirds of the cabin on Barrow-bound flights held cargo. Even at $337 for the cheapest one-way seat, MarkAir couldn't afford to give up the cargo space unless the plane was full.

But after this afternoon, the agents faced a rare problem. There were more people trying to get to Barrow than there were seats on the plane, including more than a dozen people from CBS and the other Anchorage television stations. Behind them calmly stood the local representatives of the national wire services. To them, Alaska was home. But even they could not fathom what Barrow would bring.

Crates of heavy television equipment began to pile up in front of the ticket counter. Luckily for MarkAir, Ed Rogers was in the Anchorage office and not out checking up on cargo operations at one of the airline's remote sites deep in the Alaska bush. Rogers served as the director of cargo sales for MarkAir and instantly saw both the revenue potential and logistical problems of the unexpected passengers and their baggage. He wouldn't think of turning away full-fare paying passengers along with the fees he would collect from their excess luggage; but with those fees would come costs. He ordered the preloaded cargo off-loaded to make room for seats in the front two-thirds of the Barrow-bound Boeing 737. The cargo taken off the passenger flight was flown up later in the day on a special plane. Rogers kept everyone happy and made MarkAir a handsome profit in the process.

Instead of waiting impatiently for the aircraft to be reconfigured, several of the reporters wandered to the airport's watering hole for an afternoon pick-me-up. They had no idea this would be their last chance to buy a drink legally. Under most circumstances, Barrow was dry and drinking was illegal. In the cabin, mock panic accompanied word that Barrow was dry. One of the stewardesses sought help from the cockpit. The captain's sardonic announcement confirming the rumors only fueled the fake outrage. Stewardesses quickly took their serving carts to quiet the good-natured clamoring for last shots. With one trip down the aisle, every bottle of alcohol was gone. The more seasoned Alaska hands calmly sat through the hubbub, reassured by the bootleg caches of liquor stashed away in their luggage. Once the administered drugs took effect, the cabin calmed down.

The pilot wakened his slightly inebriated passengers (it's never too early for a drink if you are a reporter) on descent to Barrow with news that he had permission from Randy Crosby's air traffic control station in Barrow to make a low-pass flyover above the stranded whales. The trapped whales were not just a national news item anymore. Now they were a tourist attraction.

The influx gathered pace for the next ten days. The Top of the World Hotel started auctioning off beds, as opposed to rooms. People in town for the long-planned mayor's conference and other business returned to the hotel after their day's work to find themselves squeezed inside suddenly shared rooms they had booked and paid in advance as sole private rooms. Making matters worse was that their new roommates weren't normal people; they were rude media types. Since the invading hordes gladly paid three hundred dollars a day for beds in shared rooms, the hotel was willing to take the heat from their displaced guests.

Barrow had never seen anything like it. The current attention, although it had only just started, dwarfed the coverage of the only other event in Barrow to interest anybody on the Outside. On August 15, 1935, a plane crashed ten miles south of Barrow, killing both of its celebrity passengers: legendary humorist Will Rogers and famed aviation pioneer Wiley Post. The few daring journalists who actually reached the remote site back then aptly named the tragic site of the crash "Desolation Point."

The world had changed by 1988. There were satellites, regularly scheduled jet flights, and ski machines. Modern Barrow had running water and a choice among Innuit, American, Mexican, and Chinese cuisine. With all its imported social ills, Barrow had so far managed to avoid one of the most pervasive problems in the Lower 48: homelessness. When the affliction struck, its source was completely unexpected. Suddenly the town was overrun by an influx of reporters with nowhere to stay.

Barrowans started clearing floor space in their homes to accommodate as many Outsiders as they could. The shivering and exhausted members of the fourth estate had little choice but to subject themselves to extortion if it meant escape from the elements. They paid a minimum of one hundred dollars each just for the privilege of sleeping on a cold floor in a private home. If you wanted accoutrements like mattresses, sheets, blankets, even running water, you had to pay for them. Many of these suddenly entreprenurial hosts were flexible in the compensation they would accept. The reporters learned quickly that what cash couldn't buy, whiskey would. Word spread back down the food chain that folks en route to Barrow should stock up on spirits to help grease their way toward a smooth and warm landing. A hundred-dollar bill wrapped around a bottle of J&B secured more than one vacant bed.

The large loophole in Barrow's prohibition was seized upon with alacrity. It was a top priority for many reporters. A not-so obscure provision allowed nonresidents to apply for temporary liquor import licenses. As everyone knew, the applications were available at the Barrow City Hall, which became the site of an almost endless line of those seeking an exemption from the harsh sentence of temperance. Locals roamed the line offering hundreds of dollars to those willing to use their permits to help them illegally resupply their own caches. Once Outsiders—in this case, reporters—got their permits, they made arrangements with their bureaus for shipments of Barrow's preferred medium of exchange. Thousands of dollars worth of beer, wine, and hard liquor were shipped overnight express by the caseload. Ed Rogers's joke was that the MarkAir cargo storage area was beginning to resemble a wholesale liquor warehouse.

Some newsmen phoned in their complaints to their more comfortably assignment editors, decrying Barrow's lack of amenities and begging for relief. Others thrived in the "hardship." In fact, it wasn't hardship as much as it was novelty. Each privation endured was a badge they could later point to as proof of their ability to report under varying levels of adversity.

For veteran CBS cameraman Bob Dunn, it was a chance to prove that not even his graying hair and expanding girth could stand in the way of his cherished bravado. Age and experience did little to temper Dunn's need to stay true to his image. For several days, he pretended to be Inuit by adamantly refusing to wear gloves. Even several severely frostbitten fingers did not put a stop to Dunn's crusade to win the "respect" of the locals. To protect him from himself, a group of Eskimo hunters gave Dunn a pair of polar bear-skin mittens. They did not want anyone to confuse their Arctic fortitude with Dunn's lunacy.

Those second-wave of reporters had commandeered the few available vans, trucks, and ski machines, so the rest had a tough time getting around. The need of so many people to get out to the whales, combined with their inability to do so, gave rise to another short-lived Arctic tradition: daily transport auctions. Ride seekers congregated early each morning outside the Top of the World Hotel and shouted their competing bids to Eskimos with ski machines and dogsleds for rides to the ice. The most enterprising locals could now fetch four hundred dollars each way. When the market finally stabilized after everyone seemed to be in it, the going rate settled at around two hundred dollars or one hundred fifty dollars in cash plus a fifth of liquor.

But, as KTUU reporter Todd Pottinger could attest, the high price did not guarantee much. Once he paid top dollar for his crew and equipment only to be dumped unceremoniously in the middle of the street after the driver somehow managed to plow into one of the Arctic's few telephone poles. Pottinger's insistence on a refund met with an incredulous laugh.

Anyone without two hundred dollars for the return trip found themselves unceremoniously stranded until Randy Crosby's Search and Rescue helicopter could arrange to pick them up. Those who could shake off the night's excess and get out of bed early enough stood shivering outside the SAR hangar for helicopter rides out to the whales.

As the Barrow sled-ride market matured, different levels of service emerged. First class transport included sleds outfitted with polar-bear blankets and down sleeping bags. Economy passengers were lucky to wrap themselves in a bloodstained but warm caribou hide. Sometimes revolted passengers had to share return sled or ski machine rides with a dead walrus or seal. Even so, it was usually the reporter's stench that outstank the dead animal's.

Just four days after the first nationwide broadcast on NBC, almost every newspaper in the United States had featured the whales on their front pages. All three networks carried daily updates from Barrow. The whales were becoming the biggest story in America. They were even competing with the final weeks of a torpid presidential election. Compounding the nonevent's absurdity, reporters outside the United States suddenly found themselves assigned to cover the story. If it was news in America, then it must really be news.

I was one of those reporters.

Moments before I unexpectedly found myself on the way to cover the story, I was good-naturedly ribbing my friend and colleague Carolyn Gusoff, who soon become one of the most respected professionals in TV news, for her interest in the story. At 6:30 P.M. on Wednesday, October 19, just as my quick call with Gusoff ended, the phone rang again. It was Takao Sumii in New York, the president of NTV, then Japan's largest private television network.

At the time, I ran a small (meaning me) television news service called N.Y. News Corp. It offered custom television coverage of news events primarily for foreign broadcasters by lining up the necessary freelance production and reporting pieces on a contractor basis. Takao asked me how soon I could get a crew to Barrow and be able to transmit reports back to Japan. I had no idea and did not know what to say. For the previous two weeks I had been in bed attempting to recover from a nasty and lingering case of mononucleosis. I was barely well enough to go to the office let alone the North Pole. I stammered in my halting (and now completely forgotten) Japanese. I could hardly turn down a job with my best customer. I told him he could count on me and ended up working feverishly to make sure that in fact he could.

Thus began my own frantic preparations to make my voyage to the Top of the World. Carolyn Gusoff had the last laugh; I was going to cover the whales. I told Sumii he could count on getting a transmission within twenty-four hours. It dawned on me as I hung up the phone that I had no idea what my first step should be. I vaguely remembered hearing NBC reporter Don Oliver refer to something called the "Top of the World" in one of his reports. When I did connect with someone there, they answered the phone by saying they had no rooms available. This was my introduction to Barrow. "Thanks for the calling the Top of the World; we are completely full."

I asked for the names of other hotels. The receptionist referred me to the only competition in town, the Airport Inn. By the time I reached the inn by phone, the hotel operator told me they, too, were full. I beseeched this second woman for help. Did she know any names? What about paying for sleeping in someone's home? I needed some accommodation before I started hiring a crew. She gave me the name of a man called Rod Benson. His brother owned the Airport Inn and he might be able to help me out.

I quickly made phone contact with Benson, who sounded like a very nice man. He told me we could stay with his family in his home for two hundred dollars per night. Unaware that the price he offered me was in fact a bargain, my response must have sounded quite ungrateful. Like everyone else, I had no choice. I asked him what we should know and what we should bring. His answer was a memorable one.

"Everything is expensive and no one takes credit cards—that is what you should know," he said directly but politely. "As for what you should bring: long johns and liquor." He laughed.

Twelve hours after getting that first call, I found myself in Anchorage, where I waited at the airport to meet the flight from Tokyo carrying Masu Kawamura, the NTV reporter assigned to story. He would be my boss while in Barrow. We decamped at the iconic Captain Cook Hotel in Anchorage to await the arrival of my hired N.Y. News Corp. cameraman Steve Mongeau, who was due in early the next morning from Toronto.

We were more worried about how to transport our liquor than we were about making sure we packed appropriate clothing. I spent about five hundred dollars on liquor from Alaska Distributors, a huge wholesale liquor warehouse and less than one hundred fifty dollars on boots that I thought would work in the coldest of climes. They were clearly better than low-top Nike, but my feet still got awful cold.

The Friday-morning flight to Barrow from Anchorage was filled with reporters as well as the regulars: the oil professionals and roughnecks heading back to their shifts at the huge Prudhoe Bay facility, which was the flight's second and primary destination. By this time, several of the oil companies had started their own remarkable involvement in what had already become a full-fledged rescue operation. I sat next to a early-middle-aged Inupiat woman with jet-black hair and deep-set brown eyes that rested atop prominent cheekbones. Her name was Brenda Itta, returning home to Barrow after participating in an Alaska Federation of Natives (AFN) conference in Anchorage.

This articulate woman was not at all upset about the coverage, but for the life of her, she couldn't understand why her tiny frontier town had suddenly become the subject of such attention. She wished the whales well of course; everyone did. But why the big deal? Whales died back home all the time just as whales are born all the time there. It's called wildlife, and in the Arctic there is so much of it, no one pays too much attention to individual wildlife. She couldn't understand why they were more important than the AFN meeting she just attended or the North Slope Mayors' Conference presently taking place in Barrow?

Brenda Itta's unknown world and its fascinating people had not as yet sparked much interest from the correspondents starting to straggle into Barrow. None of us came to Barrow to report on the story of this amazing town and its remarkable people. We came to tell the world about something that happened so often no one familiar with the phenomenon could understand our interest. The routine stranding of three whales under a patch of ice was about as newsworthy in and around the North Slope of Alaska as a deer hit by a truck on the Pennsylvania Turnpike. What made this stranding extraordinary was that nobody outside Barrow knew anything about whale strandings because they had never been seen before. But now, with a stranding just twenty miles from a state-of-the-art satellite uplink Earth station and broadcast production center, these whales' story could be seen and heard by anyone with a television, anywhere in the world.

Had the facility been located farther away, or had the whales been stranded just out of eyeshot, these whales would have met the same fate that befell untold dozens every year prior to 1988 and in every year since 1988. This brutal lesson of media obsessions was made all too tragically on Saturday night, October 22, 1988, during the height of the whale frenzy. Right across the street from the Barrow fire department, a small, poorly constructed driftwood house erupted in flames, killing three small children in the worst Barrow house fire in years. The Karluk Street fire station was empty that night. The men had gone home early for some much needed sleep—they were near exhaustion after working eighteen-hour days all week to help to save the whales.

An electrical short in the bathroom started the fire which killed eight-year-old Delia Itta, her sister Irene, two, and their baby brother Miles Steven, ten months. No one in Barrow accused anyone of negligence. The house was a veritable fire trap. Once ignited, the wall's combusted like dry tinder. The house was so quickly engulfed that even if the firemen had been on call and at their posts, there was very little chance they could have saved any, let alone all of the lives lost. The house contained neither smoke alarms nor adults at the time of the fire.

That very night Barrow played host to the highest concentration of national and international journalists and television cameras, maybe in the world. Not a single mention of the tragic deaths of the three children was made in any of the whale stories prepared for broadcast that evening or the next, including my own.

It wasn't until the saga neared its conclusion that broader, more fundamental questions about the story's real significance—that is, what was so important about a natural and not uncommon Arctic whale stranding—started to get asked. Did the naturally stranded whales deserve all the effort and attention they got? Was the coverage proportionate to the event? Little mention about our remarkable experiences in Barrow was made in our stories, packages, or dispatches. Then again, those were the days when reporters were not supposed to become subjects in their own stories. We were sent to cover the whale strandings. These were all good and important questions, but their asking would come later. In the meantime, our job was to cover the whales and their rescue.

On the plane, Brenda spoke a good deal about her family's history and the problems her Inupiat people were having coping with some of the challenges of modern life. Her people had a terrible problem with alcohol. Everyone knew that. Few tried to hide it. She didn't strike me as terribly optimistic when asked about long-term prospects. The flight's first stop was in Fairbanks, Alaska's second city, roughly 450 miles north of Anchorage. As passengers deplaned, several commented on their reluctance to get off. It sounded to them as though the rest of us were headed into quite an adventure. Brenda commented in passing at her distaste for those who tried to smuggle liquor into Barrow, as if it didn't have enough already. I nodded in agreement, hoping she had nothing to store in the overhead compartment above her, which was stocked with my own bootleg whiskey.

Only then did it dawn on me that Rod Benson's comment to me on the phone about making sure I brought alcohol was made more than in jest. Barrow was hooked. The whale extravaganza presented an unexpected opportunity to massively increase local illegal stocks and to make a killing in the process.

It seemed like everyone brought booze. Others brought it for the same reason I did, to help them do their jobs in a strange town. It didn't take long to realize why the Inupiats, and no small share of Anglos in Barrow either for that matter, had such a problem with alcohol. Two days after we arrived, we had the same problems; some would say even worse.

Life in Barrow is about one thing: staying warm. We spent six to eight hours each day on the frozen windswept ice atop the frozen Arctic Ocean gathered around small holes that grew more crowded by the day. People drank in the morning before going out to the whales to get warm. When people weren't fighting on the ice, we drank bourbon from each other's flasks to stay warm. When we got back to town, people drank until they either went to bed or passed out. The mixed blessing of an irritable stomach allowed me to live my Barrow adventure pretty much alcohol free. It wasn't that I didn't want to drink much, it was that I couldn't drink much then, or since.

"It is too cold to be sober," went a common refrain. The warmest buildings were rarely heated above fifty-five degrees in winter, because most people rarely took off their coats indoors. It would take some time before the visitors did take their coats off upon entering a home or building from the outside cold to keep the air inside their coats and close to their bodies warm.

The novelty and excitement of our new universe was short-lived. The overwhelming oppressiveness of Barrow almost immediately started competing with the wonderment. We were suddenly in a dark, cold, and inebriated environment that challenged most of the laws thought to define normal human existence.

Quick to sense a change in the attitudes, performance, and energy levels of their crews after in Barrow, the networks decided to start rotating crews in and out of town to make sure no one spent more than a week unrelieved. I wasn't relieved and didn't think myself at all unlucky. I not only endured, I loved it. This was no hardship. It was a blast. Besides, each swapped crew meant new people and new booze!

Just like the Eskimos we simultaneously patronized and romanticized, too many of the traveling television bards adopted the worst of their ways with ease. Liquor jokes, liquor stories, liquor threats—they all became the shared metaphor of the media horde. First went our sobriety, then went our hygiene. We didn't care much for our appearances—those of us who had a lifetime adjusting to our less-than-primetime looks had an easier time sliding into sloth than the on-air talent. The hassle and expense of hygiene was an annoyance to those not already preoccupied. It became a nightmare for those who were.

My first morning in Barrow, after the ordeal of undressing the layers upon layers of clothing in a freezing bathroom, I looked forward to a long and lustrous hot shower. As I stepped in, it occurred to me that the tiny cloth on the towel rack was my towel. I almost decided not to take a shower at all. Why bother? But I got in and deeply breathed in the steam. More than the warmth, it was the moisture I longed for. Barrow was one of the driest spots on earth—a frozen desert. Its cold, dry air parched the throat and cracked even the toughest skin.

My quick escape didn't last long. It ended when the hot water suddenly turned ice cold. And I mean ICE cold. Rod was none too pleased with me, and this was his way of showing me that. Water, I did not then know, was far from the ubiquitous resource so taken for granted by Outsiders. In Barrow it was the most precious and expensive of resources strictly rationed by the North Slope Borough. Rod wanted me out of the shower. Shutting off the hot water worked like a charm. Any more long showers, he told me, and he would start up charging me for our water use.

One of Rod's neighbors got a big laugh out of his ability to sell five-minute showers for fifty dollars. He claims people paid it. Who knows? Those of us unwilling or unable to afford what we previously thought to be normal use of indoor plumbing learned quickly to adapt. When in Barrow do as Barrowans does. These indignities were hardly indignant in the end. We did have indoor plumbing after all.

Certainly a far cry from the manner in which many Arctic peoples' still heard "nature's call." It wasn't just the twenty-five degrees below zero temperatures. It certainly wasn't the fear of being seen. It wasn't even the danger of freezing exposed and sensitive body parts. It was the damned dogs.

Our first night in Barrow saw those of us from N.Y. News Corp. and NTV gathered around Rod Benson's Formica bar for a late-night bull session. Rod played the fine host and basked in our excitement at finding ourselves in his world; a world we did not even know existed twenty-four hours earlier. The heavy smell of scotch and stale cigarette smoke permeated the cold, dry air. Rod got up and announced he needed a few moments but would be right back.

On the way out the door, he picked up a roll of toilet paper together with a thick wooden stick that were resting together on an old metal chair. As soon as the door slammed behind him, the sounds of excitedly barking sled dogs shattered the quiet of the Arctic night. Not sixty seconds later, Rod, his aplomb perfectly intact, was back in his house comfortably seated. What was all the racket? we asked. He just smiled. Soon enough we would find out for ourselves he promised. Whether or not Rod really needed to go, or was just having fun at our expense, we will likely never know and it is just as well.

The barking dogs were the omnipresent sound of Barrow. Whenever one was outside, no matter the time of day or night, barking and howling dogs could always be heard, either close by or in the distance. But they were always there. They were Alaskan sled dogs, much closer in temperament and genetics to wolves than to dogs. These were work dogs, not pets. They were an incredibly tough breed of dog reared especially to pull heavy sleds in the Arctic. They lived outside year-round. They were everywhere. They weren't wild dogs; they were owned work dogs. Yet they seemed to roam the town at will. Knowing that the hungrier they are the better they perform, sled dogs are purposely underfed by their owners. Consequently, they are constantly on the prowl for supplemental nourishment.

Human scent often means a dog's next meal—one way or another. Their keen sense of smell could easily locate someone attempting to relieve himself outdoors and track even the most well-hidden person at his most vulnerable moment. Almost the instant a person reached for his trousers, packs of canines were barking madly as they raced toward their victim.

Snapping their jaws without regard for what they might bite, the dogs fought among themselves just for the chance to snatch human waste within seconds of it being deposited, oftentimes before a person had to chance to pull up his britches, requiring one to finish his business with one hand while flailing the club at the snarling dogs with the other. So the story goes.

Lofty salaries and flashy bylines meant precious little to reporters assigned to Barrow. Here, skills perfected on the Outside were of little use. Those that considered long jet journeys arduous before arriving in Barrow actually looked forward to it when it was time to leave. This was not Johannesburg, Beijing, or even Beirut. There were no taxis outside the airport to whisk you to the comfortable superbly catered hotels you would call home for the duration of your story.

There was little in Barrow to remind an Outsider of the world he left behind. Nothing seemed the same. There were no trees, no grass. There was nothing higher than the ground that was not put there by man. None of the earth exposed itself above the flat blanket covering of white that concealed the ground. If it weren't for man, nothing would break the completely uniform terrain.

Suddenly the world's changeable attention focused on one of its most isolated places. Even with the miracle of instant satellite communication, Barrow seemed every bit as trapped in its harsh setting as the three whales were trapped under the ice. Three hundred and twenty miles above the Arctic Circle, each day survived was a miracle achieved. No one lived in a more unforgiving and hostile world, it seemed, than did the hearty Inupiat Eskimos.

Until the media adopted the whales as their own, it would have been both impossible and inconceivable to save them. Because it was nature at work, most Barrowans did not see the point of trying to rescue the whales. But once the story went nationwide, the decision was made for them. They had been cast by their cultural betters from the world of television news to play the role of innocent and enlightened savages in this touchy-feely state of nature. If they could be made to help save the whales, what a story it would make. Premodern noble men in the glorious state of nature working hand in hand to save a fellow creature in the state of nature. If only.

Whales stranded themselves for tens of thousands of years before the invention of satellite news gathering. They will continue to strand themselves for thousands more. Everyone assigned to the whales' story quickly learned this was a nonstory, yet it was one the world was desperate to follow. It took on a life of its own, as media stories are wont to do.

The power of television alone could not account for the spellbinding influence of this story. The herd instinct lead the news media to Barrow and that same herd instinct compelled us to darn near take the town over when we got there. When NBC found good grazing, everyone followed. The compelling struggle of the whales and those who worked hard to rescue them would lead news programs around the globe for almost two weeks. But no group of news directors could have created this huge amount of interest. That power belonged to the whales, their rescuers, and most important, the millions of people around the world who wanted them freed.

Barrow natives never did figure out precisely how to deal with the arrival of the Outside. Isolationists argued that Outsiders wanted the Eskimo and his ancient way of life destroyed. Fortunately, there weren't that many isolationists. Most Inupiat were smart enough to realize there was much in the modern world for them, too; that his life could be bettered and his prospects improved in the same ways progress helped everybody else. For the Eskimo, the real question was how to keep the best of his past alive without forgoing the benefits of progress.

6

The Tigress from Greenpeace

Autumn 1988 marked the final days of Ronald Reagan's presidency. America's fortieth president had only a few months left in office until his second term expired. While the country was naturally preoccupied with the race to succeed him, there was still much left to do.

No one knew this better than Interior Secretary Donald Hodel, who realized that the period right before the president left office was his own last and perhaps best chance to push some of Ronald Reagan's most significant land management policies through Congress—expanded access to America's abundant but off-limits energy resources chief among them.

The oil companies promised drilling in the Arctic was safe and for twenty-plus years had proven it. Environmentalists countered that a single "blowout" at an offshore oil rig could spill millions of gallons of crude oil into a fragile ecosystem, causing catastrophic damage. Oil companies agreed with them. Offshore drilling was far more dangerous than onshore drilling. Yet when oil companies argued that the best way to mitigate the risk of off shore oil drilling was to increase onshore drilling, the environmental lobby opposed them. Environments argued then, and have argued ever since that the oil industry was bad and dangerous and therefore must be stopped.

Despite President Reagan's personal popularity, public opinion seemed to side with the environmentalists. Energy was still relatively affordable and still seemed abundant. These were the days before alternative media and the Internet. The editorial biases of the establishment media, represented by the big three television networks and *The New York Times,* still held sway, and made it extremely difficult to enact proposals to reasonably expand domestic energy production. One thing can be said for environmentalists in those days that cannot be said for them today: Back in 1988 not even the oil companies had a clue as to the true size and scope of energy resources beneath our waters and under the soil and land.

Recent studies (2010) conducted by the U.S. Geological Survey suggest that the American Arctic (Alaska) could contain 90 billion barrels of oil; the second largest undiscovered petroleum reserve in the world. If true, this find would contain $8 trillion worth of oil at 2011's average price of ninety-five dollars per barrel; $8 trillion that could be spent on and in America rather than exported to countries that hate us. Other experts say the oil fields off and under Alaska and its Arctic coast are much bigger still and could extend throughout the entire Arctic region and at twice the size of USGS estimates.

With time running out, Hodel made one last effort to open up more of the U.S. continental shelf for limited offshore drilling. The biggest prize was Alaska's Bristol Bay. Separating the Aleutian Islands from the Alaskan mainland, Bristol Bay served as the home to more than three-quarters of the world's salmon, half the tuna, herring, halibut, and countless numbers of other commercial fish species. Supplying the world with more than a billion dollars' worth of fish each year, Bristol Bay was and remains the backbone of Alaska's commercial fishing industry.

The oil industry and geologists believed that some of the world's largest remaining undeveloped oil deposits lay just beneath Bristol Bay's floor. The oil companies argued those reserves could be tapped safely without damaging America's richest maritime region. From the oilman's point of view, the quantity of oil and gas waiting to be drilled more than justified the risk. However, the Alaskan fishermen, whose livelihoods depended upon the bay's renewable resources, were not so sure.

But now, something funny happened. Rather than continue its public relations and media war against the fishing industry by accusing it of destroying Bristol Bay through "unsustainable" exploitation, Alaskan environmentalists, assisted in money and support by its allies in the Lower 48, now joined forces with their former commercial fishing opponents to oppose any efforts by the oil companies to even survey Bristol Bay to find out how much oil might be below the sea floor.

Cindy Lowry was the Alaska field coordinator for Greenpeace, either the most famous or notorious of all environmentalist organizations, depending on one's perspective. Although Greenpeace was created in 1972 to stop French atomic-weapon testing, its young group of left-wing firebrands burst into the world's consciousness with their attention-grabbing stunts to save the whales. While their antics made for great TV, they were a bit late to the party. By the time Greenpeace showed up in the late 1970s, the whales were already well on their way to recovery. They had long since been saved from extinction—not by environmentalists, but by the oil industry! You read that right. It was petroleum that saved the whales, not Greenpeace.

Greenpeace etched its image using inflatable rubber dinghies. By placing themselves and their fragile rafts between the hulking keels of aging whaling ships and the whales they lumbered to kill, the daring two-man crews made a powerful impact on global opinion. By 1989, Greenpeace was a household name. Its two million members were active everywhere. From the North Pole to the South Pole, Greenpeacers fought for an ever-widening array of causes. Controversy was their calling card.

To Cindy Lowry, Bristol Bay was more than a commercial fishery. In fact, she and her organization cut their teeth on fighting the fishing industry. It was the critical pathway for Alaska's sea creatures. All the animals that migrated to and from Alaska depended on swimming through and living in a clean, viable Bristol Bay. Everyone could agree upon that.

Lowry believed that if the oil industry were given rights to develop Bristol Bay, everything that lived in it or passed through it, including two-thirds of the world's gray whales, could be at risk. Never much for understatement, Greenpeace's line of opposition to exploration rights in the bay was that a rig "blowout" could wipe out entire species.

For Cindy, it was the offensive to even weigh the commercial interests of people against the very survival of animals. The killing of whales, by whatever means, was never justifiable (did that extend to ice strandings?). Cindy Lowry's job description was to stop any human activity anywhere it might threaten nonhuman activity—anywhere. She was a true believer.

She didn't trust many people, least of all conservatives. To her, the mere mention of Ronald Reagan's name led to outrage. Bristol Bay first appeared as a target for energy development back in 1985. The Interior Department solicited bids to buy lease rights in the bay. The outcry against the plan to search for oil in the rich ecosystem was so great though that Secretary Hodel agreed to cancel the process with a caveat. Instead of voiding the bids outright, the Interior Department would keep them sealed in the event the current or next administration "changed its mind."

Three months before President Reagan was scheduled to leave office, almost everyone thought the issue of offshore oil drilling in wildlife areas was dead. Opposition was too great, support too meek. Reagan was opposed by his own vice president, George H. W. Bush, now the Republican candidate for president. Even oil companies had given up. But Donald Hodel did not. His office announced that the sealed bids would be opened and read at a hearing in Anchorage on October 11, 1988.

Cindy Lowry's distrust seemed to pay off. While no one else was prepared for the sudden change in administration policy, Cindy was. Three years earlier, she submitted Greenpeace's own bid for lease rights in Bristol Bay. As her price for rights to drill in the bay, she offered the value of the marine life that Greenpeace predicted would be destroyed if the bay was opened up. Cindy was certain that if drilling went ahead, it would be the creatures of Bristol Bay that would pay the price, not the oil companies. How risking the billions of dollars needed to develop Bristol Bay did not constitute a risk for oil companies, Cindy did not say.

Cindy didn't consider herself a left-wing anti-everything rabble-rouser; none of them ever do. But the oil companies, Inupiat subsistence whalers, and legions of others she frequently tangled with thought that was precisely what she was. Yes, Cindy Lowry was a heart-on-her-sleeve, emotion-first-reason-second animal lover. She did not just admit it, she was proud of it. When not on "assignment," she could easily be mistaken for a fashion-conscious banker. She looked younger than her thirty-eight years. There weren't many limousines in Alaska, but in many ways Cindy Lowry was

Alaska's version of a limousine liberal. She dressed in the latest fashions, wore expensive perfumes, drank expensive coffees, drove a gas-guzzling Volvo, and had a great big dog named after the tallest mountain in North America, Denali. Outsiders knew it as Mount McKinley, named for an American president who sanctioned an expedition there.

Lowry had only a few weeks to prepare for the October 11 hearing that would determine the fate of Bristol Bay and, in a sense, America's energy future. Cindy prepared for the worst. So did the Mineral Management Service of the U.S. Department of the Interior (MMS), which held the hearing. They hired fifteen extra security guards to protect the proceedings and its participants from peaceful, nonviolent types like Cindy Lowry.

Cindy dressed as she always did for professional functions. But hidden away in her black leather executive attaché case was a sleek megaphone probably bought at the Sharper Image. Before the doors were opened the security guards were warned to look out for her likes, not smartly dressed women. Suppressing a smirk, Cindy walked right past them to a seat at the back of the auditorium. She couldn't believe it. As Alaska's most notorious environmentalist, she not only expected trouble, but was hoping for it. Instead, no one even recognized her.

The hearing was a big event. Controversy was all but assured. All the Anchorage media—the newspapers and the television and radio stations— were on hand to cover it. Earlier in the week, the Interior Department in Washington sensed trouble. They instructed the moderator to find whatever excuse he could not to open the Greenpeace bids. The tension was palpable. The moderator knew he wouldn't get away with it, but orders were orders.

Again, Cindy was ahead of the game. She had locked horns with the oil companies and used histrionics too many times before to know the hearing would not go as its sponsors wanted.

She knew it was she, not they who were in charge. They were afraid of her. She was not afraid of them. She couldn't lose—if she caused trouble and was expelled, she would claim to be the victim of a rigged process; that her free-speech rights were trampled. If she was permitted to stand her ground inside and lost, she could still make the same basic charge: the process was rigged.

Cindy made sure she was flanked by friends who would protect her. Fellow activists and fishermen trying to defend their livelihoods sat next to Cindy on both sides. When the moderator announced that all bids would remain sealed, Cindy seamlessly transformed herself from well-behaved participant to activist loudmouth—literally. She slipped the high-powered megaphone she smuggled past security out of her briefcase.

"What about the bids? Why aren't you going to read the bids?" she demanded. The megaphone was louder than the auditorium's public address system. "Why don't you open the bids like the law requires?" The law, of course, required no such thing. But amid the hubub no one had the presence of mind to point that out. Hundreds of heads turned in her direction. Applause and cheers overtook the smattering of boos from Alaskans who favored development as strongly as Cindy opposed it.

The security guards sprang to life. From all corners of the hall, they ran toward Cindy's direction to stop her disruption and to restore order. They fought and struggled with the phalanx of burly fishermen who rose with broad chests to shield her. Did they know she opposed them, too? After a heated exchange, the guards overwhelmed their opposition and yanked Cindy out of her seat. The crowd jeered as the guards dragged her screaming from the hall. Camera crews captured it all for the evening news. Practice made perfect. It was a masterful performance.

Outside, the media lined up to interview the hearing's well-rehearsed animal-rights diva. The episode became that night's lead story on all three Anchorage newscasts. After answering all the media's questions, Cindy walked to her Volvo where her boyfriend, Kevin Bruce, was waiting. Kevin always tried to be on hand whenever Cindy planned any of her stunts in case he was needed to post bail. Knowing she was too upset to drive, he gave her a warm hug, took her keys, and drove her home.

Make no mistake. Cindy Lowry didn't oppose enjoying all the fruits developed and produced by the industries she made a living trying to close. On the way home, they stopped for drive-through Chinese takeout to eat while watching Todd Pottinger's 11:00 P.M. newscast from the comfort of their modern Anchorage condo, outfitted with all the latest accoutrements. They had expected Cindy's expulsion to be the top story. The surprise came when they heard Pottinger report it as a major victory. The uproar she contrived had forced the MMS to cancel the hearing.

The sealed bids went right back to the same vault where they had moldered for the last three years. Cindy and Greenpeace had won. For the moment at least, Cindy Lowry had helped keep Bristol Bay "safe." She also helped keep safe, if not strengthen, the stranglehold that foreign regimes had on U.S. energy needs.

While still a bit shaken by her ejection, Cindy's face lit up. She basked in victory not for herself, but for her good friends the otters, seals, and whales of Bristol Bay. How sweet.

Opponents sometimes accused Cindy Lowry of many terrible things, but none of her critics ever suggested that she generated publicity for her own purposes. Cindy Lowry was, heart and soul, an activist. She was a true believer and hard not to respect. Environmentalism was her life's passion, often to Kevin's chagrin. While her tactics were sometimes questioned, no one could question the sincerity of her motivation. She thought Alaska's wilderness to be in grave danger. It wasn't a passion she acquired. Cindy Lowry was born with it.

By the time she was five, little Cindy was already cutting loose the fish her family caught on pleasure trips. The adults soon learned that if they ever wanted to eat any of their catch, Cindy was better left at home. By her tenth birthday, she displayed a dangerous willingness to use deadly force to protect animals. Patrolling to protect her Kansas farm against coyote poachers, little Cindy marched with her grandfather's heavy shotgun slung over her tiny shoulder. Shoving her loaded gun's double barrels into the marauding hunters' stunned faces, she forced them to think twice before trespassing. Word of "that crazy Lowry kid" spread fast. Her militancy worked. The poachers never returned.

When it came to her own life, Cindy was no martyr. After working long weeks on the Bristol Bay lease sale, she intended to take the rest of the week off. Nothing could spoil the hard-earned and long-planned weekend with Kevin she had already postponed several times. Thursday morning, October 13, Cindy Lowry slept in. Figuring she wouldn't miss the paper she referred to as *"The Anchorage Daily Snooze,"* Kevin took that morning's edition with him to his office. While he casually glanced at the front page, one headline caught his eye. It read "Ice Traps Three Gray Whales." He decided against calling Cindy who he hoped was still sleeping after her busy week. Stage-managing raucous publicity stunts was exhausting work.

A local Anchorage reporter named Jeff Berliner wasn't so thoughtful. He woke Cindy up at home to ask what she knew about the three whales. To the Alaska press corps, Cindy's phone was referred to as "enviro quote." Whenever reporters needed a source to quote on an environmental issue, Cindy would always oblige them, whether or not she knew any more than they did.

Jeff's call was the first instance she heard about the stranded whales. If Cindy didn't know, Berliner told himself, maybe it wasn't a story. Cindy thanked Jeff for the call and promised to get back to him as soon as she found out anything. The instant she hung up, the phone rang again. This time it was Geoff Carroll calling from Barrow. The biologist figured that if anyone could help him help the whales, it was Alaska's most famous whale hunter. Cindy Lowry was his man.

All Geoff knew for sure about the whales was that they were California grays. He didn't know their sex or ages although one was a baby and the other two seemed to be adolescents. Geoff told Cindy that unless a path through the ice could be cut to the open water, the whales would die. Any ship with a strong, steel reinforced bow could probably do the job, he told her. The night before, the two biologists spent hours on the phone asking Coast Guard personnel around the country for help.

At the time, the United States Coast Guard only had two icebreakers on active duty, a fact Alaskans knew well. Many had long argued unsuccessfully for more. Neither of the ships were available to help the biologists. One ship, the *Polar Star,* was limping its way through the seventeen-foot-high ice floes to clear a commercial path through the Northwest Passage, while the other, the *Polar Sea,* was undergoing extensive repairs in its Seattle drydock.

Whale strandings were common in Alaska. When whales were imperiled near Anchorage, Cindy always tried to help. So did lots of folks. In fact, the last time whales became stranded nearby, Cindy and her dog, Denali, were almost killed trying to save them. That August, a group of Beluga whales beached themselves just south of Anchorage. They were exposed and helpless on the mudflats of Turnagain Arm, the body of water to the south of Anchorage. The Arm was known for its immense tidal surges called bore tides. Unlike regular tides that gradually ebb and flow, bore tides formed high-crested walls of water that moved at up to thirty miles an hour. The group of whales Cindy was trying to help had become stranded by a bore tide, finding themselves trapped on the Arm's mudflats. Cindy knew that if they were not helped immediately, the whales would die before the next tide could bring the sea back in to save them. Before launching her own private rescue, Cindy reported the stranded whales to the Anchorage office of the National Marine Fisheries Service (NMFS). NMFS was the federal agency responsible for enforcing the 1972 Marine Mammal Protection Act, passed by the U.S. Congress primarily to help endangered whales like those stranded on the Turnagain mudflats and, later, the three trapped whales in Barrow. Even though NMFS didn't help her as much as she would have liked, Cindy obeyed the law requiring citizens to report stranded animals.

NMFS employees took emergencies reported by Cindy Lowry with a grain of Greenpeace salt. "It's her again," they seemed to lament. "It's that crazy but lovable environmentalist again." She constantly cried "stranding." If NMFS responded every time, they would exhaust their annual rescue budget in the first quarter of the year. They told her there was nothing they could do for the beluga whales stranded on Turnagain Arm. If they were going to be saved, Cindy Lowry would have to do it herself.

Stranded out on the flats, dry skin was the biggest danger the whales faced. To a person, dry skin meant minor irritation easily alleviated by applying moisturizing cream. To a whale, it meant death. Without water to cool their warm-blooded bodies, the whales would overheat and die. Cindy called her surprised boyfriend at work and told him she needed him to help her scoop water from tidal pools over the stranded whales.

Kevin was mortified. Was he hearing this suicidal suggestion from the woman he loved? A woman he knew to lovably nuts, but thought possessed some sanity? Anyone foolish enough to ignore the huge red danger signs warning people to stay off the mudflats stood a good chance of miring themselves so deep they couldn't get out. The mudflats were more dangerous than quicksand. The more you resisted, the deeper and firmer the mud would clutch you. If the mud did not pull you all the way under, you could watch until the incoming tide consumed you in a wall of water.

With the elections coming up, this was Kevin's busy season. Kevin was—you'll never guess—a political consultant for liberal Democrats! But Kevin was more level-headed than Cindy, more practical. Then again, so were most people. He didn't want Cindy to become Greenpeace's latest martyr. After repeated but unsubstantiated assurances that she wouldn't take any unnecessary chances, Cindy still could not convince Kevin the whales were worth the risk. Only when she threatened to go alone did he relent.

Like ice strandings in the Arctic, tide strandings of the kind Cindy and Kevin were now witnessing were natural and common occurrences. But their routineness did nothing to quench Cindy's zeal. She loved animals. An animal in distress meant distress for Cindy. Before he could unfasten his seat belt, Kevin found himself screaming at Cindy out his open window. Seconds earlier, Cindy and her dog bolted out the open door and onto the deceptively solid floor of the arm. In his haste to urge them back to safety, Kevin banged his head on the window frame.

Just a few hundred feet out on the dry waterway, Cindy screamed for help. Like a stealthy predator, the oozing mud grabbed Cindy's left leg and pulled her deathward. Between her frantic cries for help, Cindy desperately tried to reassure her dog, Denali, who was fighting his own losing battle against the deadly flats.

Sinking against the encroaching and unmistakable sounds of the fast-approaching bore tide, Cindy and her dog didn't know what to do. Her final solace was knowing that her death would mean life for the beached whales.

The last thing Kevin Bruce wanted was to be eulogized as the "horn-rimmed hero." Vaulting across the protective guard rail, he bounded onto the flats in a daring effort to save Cindy and her dog. Finally reaching them, Kevin wisely ignored Cindy's appeals to help her dog first. In just three minutes, the mud had already pulled Cindy waist deep. Cindy and her dog watched the wall of water threaten to consume them.

But Kevin turned his back, concentrating instead on pulling Cindy to safety. When she was free, she grabbed Denali by the scruff of his neck and pulled him out of the thick mud with one hard yank. They sprinted back to the shore. When they reached it, the water turned from demon to savior. They cheered as it rushed over the whales.

When she heard about the whale stranding in Barrow, Cindy immediately thought they must be beached like the belugas in Turnagain Arm. Until it was explained to her, she could not understand what Craig and Geoff meant when they talked about "shore ice," "open leads," and the need for icebreakers. The Arctic seemed as remote to Cindy in Anchorage as to anyone in the Lower 48.

By the close of business Thursday, October 13, Cindy did not know nearly enough to mount an effective campaign to save the Barrow whales. But by the time Kevin got home, something told him that his long-awaited weekend would go the way of all the others. That something was the look on Cindy's face. The seeds for still another mission of mercy had been firmly planted in her. This was just the sort of crisis Cindy lived for and just what Kevin feared. Cindy loved Kevin, but truth be told, she loved whales more. He knew it. She knew it. Everyone knew it. Every time he started to think otherwise, there was another stranding to remind him.

At 6 A.M. Friday morning, Cindy's phone rang. It was Geoff Carroll in Barrow. After apologizing for waking her up, he told Cindy that the local television cameraman's footage appeared just hours before on the *NBC Nightly News.* The three stranded whales were a national story. Cindy Lowry was in business.

She jumped out of bed and into the shower. Before she could finish rinsing the shampoo out of her hair, the phone rang again. It was her boss, Campbell Plowden, from Greenpeace's Washington office. He coordinated all the organization's whale activities. While he did not see the NBC report himself, he heard about it and wanted to know if Cindy thought Greenpeace could play any kind of role. Plowden would leave the decision in Cindy's hands. If she could justify a realistic effort to help rescue the stranded whales, Greenpeace would pay the bill.

Plowden knew the International Whaling Commission's rules on the subsistence hunt allowed the Eskimos to kill any whales they could catch even though they ate only bowhead. He was afraid the Eskimos might claim the whales before anyone tried to rescue them. He wanted Cindy to find out if there were any plans to kill the whales to fill their quota.

In his long fight against subsistence whaling, Campbell Plowden knew as much as anyone about the practice and thought it awful. The ardent whale advocate knew the Eskimos were not subsistence hunters at all. He was right. Missile launchers, time-released bombs, and outboard motors did not bear much resemblance to pre-modern whaling. Plowden couldn't understand how Barrow with its $80-million high school and $400-million

Utilidor water system could even be allowed to call itself a "subsistence village." As for Barrowans, they couldn't grasp how a highly paid K Street liberal lobbyist 7,000 miles away in Washington, D.C., got off trying to tell them how they could and could not live their lives.

Cindy called Geoff and Craig back and asked them if they knew of any local plans to harvest the three whales. The biologists confessed that even if there were plans, they would likely hear nothing of them. Barrow's newcomers often charged the locals with furtively keeping to themselves, particularly when dealing with one with environmental leanings.

The IWC delegated authority to regulate the local hunt to its local subsidiary, the Alaska Eskimo Whaling Commission (AEWC). Craig called the AEWC office in Barrow to see if there was any talk of harvesting the trapped whales. Craig learned that yes, in fact, there was such interest. A few local captains had asked for permission to harvest them. A meeting was scheduled for 7:30 P.M. Saturday October 15, in a classroom at Barrow High School to hear the request.

Craig was surprised. After three days with the stranded whales, he couldn't help but feel attached to the helpless giants. These creatures had struggled against fantastic odds to survive as long as they had. His boss always reminded him never to get emotionally involved. Why did he feel so attached to three whales foolish enough to strand themselves under the growing Arctic ice? Craig knew that if presented with data on the stranding in the abstract, he would say the whales' death was a good thing: natural selection, survival of the fittest, a cleansing of the gene pool. But knowing the whales as well as he did, Craig suffered with them. He wasn't thrilled with a thought of a few greedy hunters harvesting three whales that no one wanted or would use.

Craig called Cindy and told her that the whales' fate would be decided at a special meeting the next night in Barrow. Cindy was on the move again. The national interest in the whales could only improve their chances, she reassured Craig. She told him to tell NBC's Don Oliver about the meeting. Maybe he would cover it. It was the same tactic human rights campaigners used to aid political prisoners in repressive lands, Cindy explained. The more people on the Outside who knew about the whales, the more pressure they could put on the Eskimos to spare them.

Rarely did such meetings deny whalers permission to harvest. Cindy and her allies had less than twenty-four hours to mount a campaign effective enough to block the Eskimos. If the committee voted to approve the request, the whales would be killed the next afternoon, right after church. The defiant whalers didn't yet understand the power of a few Outside television cameras. The Outsiders were always giving Barrowans a hard time about their whaling. What business was it of theirs anyway? In fact, if the meeting went as planned, some whalers would probably offer to take Dan Oliver and Russ Weston on their ski machines to film the kill.

Since she planned to take the rest of the week off, Cindy arranged to remodel Greenpeace's Anchorage office. They were busy with buzz saws and power drills and she couldn't get any work done there even if she wanted to. She holed herself up in Kevin's H Street condo and started working the phone. The simplest way to free the whales was to have a ship come in and break the ice. Campbell Plowden told her he would try to find an icebreaker from Washington while she should use her Alaska contacts.

She called Alaska Governor Steve Cowper's Juneau office. Cindy called the governor's deputy chief, David Ramseur. Sometimes he helped, more often he didn't. Cindy voiced an impassioned appeal as she told Ramseur the story of the trapped whales. Environmental activism was a lot like sales. Cindy had to convince the people in power that taking action was worth the investment in political capital.

She enticed Ramseur with some tempting political bait. If the governor could use his influence to get the Coast Guard to dispatch an icebreaker to Barrow, Cindy promised that the first-term Democrat would win brownie points from Alaska's small but noisy environmental crowd. Ramseur was unmoved after listening to Cindy's offer. "What do you want us to do?" he asked. "I'm not interested and the governor's not interested."

From previous dealings with the governor's top aide, Cindy knew Ramseur had an impatient streak that didn't mix well with her hunger for action. Instead of trying to reason with him, Cindy upset him more by barking back. While her mind told her that aggravating him was counterproductive, she went on. She knew she had lost this round. Cindy promised Ramseur she would find other means to save the three whales. Ramseur didn't want Cindy to hang up mad. He offered to listen with so long as neither he nor the Governor could be used to lure others into promising help.

Cindy's phone rang again. It was the wife of an oil executive who made Cindy promise never to identify her. Cindy jokingly called her "Jane Whale." Ms. Whale asked if she knew anything about those whales that appeared on NBC News the night before. When Cindy said she knew quite a lot about the whales, Jane Whale was thrilled.

"You see," she said, "I know a way we can get them out." Cindy's back straightened as she pressed the phone closer to her ear. The woman on the other end of the line said she knew Pete Leathard, the president of VECO, Inc., Alaska's largest oil construction company which had a huge operation at Prudhoe Bay. Jane told Cindy that Leathard saw Brokaw's broadcast the night before and was so moved by the pictures of the whales that he wanted his company to help save them.

"How can *he* help us?" Cindy asked, unable to disguise her contempt. Why would an oilman, the enemy and her moral inferior, be interested in helping three trapped whales. Only her likes were enlightened enough to love animals. It must be a stunt, a hoax, or a PR ploy, thought the master of PR ploys.

"No, no," the woman tried to reassure her. "Leathard's serious."

Jane told Cindy that VECO owned an ice-breaking hoverbarge built to supply construction materials to build offshore oil rigs in the Arctic. For all the accepted wisdom about the oilman's greed, little attention was paid to the risk that same man was willing to take to provide more oil to an expanding industrial economy. Unlike in warmer climes, drilling offshore in the Arctic is only possible during the short summer season when the ice cap thaws enough to even permit exploratory drilling, with the average cost of each sunk well—successful or dry—about $200 million.

Mukluk Island was just such an example. In 1984, amid predictions of a great discovery, three oil companies joined forces to build the only platform then stable enough to withstand the shifting ice and harsh winds of the frozen Arctic Ocean. The hoverbarge supplied materials used to build Mukluk Island, a man-made gravel island in the middle of the Beaufort Sea. At the time, Mukluk Island was the biggest and most expensive oil rig ever built, costing nearly $2 billion. All they struck was seawater. Its failure marked the end of North Slopes drilling activity for nearly two decades.

The $4-million hoverbarge commissioned to manage the ill-fated enterprise was but a rounding error of the dry well. Leathard was sure the barge could cut through Barrow's ice. It was designed to float on a cushion of air and to break through the thick ice by displacing water under it. Since it was of no use, Leathard thought VECO's chairman and founder Billy Bob Allen wouldn't object to lending it to the rescuers in Barrow.

If Allen had any doubts, Leathard thought he could assuage them by pointing to the national news coverage of the story, guaranteeing VECO some exposure. The "industry," needed positive publicity. An oil company helping rescue three stranded whales was like money in the bank. Leathard was convinced the hoverbarge would work and was determined to prove it.

Jane Whale told Cindy that all Leathard needed was a helicopter powerful enough to pull the 200,000-pound barge out of its frozen berth. The barge sank a few feet deep into the thawed permafrost during the Arctic summer, freezing it deeper into the ground each winter. Cindy's contact needed help locating a helicopter suitable for towing the barge 270 miles northwest to where the whales were stranded.

"The only type of helicopter that can pull a load that big is the Skycrane," she said. "A Sikorsky CH-54 Skycrane."

"Well, where would I find one of those?" Cindy asked.

"The only people that have them in this state are the Air Force and the Alaska National Guard."

"How long will all this take?" Cindy asked.

"Once you get the helicopter, VECO can have the barge in Barrow and the whales freed in forty hours," Jane promised, who asked Cindy not to reveal her name. "Just trust me," she pleaded. "VECO really wants to help." She instructed Cindy not to call her unless it was urgent. Otherwise, she might have to withdraw the offer. As little as Cindy trusted VECO, the favor was more than returned.

Cindy hung up the phone puzzled. Why would an oil company want to help three whales? After fruitlessly trying to come up with reasons why the plan wouldn't work, Cindy realized she had no choice. She had to trust the bad guys. She didn't know how but Cindy would get that helicopter.

She called Dave Ramseur in the governor's office. She said an oil company would donate the use of its icebreaking hoverbarge to cut a path to freedom for the trapped whales. All they needed was the one time use of two Skycrane helicopters from the Alaska National Guard or the Air Force.

Ramseur told Cindy that no one in state government could help. As for every other oil-dependent state, 1988 was a bad year for Alaska. It walked a financial tightrope, and one false move could mean sending the state into recession. Tax revenues from oil companies were way down at the moment they were most needed. After the governor had asked Alaskans to bite the fiscal bullet, why would he spend his political clout on three non-voting whales?

Only a few months earlier, Governor Cowper was roundly criticized for moving too slowly to rescue seven North Slope Eskimo walrus hunters trapped on a huge piece of ice that broke away from the shore and drifted out to sea. Ramseur correctly thought if the governor suddenly led a rescue effort on behalf of three animals after doing so little to save the lives of seven native Alaskans from Kotzebue, it would open him up to massive attack. (The walrus hunters were ultimately saved three weeks after they were stranded.)

Cindy lost her cool when Ramseur asked why she was so concerned about whales endangered not by man but by nature. Suffering is suffering, Cindy sniffed. She then reminded Ramseur that the whole country had collectively watched the 1987 rescue of a toddler named Jessica McClure from a well in Midland, Texas. Ramseur responded by suddenly remembering that the governor was out of town and couldn't be reached until Monday.

He laughed when Cindy asked him to request the assistance of Soviet icebreakers, invoking an obscure American Soviet maritime treaty. "The Coast Guard wouldn't even let us ask the Soviets for help when the Kotzebue hunters were trapped," Ramseur snapped. "You actually think they're going to allow it for three whales?"

Cindy hung up more in anger than in sadness. She called Geoff and Craig for consolation. Ramseur wasn't lying when he said the governor was out of town. He was, in fact, in Barrow—right across the hall from Geoff and Craig, in the Naval Arctic Research Lab's hearing room. For Governor Steve Cowper, his initial refusal to help marked the last time he would be asked to take any part in the drama about to unfold. From that moment until the rescue was over, Governor Cowper was neither heard from nor consulted again.

But could anybody know that this otherwise unremarkable event would turn into one of Alaska's biggest news story since the big 1964 earthquake? That it would capture the imagination of millions around the earth? That it would come to involve both the President of the United States and the General Secretary of the Communist Party of the Soviet Union? Had it not been for the real news of the the *Exxon Valdez* that spilled 11 million gallons of North Slope crude oil into the pristine waters of Prince William Sound just five months later, it might well have been the kind of blunder from which some politicians never recover.

Cowper fumbled the initial media attention that came with the rescue, but then so did everyone else. Friends couldn't connect with Cindy's despair that seemed to accompany her slightest failures. Her best political contact laid the facts bare. She could count on no help from them.

Cindy looked out her east window and gazed at the snow-covered Chugach Mountains. They seemed to stare right back at her. But it was a facade. The sun's orange afterglow lent the rugged mountains a warmth and peace that did not exist. Nothing in Alaska, Cindy mused, neither its nature nor its people, was as benign as it appeared. She thought about the three whales as if she already knew them. She had not even seen any of the pictures of three California grays. Yet she started to cry, the first of many tears to come. Kevin rolled his eyes.

It was 7 P.M. on Friday, October 14, 1988, exactly one week after the whales were first found. Cindy Lowry was at her lowest ebb of the crisis. A man named Kent Burton was on the line. He identified himself as the Under Secretary for Oceans and Atmospheres for the U.S. Department of Commerce. He was calling from his Washington home where it was 11 P.M.

"Hello, Cindy?" he said. "Commerce Secretary William Verity suggested I call you to offer our help in your efforts to save those three whales."

Who said the nature gods didn't offer miracles? This was *the* critical call of the entire event. Without that call, no rescue would have proceeded. Kent Burton got involved at the request of Alaska Senator Ted Stevens. Even then, Stevens was one of the longest-serving members of the United States Senate. Anonymity was the tool Stevens used for twenty years to build his unique position of quiet power. It was the tool he would use for twenty more years until he was narrowly defeated in his bid for a seventh term just eight days after being found guilty in a high-profile federal corruption trial. He was convicted of accepting unreported contracting services from none other than Bill Allen's VECO. A few months later, Stevens's convictions were all dismissed on grounds of "gross prosecutorial misconduct." Stevens was killed in an August 2010 plane crash deep in the Alaskan bush.

It was Stevens more than anyone else who leveraged enough power to save the three whales. Stevens answered almost every reporter the same way. In his native Hoosier twang, Stevens repeated his maxim. "If you're gonna get things done next time, you better keep your mouth shut this time."

The Commerce Department was the critical arm of government responsible for dealing with endangered species and animal protection. Unlike Outsiders, nearly every Alaskan has experience with wild animals. Even in the heart of Anchorage, moose graze in public parks and bears pick through curbed garbage. Just outside town, grizzly bears stand comfortably in any of the hundreds of salmon-rich streams.

Senator Stevens wasn't the only one to lobby the Commerce Department that day. Earlier, Campbell Plowden had done the same. He told Burton that Cindy was trying to get an icebreaker to cut a path for the whales to swim through. It worked. Commerce was interested in helping Cindy Lowry with the whales. Who needed the governor? Now, she had big oil and Ronald Reagan on her side. With allies like that, how could she lose?

7

Billy Bob's Last Frontier

Alaskans call their state the Last Frontier. Kind of an "America's America," it is a place where a dark past, or even no past at all, do not prevent a better future. The Alaskan ethic venerates those who overcome adversity. There weren't many who embodied that ethic better than William "Billy Bob" Allen. Few Alaskans would impose their own tales of hardship on Bill Allen. When he disembarked at the Port of Anchorage in 1968, there was not much to distinguish him from other Lower 48 migrants flocking north in search of a better life. A difficult past and a burning desire to stake his own claim were his only possessions. Alaska was the last place big enough to accommodate ambitions the size of Bill Allen's. Alaska was his last, best hope.

The poverty of hard-scrabble New Mexico helped fuel Allen's hopes. The day Allen's father walked out on the fourteen-year-old Bill and his family was Allen's last day of school and his first day of work. The hungry youngster found work helping a local welder lay oil and gas pipelines. After fifteen years of toiling under a hot desert sun, Bill Allen examined his life and determined it would lead him nowhere unless and until he changed. His dreams sprang back to life with stories of an Alaskan oil boom. It was 1968.

Alaska was about to take off and Bill Allen wanted to get in on the ride. He and a partner founded a small oil-supply business called VE Construction. His partner had the money; Allen had the brains. Before long the thirty-one-year-old leather-necked New Mexican landed his first contract building a small offshore oil platform in waters near Anchorage. He was so good that, in less than a decade, Bill Allen had built Alaska's largest oil construction company.

No one could tell by looking at Allen, but in 1988 he was one of the richest men in Alaska. Only after he achieved great success in Alaska could Allen find much time to spend at his ranch near Grand Junction, Colorado.

On Saturday morning, October 15, 1988, two days after the whales first appeared on NBC News, Allen and a number of his ranch hands were checking and fixing the shoes of some of his fifty thoroughbreds. Through the back legs of one of his horses, Allen could see his ranch manager's pickup approach the paddock. He brushed off his Wrangler Jeans and pulled out a faded red bandana to wipe the sweat from his dusty face.

"Mornin' boss," the ranch manager said. "Pete Leathard's on the phone from Anchorage. He said it's important."

Allen told his men they could go to lunch as soon as they finished shoeing the horses. He walked across the meadow toward the heavy black rotary phone that was probably older than the stable it was in. Allen knew Pete Leathard would not have bothered him unless it was necessary. In the "all bidness" (oil business), unexpected news is almost always bad news. Allen's mind raced to concoct the worst possible scenario. Perhaps there was a blowout at one of the offshore rigs built by VECO. He wondered how many men had died. Therefore, Allen thought he was hearing things when Pete asked him for permission to authorize the National Guard to tow the hoverbarge to Barrow on a whale rescue mission.

"You wanna do what?" Allen asked incredulously.

Not only had Bill Allen not heard about the whales, even if he had, he wouldn't have given a Texas damn. He loved horses, not whales. Those damned environmentalists always hid behind whales whenever they tried to stop any of his new projects—projects that employed thousands, and funded the very Alaskan government Lowry and others used against him.

Allen listened while Leathard tried to convince him that VECO might get some benefit from helping free the whales.

"Bill," Pete said. Allen had only recently begun to insist on a single, more dignified first name. "That barge can do the job. It can free those whales and win us some points with the public. I hate to do this to you, Bill, but we need you back here to take charge. The media's all over this one."

Allen didn't need to be reminded that the hoverbarge was a VECO disaster. It was his $4 million that paid for it. No one liked losing money more than Bill Allen. Better to use the barge rather than let it sink further into the tundra. Pete Leathard was right. The moment Allen signed on, the rescue was on.

Allen canceled the rest of his stay at the ranch and booked a flight back to Anchorage. He stored his cream-colored ten-gallon Stetson in the overhead compartment and stretched his long legs in his specially requested bulkhead seat of the 757 widebody jet. During the six-hour flight from Denver to Anchorage, he started having second thoughts. What in the "hail" was he thinking, he asked himself. An oil construction company doing environmentalists bidding to save three whales? Whenever someone from the Outside asked him how folks in his business got along with the state's environmentalists, Bill Allen used an industry metaphor. "Since 'all' don't mix with water," he would say, "we don't mix."

Just about the time Pete Leathard called Billy Bob Allen in Colorado, Kent Burton from the Department of Commerce got in touch with Cindy Lowry in Anchorage. Burton was waiting for instructions on how to help save the whales. Cindy told him she still had not heard that VECO had officially donated the barge. The phone rang again. It was Pete Leathard from VECO. He told her that Bill Allen not only authorized use of the barge and himself was on his way back to Anchorage.

Cindy Lowry's acceptance of VECO's offer created one of the oddest coalitions in the history of modern environmentalism: VECO with its barge and Greenpeace's Cindy Lowry with her contacts to save three California gray whales. Cindy called Kent Burton at the Commerce Department in Washington to tell him the good news. She asked him what she could do to get the helicopter that the governor turned down. Burton informed her that this could only be obtained with the request of an authorized elected official. Once that was done, Burton could take the next step.

Why bother with senators? Cindy asked herself. She expected even less help from them than from Governor Cowper. When was the last time, Cindy wondered, when either of Alaska's senators, or its lone congressman—all of whom were Republicans, who everyone knows hate nature and all that's in it—ever supported anything she worked for? Surely, if any of Alaska's four statewide office holders would help, it would be Governor Cowper. He was the only Democrat.

Still, Cindy took Kent Burton's advice and called Senator Ted Stevens's office. She realized she might have misjudged the demonized Stevens when the senator's assistant, Earl Comstock, told Cindy they were anxious to do whatever they could to help. Stevens had been following the story of the trapped whales on television like everybody else. Republicans could love whales, too!

On Saturday, Comstock called the senator at home to ask if he would be interested in relaying Cindy's request for National Guard helicopters to tow the frozen barge. The senator was more than interested. To his wife's chagrin, he canceled plans to spend a quiet Saturday with his family and rushed to his office on Capitol Hill.

Cindy wanted to find out for herself who had the helicopters and how long it would take to make them operational once they were put on active duty. She called National Guard headquarters in Anchorage, expecting to get another answering machine. Instead, she reached General John Schaeffer.

General Schaeffer was more than the highest-ranking military officer in the state; he was an Alaska legend. The full-blooded Inupiat Eskimo from the small subsistence village of Kotzebue on Alaska's northwest coast was the unrivaled hero of his people. The fifty-one-year-old general was the highest-ranking Inupiat in Alaska state history. His achievements were taught in all of Alaska's schools. As an investment manager turned a half-million-dollar grant to his local Native corporation by the 1971 Alaska Land Claims Settlement act into more than $50 million. Schaeffer managed it all in less than a decade, and he did it by employing seven hundred people in a village that had never before used money.

His military career was just as impressive.

Two years before statehood, a twenty-eight-year-old Schaeffer enlisted in the famous Eskimo Scouts, officially known as the Alaska Army National Guard's First Battalion. By 1988, General John W. Schaeffer was adjutant general for the Alaska National Guard and commissioner of the

State of Alaska Department of Military and Veteran Affairs. Many Alaskans felt Schaeffer's next stop would be a term in Juneau as Alaska's first native governor. Opinion polls showed Schaeffer winning almost any political office he sought.

Cindy was startled to hear his unmistakable voice answering the phone that Saturday morning. Before she could respond, the general had to repeat his greeting a second time. Cindy didn't know at the time that General Schaeffer had gone to his office because of the whales. Ted Stevens had beat her to it, and had already asked the general to coordinate the logistics needed to support a rescue operation.

"We're here trying to save those whales," the Inuit general told Cindy. She was impressed. She didn't know how or why, but all of a sudden, the "bad guys" were marching to her tune—or perhaps she was marching to theirs?

In less than twenty-four hours, Cindy Lowry had enlisted the support of a giant oil construction company, a U.S. Senator, the U.S. Commerce Department, and Alaska's highest-ranking military officer, all to help save three stranded whales at the top of the world. But this was no time to celebrate. The rescue hadn't even begun. The constantly ringing phone never let Cindy's exhaustion catch up with her. If it wasn't the National Guard, it was Senator Stevens. Her boyfriend's bedroom had become the makeshift headquarters for most massive animal rescue in history.

She couldn't grab a much-needed cup of coffee before the phone rang again. This time it was Ben Odom, Bill Allen's biggest client. Odom was a senior vice president for the Atlantic Richfield Oil Company (ARCO), one of the largest, oldest, and richest oil companies on Earth. Established in 1866, ARCO was a driving force behind John Rockefeller's Standard Oil Trust, which developed the modern petroleum industry and, in many ways, the very world we inhabit today. In the intervening century and a quarter, ARCO had grown to become the largest gasoline retailer in the United States with huge oil operations all over the world, including Alaska.

It was Ben Odom's ARCO, together with partner Exxon, that discovered North America's largest oil field on March 12, 1968, at Prudhoe Bay, on Alaska's North Slope. Odom was responsible for all of ARCO's in-state operations, which made him one of the most powerful men in Alaska. (ARCO merged with BP in 2000.)

Although Ben Odom and Bill Allen had become close friends, the two men were cut from very distinct cloths. Both were born into the oil business, but at opposite ends of it. Whereas Allen had a tough childhood, Odom was born into the elite world of the great Oklahoma oil boom of the 1930s. Refined and educated in the ways of the industry, Odom was groomed to rise to the top. After thirty-five years at ARCO, his style and charm were frequently compared to his lifelong friend James A. Baker III, who in just a few weeks would be nominated to be U.S. secretary of state by yet another old Texas oilman friend, President-elect George H. W. Bush.

Early Saturday morning, the casually dressed Odom had arrived in the elegantly appointed executive suite atop the twenty-three-story ARCO Alaska Tower in downtown Anchorage. The night before, Pete Leathard had asked permission to use some ARCO equipment to remove the hoverbarge, which sat at ARCO's East Dock in Prudhoe Bay. Odom was intrigued as much by the technical challenges of a rescue as he was by the whales. The Arctic was the world's most difficult work environment. Any chance to try something new could only help. He built his career by accomplishing things people said couldn't be done in such harsh conditions. Odom also knew it wouldn't hurt ARCO's image to look like the good guy. (As though providing cheap, reliable, abundant, and safe energy wasn't enough to be called a good guy.) Trying to save whales could only win points in a much larger industry battle.

For almost a decade, ARCO and all the major oil companies had lobbied hard for the right to drill for oil in the Alaska National Wildlife Refuge (ANWR). At twenty million acres, ANWR was one of North America's last virgin wildlife santuaries. The oil companies wanted permission to drill on just one 2,000-acre site inside the gigantic refuge. Environmentalists argued that this spot was right in the heart of 200,000 strong Porcupine Caribou Herd's central calving area. The oil industry responded by reminding environmentalists that they said the same thing when they tried to stop development at Prudhoe Bay, which turned out to be the most environmentally sensitive oil operation ever built. Caribou frolic and play by the pipeline, and the herds have thrived.

Ben Odom and Bill Allen knew that refusal to allow exploration in ANWR would only increase America's dependence on foreign oil produced with far less concern for environment safety. They also believed development of Alaska's oil could make their companies lots of money. Both

President Ronald Reagan and candidate George Bush felt that refusing to tap the last remaining domestic sources of oil would ultimately weaken the United States, something they promised not to allow.

Environmentalists like Cindy Lowry argued that the threat to the environment had become too great—even though it was cleaner than it had been in decades. Allowing oil drilling in a National Wildlife Refuge was an obscenity—then again, anything that Cindy didn't like was an obscenity of one sort or another. Before the *Exxon Valdez* spill of March 1989, the oil companies bragged about their well-deserved reputation for outstanding environmental management in the Arctic. But that same year, the Environmental Protection Agency (EPA) charged that the oil companies regularly violated many strict federal standards. The EPA claimed that oil and chemicals had spilled over and "ruined" 11,000 acres of tundra. They never bothered to explain what "ruined" actually meant.

During the 1988 presidential campaign, George Bush claimed that caribou "loved the pipeline." Naturally, he was mocked by the elites, egged on by his detractors in the environmentalist camp, as being environmentally insensitive. The U.S. Fish and Wildlife Service translated Bush's malapropism into acceptable, politically Jargon and said that the negative impact on the migrating caribou was far less than originally predicted.

At the time of the whale stranding, it looked like the oil industry had gained the critical upperhand in the decade-long battle to open the Arctic National Wildlife Refuge (ANWR). Ben Odom, Bill Allen, and the U.S. government hoped some positive coverage of oil companies working to rescue whales might help. Good public relations could sway the few fence-sitting senators whose votes were needed to start drilling.

Odom didn't want to take any chances. He offered more than the use of some facilities. He told Cindy that ARCO would be delighted to donate all the fuel the National Guard helicopter would need to tow the 200,000-pound hoverbarge. Based on Pete Leathard's estimates, Odom figured it would cost ARCO $35,000 to provide the fuel needed to pull the barge out of the ice and tow it on the forty-hour trip to Barrow. For a company that did twenty-five million dollars of business a day in Prudhoe Bay alone, that wasn't even a rounding figure.

Odom told Cindy that he would meet with Allen as soon as he got back to Anchorage. If all went well, the hoverbarge could be on its way to Barrow as early as Monday night, October 16. Two days later, the whales would be free.

Not quite.

Cindy anxiously wanted to talk to Geoff and Craig. In just a few hours, Barrow was scheduled to hold a special meeting to decide the whales' fate. The International Whaling Commission granted the local representative, the Alaska Eskimo Whaling Commission (AEWC) the right to control their own IWC quota. They could continue to hunt as long as they made sure Barrow whalers obeyed the law. If they didn't, the IWC had the power to impose tough sanctions, including probation, heavy fines, and—most severe of all—reduced quotas in upcoming seasons, a cultural death penalty for a village whose culture many believed was already long extinct.

The AEWC board included all of Barrow's top whaling captains. The consensus approach made sure that each captain shared an equal stake in the committee's decisions. Every so often, the captains met informally over Chinese food. Visits by IWC representatives marked the closest thing to a formal event Barrow ever hosted. Whalers reluctantly stepped out of their heavy native garb to dress uncomfortably into ill-fitting Western clothing that hadn't been worn since the last time the IWC was in town. No one in Barrow, Inuit or non, were much for Western-style meetings. Only the most unusual situation could get them to participate in one; the stranding of the three California gray whales had become such a situation.

Nuiqsut whalers wanted the three animals harvested, and offered Barrow whalers the chance to make some money in the process. The quota and IWC regulations allowed it; state law allowed it; so did tradition. But the whales were quickly becoming a national media story How would the whalers appear to Outsiders if they killed animals the world wanted saved, and all for a just few thousand dollars? The leaders of the whaling crews knew they possessed the power to decide whether they would harvest the trapped grays or let them die and become part of the normal food chain. But what they did not know was that they also had the power to create or abort one of greatest media nonevents of all time.

To Alaska Wildlife Management professionals, harvesting the struggling creatures seemed the proper thing. Most Barrow lay people agreed. Conventional wisdom convinced them that an extensive rescue would doom the whales to prolonged suffering and the taxpayer to wasted expense. Geoff and

Craig knew little chance existed that the whales would survive. Cindy also was not convinced that the whales could be rescued. But she had to try. She was afraid the whaling captains wouldn't give her the chance. She did not want them to change their lives or ways. All she sought was a little time to learn whether a successful rescue could be mounted.

Dr. Tom Albert, the North Slope Borough Wildlife Management Director, asked Cindy for a progress report. Were the prospects for rescue real? His job was to work with the Eskimos—if they wanted to harvest the whales. Albert didn't want his men, Geoff and Craig, preventing a harvest if the chances of a rescue were slim. Provocation without cause could only sour relations with his Eskimo employers.

When Cindy told Albert about the plan to break the ice with VECO's hoverbarge, she said enough to convince him to side with her attempt to save the whales. He knew that Geoff and Craig would have to take on a new, broader mission. Research was still important, but their task was no longer aloof observation. Now Geoff and Craig had to do whatever they could to keep the whales alive. For the first time since the animals were discovered ten days before, man was about to take his first active step toward freeing them.

Although Cindy had the rough outline of a rescue, it still had to be implemented. Lowry had to follow up on the promises of support to ensure they were delivered. Even though the efforts of the rescuers could be rendered moot by an Eskimo decision to use their remaining quota of strikes to kill the whales, it was time for everyone on her side to get to work.

The organization that was born on Saturday morning, October 15, 1988, needed a leader and a name. Kent Burton of the Commerce Department provided both. The U.S. government would lead the rescue and it would be called Operation Breakout, a name that would be changed to Operation Breakthrough on the eve of the whales' eventual rescue.

As undersecretary for Oceans and Atmospheres, Burton oversaw the National Oceanic and Atmospheric Administration (NOAA). Under the Endangered Species Act of 1973, NOAA was the final legal authority on any matter concerning all marine mammals, including whales. Burton wanted a NOAA representative on the ground to coordinate the government operation. He needed someone competent enough to manage NOAA's role as rescue coordinator.

Tom Albert told Burton he had already spoken with someone from NOAA Fisheries' Anchorage office named Ron Morris. Albert solicited Morris's help at that evening's Barrow whaling captains' meeting. Morris thought the overnight trip to Barrow would be pleasant diversion. He packed a few things and drove down Minnesota Drive to Anchorage International in time for MarkAir's noon flight to Barrow.

Bill Allen's plane landed in Anchorage two hours after Morris's left. Pete Leathard met Allen at the gate. The National Guard was busy putting together a team, Pete told Allen. NOAA assumed a federal role and already had a man on the way to Barrow, and ARCO promised to supply the fuel for the whole operation. On the way in from the airport, Allen nodded his head and pointed the rough-edged tip of his Tony Lama cowboy boot resting on Pete Leathard's dashboard in the direction of Alaska's tallest building. It was Allen's way of saying he wanted to see Ben Odom. Odom was in that Saturday afternoon, busy at work on his company's role in the rescue. The three of them began mapping out the operation.

Odom asked how much labor would be needed to break the barge free of ice and how much it would cost. Leathard reminded them that at fifty dollars an hour, labor alone could soon cost VECO tens of thousands of dollars. Earlier that day, Allen committed himself and his companies to help and that is exactly what he intended to do. The three men called General Schaeffer, who told them he was having trouble assembling a logistics command to run the operation from Prudhoe Bay.

General Schaeffer wanted a sharp forty-year-old colonel named Tom Carroll to head the operation. Carroll was the best field commander in the state. However, he had taken the weekend off and wasn't scheduled to report to HQ until 0800 Monday morning. General Schaeffer wasn't going ahead with the operation until he could account for his man.

8

A Great Eskimo Hunter
Saves the Whales

There was nothing Tom Carroll loved more than the smell of fresh-cut wood. When he wasn't covered in military fatigues, he was usually covered in sawdust. At headquarters, they joked that the only way to keep Colonel Carroll clean was to keep him green. Saturday morning, October 15, was no exception. The boyish-looking colonel's glasses were covered with a layer of dust so thick he had to use his hands to "see" along the edge of the cabinet door he had just put through the lathe in his Anchorage garage. Carroll, his glasses opaque, knocked over nearly everything between him and the ringing phone.

It was General John Schaeffer calling to tell him the National Guard had been asked to help save those stranded whales everybody was talking about. "They're calling it Operation Breakout," the general said. "Are you interested?" Carroll knew the question was rhetorical. When your superior suggests an assignment, the well-trained officer accepts. But he was happy to. Carroll loved field operations—it was why he remained in the military after he returned from his decorated tour in Vietnam as an infantry commander. He welcomed any opportunity to leave his cloistered desk in the Anchorage's Frontier Building. The General told Carroll to report to headquarters.

Carroll hung up the phone, showered, donned his standard issue Alaskan National Guard Colonel's fatigues, and headed out the door. Colonel Tom Carroll was an unflappable professional. His father was a military man, a legacy passed onto Tom. The colonel evoked Alaska and the military's can-do spirit. Adventure, risk, and daring were nothing new to the colonel. Neither was loss. He first learned what loss meant the hard way and at a young age.

On the morning of March 27, 1964, when Carroll was a fifteen-year-old boy, Prince William Sound erupted as the epicenter of the most powerful earthquake ever to strike North America. Its 9.2 reading was the highest ever recorded by the Richter scale, eighty times more powerful than the 1906 San Francisco earthquake. It made history for moving the earth farther and faster than any other one on record. Its force was so devastating that it killed people seven hundred miles apart. The Good Friday earthquake was Alaska's greatest modern tragedy. From Port Ashton to Nellie and Anchorage to Seward, 131 people died that morning. Tom Carroll's father was one of them.

Carroll was one of the few people in the Last Frontier of the late 1980s who was actually born and raised in Alaska. He was called a sourdough. Alaska's earliest white pioneers used to cherish this hardy yeast and carry it with them to make bread and biscuits. Since the dough would replenish itself after each use, it stayed fresh indefinitely, just like those early pioneers who settled and remained in Alaska. It became the state's namesake. Becoming a sourdough required a rite of passage no other state could match. Other than birth, sourdough status could only be conferred to those who had survived at least twenty-five Alaskan winters.

Colonel Carroll drove down C Street through one of Anchorage's many strip malls built in the oil-boom days of the early 1980s. He thought about the strong images of the whales he saw on Todd Pottinger's newscast the night before. Carroll was no environmentalist, but like almost everybody in Alaska, he wished the creatures well. But he wondered why the National Guard had joined the rescue.

Civilian passersby didn't stare at Tom Carroll as he dashed through the lobby of one of Alaska's modern office buildings dressed in jungle combat fatigues. Alaska had one of the highest military-to-civilian ratios of any state in the country.

When the colonel walked into his office he was surprised to see General John Schaeffer sitting in his chair, using his phone. Senator Stevens was on the line from Washington. Like an unexpected visitor, Carroll offered an apologetic salute to his superior and gingerly backed out of his own office.

Eight days after the whales were first discovered trapped in the ice, General Schaeffer joined Colonel Carroll, a contracting officer, two Arctic logistics specialists, and a press aide in the conference room down the hall from his office. He explained to the hastily assembled group that the purpose of their mission was to tow a 185-ton hoverbarge from Prudhoe Bay to Barrow. Tom Carroll, whom Schaeffer had put in charge, had to decide what equipment was best suited for the massive tow. Carroll knew that pulling 185 tons over nearly three hundred miles of jagged ice could prove to be quite a tricky operation. Privately, he wondered whether it was even possible. But Colonel Carroll was paid to do, not to doubt.

Pete Leathard assured General Schaeffer that the most difficult part of the task would be digging the barge out of the frozen tundra where it idly sat for the last four years. Once free, the barge could easily be towed across the ocean's solidly frozen surface ... or so everyone thought. Carroll checked with all the armories across Alaska to determine what equipment was available and best suited for the job. In calligraphic script, Colonel Carroll listed the options on a yellow legal pad christened for his new assignment. The colonel weighed his options and, like all good commanders, sided with caution. He chose the Sikorsky CH-54 Skycrane helicopter. The Skycrane was capable of lifting more weight than any other helicopter. If it couldn't do the job, nothing could.

Carroll wanted to make sure that the necessary fuel, the Skycrane's biggest requirement, would be available. It guzzled a staggering 650 gallons an hour. That meant it would take at least 30,000 gallons to get the barge out of the frozen earth and across the ice to Barrow. Before he ordered the helicopter, Carroll checked with Schaeffer to see whether he was authorized to use that much fuel. The general told Colonel Carroll to guzzle away: ARCO was donating all the fuel he would need.

When Ben Odom learned his offer was being taken seriously, it was too late to turn back. By the time the rescue was over, ARCO would become by far Operation Breakout's largest private cash contributor, donating more than at least half a million dollars' worth of fuel alone to help save the three whales.

Next on Colonel Carroll's checklist was office support. Between the pilots, public affairs, and ground personnel, Carroll would need a command post and living quarters for nearly a dozen people. After checking with Ben Odom, Carroll learned that ARCO would also provide office space, telephones and rooms for the National Guard and VECO in the company's ultramodern Prudhoe Bay installation 1,700 miles from the North Pole.

ARCO spent hundreds of millions of dollars to build a superb habitat for their workers on the North Slope. To keep up morale, the heartless oil barons made sure their hard-working employees were extremely well paid and provided with every conceivable comfort while on the job—movie theaters, maid and room service, bowling alleys, and cafeterias that served the finest steaks and lobster flown in fresh from Anchorage. Until the Eskimos in Barrow spent $15 million to build a swimming pool in 1986, Prudhoe Bay had the only one above the Arctic Circle.

It took several hours for Colonel Carroll and his men to arrange for the aircraft and personnel to support the Skycranes. When they finished, the colonel told his men to go home. "Don't forget to get some sleep," he reminded them. "You're all due back here at 0500 hours." He wanted to get an early start. "Wheels up at 6:00 A.M." Tom Carroll had asserted his command. Carroll wanted to check the ice conditions around Barrow himself before making a final decision to okay the hoverbarge tow. For all the talk about how smooth and solid the Beaufort Sea ice was between Prudhoe and Barrow, no one had actually examined it. Carroll was a man focused on details. Details make or break missions.

Pete Leathard promised that the barge could break ice up to two feet thick. Any ice thicker than that would have to be cut by something else. He didn't have to elaborate. There was nothing else available capable of cutting ice more than two feet thick. Tom Carroll was not about to risk his men, equipment, and his own rank on an operation that didn't have an excellent chance of success. If he ever thought the deck was stacked against him, Operation Breakout would end.

General Schaeffer walked with the colonel to the copy machine across the hall. Carroll glanced at the document the general was about to copy, which contained Schaeffer's handwritten call sheet with the names and numbers of everyone involved in the rescue. The colonel was prepared to find the names of some of Alaska's most prominent citizens: Senator Stevens, Governor Cowper, Bill Allen, and Ben Odom. But he was taken aback by the name on top of the list: Cindy Lowry.

"Isn't she the Greenpeace gal with the bullhorn?" he asked the general.

"Yup. She sure is," Schaeffer responded. "And, like it or not, you'll have to work with her. She's the one who started this whole thing in the first place. We're on her side in this one, Tom."

Colonel Carroll had nothing against Cindy. He didn't know her personally. But he wondered how someone so well known for her rabble-rousing against the United States Armed Forces in Alaska could be so suddenly interested in participating in a top down military operation.

Tom Carroll tried to call Cindy Lowry, but he couldn't get through because she was on the phone to Geoff and Craig, who had just gotten back from a day on the ice with the whales. They were discussing strategy for that night's critical Barrow whaling captains meeting. They confirmed what she had been watching all morning on her television. The whales were fast becoming a local phenomenon, a tourist attraction, and a national news event all in one.

By Saturday afternoon, October 15, a week and a day after they were first discovered, the whales now had almost round-the-clock company. Some Eskimo hunters and the few media crews already in town joined Geoff and Craig to spend the entire day with the animals. The whales would never again go unattended during daylight hours. Geoff and Craig told Cindy that as they were about to leave, they discovered the youngest whale had trouble breathing. The baby whale wheezed, coughed up lots of water, and looked exhausted. Until that moment, Geoff and Craig were ordered to observe the whales, not to interfere. The whales needed more room to breathe. The hole they depended on for survival was once sixty feet by thirty feet. In the eight days since the whales were first discovered, it had shrunk by two-thirds. The hole would soon completely freeze over.

The two biologists wanted to help. If they could just slightly expand the hole, the whales could breathe easier and buy some precious time. They shouted their ideas for expanding the holes over the deafening whine of their ski machine as it raced across the bleak Arctic landscape on the long, cold ride back to Barrow. Before ending the conversation to clear her line,

Cindy asked Geoff and Craig if they had heard anything yet from Ron Morris.

"Who is Ron Morris?" they asked.

"Ron Morris, from NOAA Fisheries. He's the project coordinator," Cindy answered. Morris was due in on the 3:30 P.M. flight. She didn't know if anyone had arranged lodging for him. There weren't many hotel rooms left. This wasn't Morris's problem alone; Cindy would find herself in the same spot before she knew it. The next call came from Campbell Plowden in Washington. He told her to get up to Barrow on the next available flight.

"Don't worry about packing," he instructed. "Just throw some things in an overnight bag. You won't be up there but a day or so."

It was too late for the last flight to Barrow, which left Anchorage at 3:40. The next flight was not until tomorrow, Sunday morning. About the same time Cindy got her marching orders, Ron Morris's plane began its descent. He was about to enter a world that after many previous visits still remained a mystery. Just five years short of becoming a naturalized sourdough, the fifty-four-year-old Morris could never quite figure out how a town like Barrow ever got started. Morris couldn't imagine a more depressing place.

When the pilot turned on the NO SMOKING sign signaling the final approach into Barrow's Wiley Post–Will Rogers Memorial Airport, Morris leaned back to finish his Bloody Mary mix. Morris popped a couple of Tic-Tacs and was ready to face the world. He wanted to make a good first impression. He stroked his beard as the plane taxied. He took good care to nourish his rakish nautical air. With his thinning silver hair, someone commented that Morris looked like one of those little wooden carvings of Maine lobstermen sold in souvenir shops across the country. All he lacked was the bright yellow slicker.

If he wasn't convinced already, Morris needed no further reminders of where the 737 landed once he stepped off the plane. It was nearly fifty degrees colder in Barrow than it was in Anchorage. Barrow and Anchorage seemed like two different worlds. In many ways they were. Anchorage was closer to Seattle than to Barrow. Separating them were more than a thousand miles of wilderness. Man and his ability to fly over it were all that connected the two vastly different realms.

No one was waiting for Ron Morris at the airport. Like everyone else who arrived in Barrow for this during the surreal days, he had no idea where to go or what to do. After grabbing his frozen nylon bag from the rickety stainless-steel luggage chute, Morris looked out the smoke-stained terminal window into a Barrow street scene shrouded in the steam emanating from the buildings and passing cars around him. He made out an AIRPORT INN sign across the street. As he pushed open the light lacquer pine door, Morris noticed no trace of his breath condensing on the window just inches from his face.

Must be Arctic plastic, he thought. Ordinary glass would have shattered in the bone-chilling temperatures. The first blast of Arctic air hit him, as it does every visitor, square in the face. Grimacing, he sarcastically mumbled, "Not a bad day." Remembering earlier visits when things were really bad, he regained his perspective. At least they haven't lost the light.

Ed Benson still had a couple of empty rooms at the Airport Inn. But by the time Morris showed up, Benson could ask and get $225 a night for a warm bed and a shower. Born and raised in New York City, Morris knew when he was being conned. But he also knew when he had no choice. He dropped his American Express card on the shelf atop the half-open Dutch door to the service counter.

While Morris unpacked his overnight bag, Ed Benson shouted to him from the bottom of the stairs. Tom Albert from the Department of Wildlife Management was calling to tell him about the whaling captains' meeting that night at Barrow High School. Before hanging up, Ron asked Albert where he could get a bite to eat before the meeting. Morris wanted to find out more about the whole harvesting issue. He saw reports of it on the news and on his desk back in Anchorage. If a competent Eskimo could convince him there was no hope of saving the whales, and Geoff and Craig would agree, then Morris would not stand in the way.

Tom Albert, the director of wildlife management for the North Slope, arranged for the newly assembled rescue team to get together at Pepe's before going to the high school for the whaling captains' meeting at 7:30. Over dinner, Ron Morris could debrief Geoff and Craig. If the whalers voted to spare the three California grays, Ron wanted to make sure everyone knew that he would be in charge. NOAA appointed him coordinator of a rescue, should it be approved by the whalers.

Geoff and Craig looked exhausted as they pulled up their chairs in the crowded restaurant. Five days on the frozen surface of the Chukchi Sea at thirty-five degrees below zero had started to take its toll. The human body needs at least seven thousand calories a day to stay warm outside in the Arctic. Morris watched in wonder as the two men devoured more of the world's most overpriced Mexican food in a single sitting than he could afford in a week. Between the two of them, their bill came to almost one hundred dollars. A couple fresh reporters spotted the biologists. Now that they were off duty, they couldn't refuse to answer a question or two, could they? Whenever asked, Geoff and Craig always answered that the fate of the whales lay not in their hands or any state officers' hands, but in the hands of the whaling captains. No one could help the animals if the Barrow elders decided to kill them.

"But what if they decide not to kill them?" NBC's Don Oliver asked in a gravelly voice. "Could anything be done to save them?"

Before either Geoff and Craig had a chance to answer, Ron Morris faced directly into the blinding glare of the NBC crew's lights and calmly but confidently introduced himself.

"My name's Ron Morris," said the man from NOAA. "I was appointed earlier today as the coordinator of Operation Breakout. As you know, the whaling captains meet in just about an hour to figure out what they are going to do. The meeting is open and you're invited to attend. Once it's over, I'd be happy to answer any questions you might have, if I can."

Finally, someone had arrived on the scene who could handle Oliver and his constant questions. They were impressed with the way Morris invited him to the whaling captains' meeting. Morris seemed a natural.

No matter how badly some of the younger Eskimos wanted to harvest the three trapped whales, none could ignore the presence of the media descending on Barrow. All three major networks were getting their acts together. By the next night, Sunday, October 16, they would all be in Barrow. Even cash-strapped CNN found a way to send its own crew to cover the stranding. Malik wanted to arrive at the meeting early. He sought to talk some sense into the brash young Eskimos clamoring for a chance to strike the stranded whales. Malik knew that killing the animals could shake subsistence whaling to its very core.

To the newly arrived press corps, Malik might have been just another Inupiat Eskimo living at the Top of the World, but he was smarter than any Outsider would realize. Walking into the high school on Takpuk Street,

Malik wore a warm outer garment called a parkee. It was made from the skins of light brown caribou fawns and the shimmering gray fur of male Arctic squirrels. His traditional lightweight boots, called mukluks, were made of bearded sealskin, or Oogruk.

When Malik entered the school, several reporters were already there. Most of them had just gotten to town and stopped by the high school. Few thought the meeting worth more than superficial coverage. Almost none had ever seen anyone dressed like Malik. As he walked out into the hall way to pour himself a cup of hot coffee, NBC cameraman Bruce Gray lifted his heavy equipment back onto his shoulders. The powerful lights affixed to his camera nearly blinded a stunned Malik when he came back into the room. Gray focused his lens on Malik's mukluks, then on his parkee, while at the same time preparing to take pictures of Malik's archetypal Inuit face.

Before Barrow's top whaling crews could make their way into the classroom assigned to them, it was clear they would have to move to accommodate all the people interested in attending the public meeting. There were more than a dozen Outsiders and around fifty Barrowans anxious to see what would happen to the trapped whales. They moved across the hall to a state-of-the-art semicircular audio visual projection auditorium filled with around a hundred padded theater chairs. That room was just big enough to seat everyone.

A short, powerfully built Eskimo man, wearing wide silver-frame glasses over dark sunken eyes and a rounded robust face, waited patiently to start the meeting. His name was Arnold Brower Jr., and he was one of the most successful whaling captains in Barrow. He was one of the top young "subsistence" whalers. His crew killed five bowhead whales during the spring season alone; an almost unheard of accomplishment, even for his mentor Malik.

Arnold Brower Jr., was part of one of the world's largest Inuit families. In fact, many of the hundred or so people in the auditorium were named Brower. It seemed that nearly every Eskimo in Barrow was either named Brower or had close relatives that were.

The Browers could trace their Eskimo lineage back thousands of years, but their name came from modern times. Their patriarch was a brash young explorer from New York City who came to Barrow in the

1880s in search of adventure. Brower discovered much more than even his burgeoning dreams could fathom. He found an immense fortune and a stunning legacy. The former came from selling coal to new steam-powered commercial whaling ships plying through cold Arctic waters in search of bounty. The latter, legend has it, came from Brower taking prodigious advantage of the Eskimo's most enticing cultural trait: spouse sharing.

No one knew for sure how many Inupiats were actually sired by Charlie Brower, but within a generation, there were literally hundreds of them. They were everywhere. Brower had dozens of "family" trading posts stretching all along Alaska's North Slope. They were all run by people who claimed to be Browers. Soon there were so many Browers in and around Barrow, they built their own section of town and named it, aptly, Browerville.

What started as a haphazard collection of traditional sod and whalebone huts had become a veritable Barrow suburb by 1988. Browers of all shapes and sizes lived in heated homes with running water. There was even a shuttle bus to take them the four hundred yards to "downtown" Barrow. When they died, Browers were laid to rest in their own family burial ground.

Like many of Barrow's subsistence hunters, Arnold Brower Jr. took pay from the North Slope Borough. But unlike many others, Brower actually worked for his living. He was one of Mayor George Ahmaogak's top aides. Since the mayor was out of town attending an Alaska Federation of Natives meeting, and the deputy mayor, Warren Matumeak, was unavailable, Arnold Jr. was left to run the whaling captains' meeting. Emergency whaling meetings were rare, but if ever there was an occasion that could be called an emergency, this was it. No Barrowan was threatened with starvation. Nor were there massive fleets of commercial whaling vessels just offshore killing all the whales Barrow used to depend on for survival. This threat was uniquely modern.

To the reporters dazzled by his strange-looking boots and classic Inuit face, Malik appeared to be a primitive Eskimo whose features would make colorful national news footage. They would soon learn that Malik was much more than a great video sound-bite.

Malik knew that, for whatever reason, tens of millions of people in the Lower 48 were glued to the saga of the three stranded whales gasping for breath at the top of the world. This was Barrow's first and probably last chance to make any kind of impression on so many Outsiders. Malik also realized that if the cameras captured the image of a cruel band of Inuit hunters, no matter how small, out to kill a few more beloved whales, it could mean the end of Eskimo whaling, and hence the end of traditional Inuit life. Once the gruesome pictures came down off Aurora I, the damage would be done.

The only question left to answer would be the severity of the consequences. Malik had to do all he could to make sure it never happened. Just before Arnold Jr. moved to open the meeting, Malik gently but forcefully pushed the startled Brower into a corner. Malik insisted on talking privately with a group of four stubborn young whalers still clamoring to slaughter the trapped animals. Speaking in his native Inupiat, Malik told the young men, his own disciples, that the stakes of their impetuous action were far too high. Shaking his head in stern, somber rebuke, Malik demanded they cancel their request to harvest the whales.

The young whalers huddled together and quickly reached a consensus. One of them approached Arnold Brower Jr., and whispered something in his ear. Brower sat down in front of the three television microphones hastily taped down on the table. "Is everyone ready?" he asked.

"The whaling captains of Barrow have decided to use our best efforts to save the three Agvigluaqs," he said, using the Inupiat word for gray whales. The room broke into a wild cheer. Arnold Brower's short declaration removed Operation Breakout's last and biggest obstacle, the local Eskimo whalers. For all of Colonel Carroll's military expertise, Ron Morris's camera presence, and Cindy Lowry's fearless determination to mount a rescue, the critical move belonged to the Eskimos. As an increasingly anxious world would soon see, the Inuits would do far more than approve the rescue. They would carry it out.

9

Colonel Carroll's Impossible Task

The instant Arnold Brower Jr. made his unexpected announcement, he completely changed the local debate about what to do with the three stranded whales. The media on hand would record the whalers' 180-degree turn. It was no longer a question of whether to kill the whales but how to save them.

Roy Ahmaogak, the local hunter who discovered the whales eight days earlier, nervously leaned over to speak into the portable public address system. His words were the first spoken after the whalers decided to help free the three leviathans. Speaking in the thick guttural accent character-istic of Inupiat Eskimos, he said, "It seems to me that before we can free the whales, we have to figure out a way to keep them alive until the barge gets here. Does anybody have any ideas?"

Geoff, Craig, and Ron Morris sat together facing the whalers. Unac-customed to speaking in front of bright lights and rolling television cam-eras, Craig George looked around apprehensively before mustering the courage to offer his suggestion.

"Arnold, what about the saws you used today?" Gaining confidence with the nods of approval from people around him, Craig continued. "Arnold Jr. was out there today and his chain saw opened up the hole real good. I can't see why they couldn't go right on doing it for the next couple of days until the barge gets here."

Chain saws were among the first tools Barrowans bought with their new oil money back in the early 1970s. They have been one of the most important weapons in the Inuit arsenal ever since. Unlike the lumberjack who viewed the chain saw as a time-saver, the Eskimo saw it as a lifesaver. Ice was more than an inconvenience; it was the constant barrier separating the hunter from the food and furs he needed to survive. The buzz saw not only saved the Eskimo from the arduous chore of manually chopping through thick ocean ice, it saved him much precious energy which allowed him to hunt for longer periods of time.

On Friday afternoon, Brower had an idea. If he could cut holes in the ice with his chain saw to hunt seals, why not use it to enlarge the whales' hole? The lone hole was shrinking several feet each day. By Friday, it was only ten feet wide by twelve feet long, barely larger than the head of a single whale. Unless the rescuers did something fast, the hole would completely freeze over.

Without bothering to tell anyone, Brower loaded one of his chain saws and a rusty gas can onto a wooden dogsled and hitched it to the back of his ski machine. Impervious to blinding winds and bone-chilling temperatures, the hardy Eskimo drove out to the whales.

After fiddling with the carburetor, Brower brought his rusty chain saw to life with a roar in the minus 25 degrees cold. He carried the saw to the middle of the longer side of the rectangular hole and cut several blocks of ice from the edge. After Craig described Arnold's success earlier in the day, the whalers decided to use a couple of their own saws to further expand the hole.

Ever since they found themselves imprisoned in a small hole in the ice, the whales had to make a choice. They could learn to dramatically alter their standard breathing pattern, or they would die. They chose to live.

Because of its distinct habitat, the gray whale developed an equally distinct breathing pattern. Rarely, if ever, would the gray whale swim more than a mile from shore. Hugging close to the ocean's edge, it lived almost exclusively in shallow waters. Gray whales spent most of their lives in water not much deeper than the length of their bodies. Other whales, like the magnificent humpback, lived farther out from shore. Their immensely powerful breaches could vault 80,000 pounds and forty feet of whale clear out of the water. The force of the humpback crashing back into the water smashed off more barnacles in a second than a gray whale could shake off in a year of gravel rolling. This spectacle delighted increasing numbers of tourists who came to Alaska. Their hosts became flourishing entrepreneurs in a growing industry Outsiders called whale watching.

Biologists long thought gray whales didn't breach because they lived in shallower waters than other whales. They never deviated from their traditional pattern of arching their backs just enough to expose their blowholes above the waterline and breathing horizontal to the surface. The moment Roy Ahmaogak spotted three heads popping in and out the one small hole eight days before, he learned something new. A gray whale could lift its huge head clear out of the water if it meant survival.

On Sunday morning, Geoff revved up the power saw to cut the ice around the middle of the hole. Malik vigorously motioned for him to stop. Geoff knew more about whales than most whites, but Malik knew more than Geoff. Shoving a buzz saw into the middle of the water where the whales needed to surface would surely drive them away. With nowhere to go, the whales would swim to their deaths, unable to breathe. Malik wanted to proceed cautiously. He sensed the whales had to become accustomed to the roar of the tools man would use to free them.

Malik took two running saws and placed them on the ice at opposite ends of the hole. Then he motioned the few onlookers to wait quietly. If the whales saw that the water above them looked unchanged from the last time they surfaced, they might take a chance.

Malik was right. After an abnormally long dive, the whales approached the open hole with trepidation. They tentatively lingered just a few feet below the surface before cautiously breaking the water's roiling plain. This time, there was no lounging in the open water. Just as they had breathed in shifts when they were first discovered, the whales started to do so again, first the two larger whales, then the baby. Each whale breathed deeply and quickly dove back down under the ice.

Only when the whales started to grow accustomed to the saws' loud vibrations did Malik figure it was okay to start using them. He slowly pushed his saw's sharp point into the edge of the thick ice. Malik, perhaps the most seasoned Eskimo whaler alive, was unprepared for what he saw. Moments after shying away from the sound, the whales seemed to relish it.

Perhaps, Malik thought, they sensed that the loud and ungainly surface instruments were miraculously splitting the ice threatening to entomb them. Malik had a new worry: how to keep the three whales from accidentally rubbing up against the lethal blades of a chain saw at full throttle.

Geoff, Craig, and Ron Morris were relieved when they saw how quickly the whales seemed to reconcile themselves to the presence of the power saws. But they were astonished at the way the whales seemed to embrace the tools as their salvation. Craig mentioned to Geoff how much Cindy Lowry would regret not having been there to see it. But by early that Sunday morning, Cindy was already en route to Barrow. Her anxious wait the night before paid off.

As soon as the whaling captains' meeting had adjourned, Geoff and Craig excitedly rushed to call Cindy from one of the newly installed touch-tone pay phones in the bright lobby of Barrow High. It was the call she and Kevin had nervously awaited all night. She had told the biologists to call the minute there was any word. She tried not to watch the phone as she breathlessly waited for it to ring. Kevin left to pick up take-out food and a movie. He was glad to get out if only for a few minutes. Watching Cindy strut so anxiously about was more than he could bear.

Anticipating Cindy's mood, Kevin scanned the shelves of the local video shop looking for anything that would distract her. He heard Cindy mention she wanted to see *No Way Out,* about a young naval officer's relationship with a beautiful Washington politico. Only after the rescue would that seem a prescient selection.

"They want to save them," Craig exultantly told Cindy. Already clutching Kevin's elbow, she almost punctured his skin with her fingernails. Not only was she denying him his long-promised weekend, now she was causing physical harm.

Later that night, Cindy tossed and turned. She was booked on the noon flight to Barrow and she hadn't even started to get ready. Although she lived in Alaska, Cindy didn't have the proper clothes for the Arctic. She didn't have any food, either. For all she knew about Barrow, which was precious little, Cindy thought if she didn't bring her own food, she would only have whale, walrus, or seal meat to choose from.

Cindy had not read a newspaper since she first devoted herself to saving the three whales. Her only source of news came through a cable hooked to the back of Kevin's television. None of what she saw or heard prepared her for the remarkable and unique stage upon which the drama was being played out. There was no mention of the ironies or the Eskimos, and there was certainly nothing about Pepe's Mexican restaurant, Arctic Pizza, $200-dollar ski machine rides, or toilet paper with wooden clubs. It was as though there was no human existence, just the forlorn images of an endless white ocean melting imperceptibly into an equally infinite white tundra. Although she was the one to propel the three naturally stranded whales into the national spotlight, Cindy Lowry had not learned a thing about the Arctic's largest and most important town where she would arrive nine days after the whales were first discovered.

As she climbed into bed, Cindy realized she did not have to reset her alarm clock. She got up at 6:30 every morning to train. Running marathons was one of her hobbies. Sunday morning, however, Cindy would get plenty of exercise racing to complete last-minute chores in time to catch the noon MarkAir flight to Barrow. Kevin had his own errands. He worried about what Cindy would eat in the remote whaling village, but for different reasons. He knew that if her culinary selection was limited to an assortment of marine mammals, Cindy would die of starvation.

Cindy liked to tell people she ate only health foods. Kevin knew that wasn't exactly true. She secretly craved preservatives, cholesterol, and lots of sugar. Kevin wanted to avoid another argument about Cindy's diet. Shortly after she left the house to buy a hat, gloves, and boots, he slipped out to quickly buy some foods she might eat. Fruits, vegetables, and high-energy peanut and raisin trail mix would be Kevin's final present to Cindy as he kissed her good-bye at the gate.

Like most MarkAir flights to Barrow that weekend, reporters filled Cindy's plane. And, like all MarkAir flights to Barrow, this one made an intermediate stop in Fairbanks. An hour by jet north of Anchorage, Alaska's second largest city marked the northern end of the state's limited road system and the completion of slightly less than a third of the journey to Barrow.

Walking around the world's most northerly modern airport terminal, Cindy figured she'd parlay the twenty-five-minute layover into her last meal before descending into the dreaded netherworld of Barrow. Seeing a

Mexican food stand across the concourse, she briskly walked over, looked at the menu, and ordered a taco salad. Surely, she thought, this would be her last chance to indulge in her favorite cuisine.

While Cindy waited in Fairbanks for her flight to continue onto Barrow, Ben Odom and Pete Leathard were flying high above the Alaskan frontier in one of ARCO's executive jets. VECO's North Slope operation had been hard at work. En route to Prudhoe, Leathard talked regularly by phone with Marvin King, VECO's ground operations manager. King and his men had spent the whole night out in the minus thirty degrees temperatures. First, they had to determine whether the barge would even work. Then they tried to free the 185 tons of sunken barge from its frozen berth at ARCO's East Dock.

King told Leathard he could make the barge seaworthy, but he needed the one thing Leathard didn't have: time. He knew the boss was on his way and assured him he would keep the operation fully staffed until the job was done. Using chain saws, ice axes, and picks, King and his dozens of men worked feverish shifts in the bitter cold, chopping, sawing, and chipping away four years of impregnable Arctic ice that had built up around the barge's hull. These hardy men were specially trained to perform manual labor in the world's most hostile climate.

At up to $100,000 a year, they were among the highest paid laborers in the world.

Each man knew it was foolish to measure the tasks he performed in the Arctic by what he could accomplish under normal conditions. Here, the rules were different. Man and his vast powers were severely diminished. The Arctic was the last place on earth where nature defied his mastery. If a white man wanted to call the Arctic home, he either accepted the limits of his adopted habitat or he died. A man could endure such taxing elements only so long. The two VECO crews working in shifts in the brutal cold arrived at the same predetermined fate: quick and inexorable exhaustion. After only a few minutes, even the ablest could work no longer. The battered men took sanctuary in a prefabricated shed that was supposed to provide the wearied laborers with warmth and nourishment.

The doughnuts, coffee, and cigarettes were about as nourishing as the forty-degree temperatures were warm. Not unlike the creatures they were spending themselves to free, the men entered the shed bewildered by their own numbness and pain. Their lungs were singed by the bitter cold. They doubled over coughing, gasping for breath.

The shed's only sounds came from the footsteps and wheezes of the exhausted men. They didn't say a word. Their jaws felt frozen. Moving their frozen joints even slightly hurt. By the time their jaws thawed enough to allow recognizable speech, it was time to get back to work. On their way out, the mildly rejuvenated workers were met and replaced by the other beleaguered crew struggling to escape the cold. At great personal peril, VECO's Arctic construction workers toiled through the night to pry loose an ungainly device that would attempt to free three whales stranded 270 miles away.

By now, all four American television networks were either in Barrow or had crews on the way. Tens of millions of Americans who were already following the story were anxious for action. The whim of a few Outside news executives had transformed a routine gray whale stranding into a serious rescue campaign. Now, for the first time since they were discovered eight days before, a tangible step was finally being taken to free the three whales. But, ironically, none of the media that generated the interest to justify the rescue could find a way to get to Prudhoe Bay in time to cover the rescue's first real story. It would not be the last time the TV reporters missed the real story.

Don Oliver and his NBC crew were the first reporters on the scene. Frantic for a way to get there, producer Jerry Hansen rented the Arctic's only available helicopter at the going rate of six thousand dollars per day. But by the time they arrived, it was too late. Most of VECO's backbreaking work was already done. The first footage to appear on American television showed the hoverbarge seemingly free of ice. Since no one could compare that event against what the barge looked like frozen and buried, the American people would never know how much the VECO crews sacrificed and accomplished.

Billy Bob Allen appreciated his men's effort. "There is no substitute for it," he preached. His men believed him because he never let them forget that he was one of them. At first, Allen told friends he wanted to help the whales because "it seemed like the right thing to do." For the next two weeks, Bill Allen and the company he built concentrated on virtually nothing else. Pending business was shelved while anxious executives throughout the industry wondered why Allen and his people were so passionately committed to something that had nothing to do with helping clients pump oil. And besides, wasn't everyone in the oil business heartless and greedy?

Allen worked well into Saturday evening in his Anchorage office familiarizing himself with the operation's evolving details. The first crisis occurred when Marvin King called from the workers shed out at the East Dock. He told Allen that the ice removal was going better than planned but his men were exhausted.

"Rest 'em up," Billy Bob answered. "We can't have none of them dropping dead on us." King told Allen there were many things left to do before the barge would be ready, not the least of which included the removal of six hundred tons of ice entombing the vessel. The ice could only be cleared by hand. King didn't know what to do first. Colonel Carroll and his special National Guard unit were due to arrive in Prudhoe late the next morning. Allen told King to combine whatever tasks he could. Any tests that didn't require the barge to be ice free should be performed as soon as possible. It didn't take long for King to figure out his boss was right.

King had just started to put the engines through their paces, before he discovered his first problem. One of the turbochargers which gave the barge enough power to hover above the surface of the ice was dead. Allen thought finding a replacement would be damned near impossible. His hoverbarge was the only one like it in the world. Allen called the barge's Japanese manufacturer to see whether they might find a replacement. When he told them he needed it immediately to help save three stranded whales, they thought their cowboy client had lost his mind.

Two hours later, Allen had received no response. He lost his patience. It was early Sunday morning Tokyo time when he called the president of Mitsui Engineering & Shipbuilding Co. Fifteen minutes later, Mitsui's equipment network located a machine in Long Beach, California, that could be airlifted to Anchorage. The amorphous effort to save the whales was still a marginal operation. Any minor obstacle could have provided a perfect excuse for any party to back out, leaving the whales to their fate. Since the hoverbarge was the rescue's only option, the inability to find a turbocharger would have been sufficient grounds for VECO to abort the rescue.

Learning he would need to charter a special cargo aircraft to fly the turbocharger to Prudhoe, Allen pressed both his thumbs firmly against the side of his balding head in a fruitless attempt to ward off the headache he invariably got whenever he ran into major unexpected expenses. The smallest plane that could fit the huge engine was the C-130 transport, a military mainstay. If the Hercules, as the C-130 was known, could transport troops and tanks in and out of trouble spots around the world, Allen knew it could get his turbocharger safely to Prudhoe.

Five minutes had passed since the turbocharger crisis was resolved when King called Allen again with still another disaster. No one in Prudhoe knew how to operate the hoverbarge. Only one man at VECO had operated the ice crusher and now Allen had to try to find him. No one at VECO had heard a word from barge captain Brad Stocking since the billion-dollar exploratory well at Mukluk Island turned up dry in 1984. Using electronic databases listing the whereabouts of oil construction sites and their employees, Pete Leathard initiated a worldwide manhunt to locate the elusive captain. After three days of intensive search, VECO gave up. Brad Stocking was never found.

Bill Allen called around the state to find out what could pull a 185-ton craft from Prudhoe to Barrow. The answer he got most frequently was uniquely Alaskan: the "Cat train."

Cat trains were Caterpillar tractors that resupplied remote inland villages during the nine months of winter, by using the surface of Alaska's frozen rivers as its roadway. In a state with no roads, the rivers were the resupply lifeline for settlements and homesteaders that otherwise could not be reached. Long snow sleds crammed with supplies and provisions were attached to heavy Caterpillar earth movers fitted with extra-wide tank treads to grip the ice and pull their cargo across the surface of frozen rivers.

But the size, weight, and destination of Bill Allen's icebreaking hoverbarge ruled out the Cat train almost as soon as it was mentioned. Even if there was a wide-enough river close by to pull it along, the barge was much too big and heavy to be towed by a Caterpillar. The nearest river leading toward Barrow was sixty-five miles west of Prudhoe and its mouth had not completely frozen. In the event Colonel Carroll and his CH-54 Skycrane helicopter could not do the job, Cindy Lowry would have to find some other way to save her whales.

Colonel Carroll had plans for that Saturday night and he was not going to cancel them just because he had to lead a mission to the Arctic early the next morning. The forty-year old was filled with boundless energy. He capered about Anchorage reveling in temperate R&R until well after 0300 hours. He waited to get home before indulging in his one noticeable vice: coffee. He drank the day's final cup, reached into his fastidiously kept closet, and pulled out a couple pairs of Army-issued long johns and other cold weather gear he figured he would need for the two-day trip "up to the Slope." He neatly packed it all into a large green canvas duffel bag. Carroll quickly fell asleep.

When his alarm rang forty-five minutes later, the colonel woke up rejuvenated. He leapt out of bed and poured himself the day's "first cup" from the still fresh pot of coffee he made less than an hour earlier. He showered, shaved, and quickly cleaned up what little mess he made and left the house. He met up with his crew of six and boarded the Alaska National Guard's C-12 King Air executive turboprop for the five hour flight to Barrow. Before pulling the hatch closed behind him, Carroll ordered the two Skycranes moved out of their Elmendorf Air Force Base hangar to be readied for a quick sendoff.

After a short nap, Carroll contorted his athletic frame around in his front-row seat to pass back sweet rolls and coffee while briefing his men about Operation Breakout. Knowing he was about to enter the fray of a developing national news event, Carroll brought along Mike Haller, the National Guard's public affairs officer to "handle" the media. Colonel Carroll told Haller his mission's purpose was to keep a competitive press from interfering too much with the rescue.

The best way to do that, Carroll said, was to befriend the media. Haller planned to hold regularly scheduled press conferences so the media could feel like they were getting all their questions answered. Carroll warned Haller to avoid giving the press the idea they were being manipulated. The minute that happened, the coverage of the National Guard could turn nasty. They knew that everyone would immediately seek to get on the barge. They discussed setting up and coordinating press pools so only one television crew, still photographer, and print reporter would be allowed access at a time. Any footage, pictures, and quotes taken by the pool reporters would be made available to every news agency.

Carroll's pilot checked with Barrow air traffic control to see if he could get clearance to do a flyover above the whale site. The colonel wanted to inspect the ice conditions from the air. Not having seen a trace of man for over three hours, the colonel was incredulous when the pilot told him that the air space around the site was restricted due to heavy traffic. "Heavy traffic?" Carroll mused.

Flying westward, they descended rapidly from their cruising altitude over the frozen coast of Elson Lagoon. The aircraft banked steeply to the right, pinning Carroll and the crew deeper into their seats. In the split second it took the speeding plane to cross the narrow sandspit, they flew directly over the whales. From two thousand feet in the air, the dozen or so people huddled around the small breathing holes looked like misplaced ants against a uniform, motionless backdrop of snowy white.

Carroll stared wondrously at the remarkable site below him. He shook his head in amazement as the plane touched down at the Wiley Post–Will Rogers Memorial Airport. From the ergonomic seat of his plush plane, the bitter, lifeless elements outside his window looked deceivingly like a fairytale wonderland as the plane taxied toward Randy Crosby's Search and Rescue hangar at the opposite end of the 7,000-foot runway. Before the pilot could cut the engines, Carroll and Haller watched in bewilderment as the SAR hangar bays slid open, letting loose a stream of television cameramen and entangled technicians racing each other in a mad dash for position at the bottom of the airplane's steps. No longer did it seem like such a wonderland.

"This happens wherever I go," Carroll deadpanned.

Like a seasoned political campaigner, Carroll smiled broadly and briskly waved as he stepped off the plane. Nonplussed by the cluster of microphones stuck in front of his chest, he warmly shook hands with Ron Morris who was clearly freezing cold. The much larger Carroll put his arm around the man's shoulder. As they walked across the tarmac, the cameras captured Colonel Carroll as he listened to Morris. They walked together into the "secured" part of the hangar, leaving Mike Haller to deal with the media.

Once inside, Colonel Carroll asked to meet the man in charge. He figured it was the big smiling man standing in a blue flight suit in the back of the room. His confident aura matched with his Grizzly Adams look gave Carroll the sense that this man was the boss. He was right. It was Randy Crosby, director and chief pilot of the North Slope Search and Rescue command. When Carroll watched the burly rescue pilot pour him a generous mug of hot North Slope coffee, he knew they were destined to get along just fine.

Carroll boarded Randy's second chopper and flew out to the site. Carroll caught his first glimpse of the whales when the red, white, and yellow helicopter prepared to touch down on the frozen surface of the Chukchi Sea. By mid-morning Sunday, Randy had already flown enough people out to the ice to know how excited they became the first time they saw the whales. Carroll was no exception. When he stepped out of the chopper, Randy motioned to the colonel to duck his head until he was clear of the swirling blade. Although the ice seemed like it was rock solid, Crosby could not take any chances. He kept the chopper on half power. If the ice started to buckle beneath him, Crosby had just seconds to raise the helicopter into the safety of the air. Those on the ice would have to fend for themselves.

Carroll walked toward the whales while trying to listen to Arnold Brower Jr. describe the ice conditions over the loud commotion of the television crews following them. He asked Brower how far it was to the ridge and if anyone had been out there yet. Brower said the closest paths through the ice were four to five miles away, twice as far as they were when the whales were first discovered nine days earlier.

Each day the whales were stuck beneath the ice, the farther they were from the safety of the lead's open water. But even that safety was rapidly vanishing. The open water lead that separated the growing formation of new ice from the encroaching polar ice pack was shrinking almost a mile a day. When Carroll and Crosby saw it Sunday morning, October 16, they figured it was less than fifteen miles wide. If they couldn't free the whales before the two ice formations met and closed off the lead, the whales would die. Brower walked with the colonel to the edge of the crowded hole. Not seeing any whales, Carroll tentatively leaned his tall frame to peer straight down into the bubbling dark gray sea. Just as his head broke the water's parallel plain, one of the whales burst out of the sea spraying water all over the startled colonel. That night's newscasts and the next morning's papers carried comical pictures of the decorated war veteran struggling to wipe crystallized whale breath off his face.

When they met him, Geoff and Craig had one message for the colonel: Get that hoverbarge to Barrow. They told him that the whales he was fondly admiring didn't have much time. Although the chain saws could be counted on to help keep the hole open, the biologists didn't think it would be long before the whales started showing signs of fatigue. Carroll promised to do his best. Holding his hat so it wouldn't blow off, he offered the two biologists a customary salute and ran back to Randy Crosby's waiting whirlybird.

Crosby, Carroll, and Brower flew west to inspect conditions at the ice's outermost edge. When Crosby lowered the 214 Lone Ranger into position for landing, the newest and most forbidding obstacle came towering into view. Powerful ocean currents had heaved up huge walls of ice. In some places, the pressure ridge rose as high as thirty feet above the ocean's surface. In the midst of all the shards, Crosby looked intently for a safe place to touch down.

Carroll and Ron Morris saw that the ice around the whales was not thick enough to challenge the hoverbarge's purported ice breaking ability. But the pressure ridge proved to be another story. There was no way the hoverbarge could break through it. Hoping to find weaknesses, the rescuers flew along the ridge to look for breaks in the ice wall where the barge might be able to sneak through.

The colonel could have canceled the National Guard plan to tow the hovercraft. If the barge couldn't break the pressure ridge, why bring it from Prudhoe? Instead of giving up, Morris, Brower, and Carroll agreed that the National Guard should proceed with the hovercraft operation. Brower was asked to help find Eskimos willing to scout the area for suitable routes the hovercraft could take through the pressure ridge. After flying back to his waiting aircraft at the Search and Rescue hangar, Carroll gathered his men, thanked Randy Crosby for his tour and told Ron Morris to keep those holes open.

"We'll see you in a couple of days," he said confidently to the cameras as he leapt up his King Air's aluminum stairs. He would be back, but not as a hero. With Carroll gone, Morris had less than an hour to prepare for the arrival of the next contingent of VIP rescuers, the oilmen. The ARCO jet carrying Billy Bob Allen and Ben Odom followed Carroll's previous flight path. It made the same banking turn and was met at the hangar by the same chorus of reporters. For Randy Crosby, it was "déjà vu all over again." Allen climbed aboard Crosby's helicopter, promising Odom and Leathard he would be a good sport. He went along to show Pete he supported his efforts and would earnestly help him pull the rescue off. The remarkable scenery of Barrow and the Arctic left Bill Allen unmoved. He had seen it hundreds of times in the past twenty years. This is where he made his fortune. He was sure he had seen all there was to see. But the impatient oilman and his patrician colleague were in for a sight that would change them forever.

Billy Bob stepped off the helicopter intent on concealing his lack of interest in the whales to the very end. He would tell the reporters how he hoped the three creatures could be freed. He would commend everybody who helped with the rescue, then return to the hangar, pour himself a cup of coffee into a Styrofoam cup, and fly off. When the helicopter set down, it blew away the snow covering the foot thick floor of glaring, bluish-gray Arctic ice.

Morris introduced Allen, Odom, and Leathard to Arnold Brower Jr., who had been busy at work with a crew of men trying to expand the whales' lone breathing hole. Allen and Brower conversed over the helicopter's loud roar. It was a few minutes before Billy Bob even realized he had not seen the whales. He did not know how long it would be before they appeared but he wasn't interested in hanging around in minus twenty-five degrees weather to wait for them.

The first whale rose just as it had thousands of times before in the nine days since it was first discovered. But for Bill Allen it was an indescribable revelation, an epiphany. A look of youthful wonder swept across his face. Pete Leathard had never seen him so animated. The middle-aged oilman abandoned all his inhibitions and for a brief moment became young Billy Bob again. He ran to the edge of the hole and quickly dropped down to one knee. Eagerly reaching out across the open water, Billy Bob stroked his hand across the side of the battered whale's face. The whale moved still closer to Allen and jutted its head over the edge of the hole. In an irresistible appeal for more attention from its new friend, the whale knocked Billy Bob down when he playfully butted its huge but battered snout into his chest.

The whales worked their magic yet again. For Allen, as for most non-Eskimos, the whale's magnificence was a relatively recent discovery. Well into the twentieth century, the only people ever to get so close to whales did so to kill them and at great personal risk. But man's transformation from whale killer to whale saver was so quick and so universal that by the end of that same century, hundreds of millions of people around the world would watch as great nations committed millions of dollars and hundreds of men to free three whales trapped at an isolated edge of the universe.

In the eyes of almost all seafaring cultures, the whale has always stood atop the pantheon of animal mythology. Throughout history the whale has played the part of legend, myth and allegory. From Jonah's punishment-cum-repentance in the mouth of the whale, to Ahab's battle of wills with Moby Dick, there has never been another creature quite like it. The leviathan has run the gamut of human emotion while never falling from consciousness. The whale has been everything but ignored.

For most of human history, one word has best categorized man's relationship with a creature it barely knew: fear. Whales are the biggest creatures ever to inhabit the earth. The hundred-foot blue whale is bigger than even the largest dinosaurs. Its gargantuan size convinced generations that the whale was evil. Ascribing evil powers that the whale did not possess, people avoided them at all costs. According to some legends, those who even saw them from a distance were marked for early death. For so long, man knew so little about the whale, he thought it was a fish. By the second half of the nineteenth century, the great beast was finally conquered. The once proud behemoth was no match for whaling fleets armed with harpoon guns. As man became more familiar with the animal he now relentlessly hunted, his conception of it began to change. The whale's long unknown attributes started to surface. Its remarkable intelligence, its grace, its unjustified trust of man confounded the age-old stereotypes. But, more than anything else, the whale had a certain undeniable charm, a charm of remarkable gentleness. Old myths died quiet deaths.

But only after slaughtering virtually every one of them did man first take note of the whale's greatness, a greatness he knew might vanish from the face of the earth. Perhaps out of guilt for having so long misunderstood and sought to undermine the creature, did man embrace the whale, now nick-named the Gentle Giant, as a symbol of his own concern for a world he was destroying. Saving the whale was a first step toward saving ourselves.

After seeing the whales, Billy Bob Allen couldn't explain it in words any better than before. But he knew whales were special.

10

From Kickers to Leads

News, by definition, is unpredictable. If it is expected, it's not news. To people in Barrow, the stranding of the three California gray whales was not news. It was expected and predictable. But to those on the Outside, it was an unprecedented chance to think of themselves as part of an effort to help rescue one of man's favorite animals. Once Oran Caudle's first pictures of the trapped whales reached Todd Pottinger's editing machine at KTUU-TV in Anchorage, it unleashed an outpouring of interest and concern rarely experienced in the human species.

In many ways, this was the story television was created to cover. It offered an abundance of spectacular natural imagery with almost no need for analysis. A picture of the rising, spouting, and surging of desperate whales confined to a tiny hole in the middle of a frozen Arctic Ocean said infinitely more than the couched words of a television commentator. It captured the imagination of millions of people in a way network executives had rarely seen. Only the immediacy of television could convey the whales' almost hypnotic allure. Somewhat the same way that a cat stuck in a tree could mobilize an entire town, three gray whales stuck in Arctic ice mobilized an entire world.

Within hours of the first NBC broadcast on Thursday, October 13, six days after the whales were first discovered, the network's New York switchboard was jammed with hundreds of calls from ordinary citizens around the country. They wanted to know how they could help. Friday morning, Greenpeace's Washington office handled hundreds more from concerned members.

The people had spoken. What started out as an ideal story for NBC to use as a "kicker," a lighthearted piece used to close a newscast, for a brief time became a national obsession. Suddenly, America clamored to see more of the whales. Through jammed telephone switchboards and higher ratings points, the networks got the message. They rushed crews to Barrow to try to meet the growing demand.

The whales didn't stay "kickers" for long. By Sunday night, October 16, they were news "leads." Just three weeks before a presidential election, and three days after they were first reported, the stranded whales became the top story on each network newscast. Among the estimated thirty million people who watched the whales gasp for air on Sunday's evening newscasts was President Ronald Reagan. He penned a note reminding himself to ask about the whales the following morning at his daily 9:00 A.M. briefing with senior White House staff members. Perhaps "helpless" was not the best word to describe the three whales. They clearly had done something that most other creatures could not do. Nine days after discovery, the whales compelled the most powerful man on earth to action.

Monday morning, October 17, the president told his chief of staff, Kenneth Duberstein, that he wanted regular reports on the rescue's progress. The daily written summary of the meeting circulated to every office in the West Wing, included a reference to the president's interest in the trapped whales. The memo quickly made its way to White House Press Secretary Marlin Fitzwater, the president's spokesman. Almost instantly, Fitzwater saw an opportunity. Mentioning the whales at the President's morning briefing would demonstrate that Ronald Reagan was just as concerned about the stranded creatures as millions of other Americans. Since no one wished the whales ill, the White House could not lose. After clearing the whales with the chief of staff's office, Fitzwater inserted a few words about them into the statement he was preparing to read to the White House press corps concerning the president's activities.

Ronald Reagan was wrapping up one of the most successful presidencies of the modern era. He enjoyed the highest approval rating of any president that late in his term. Kenneth Duberstein's job as White House Chief of Staff was to ensure this legacy was not squandered in the final days. No last-minute missteps. The longest economic recovery in American history, pushing the Soviet Union to the brink of extinction without a shot being fired, a renewed sense of American pride—all were his legacy.

Nonetheless, there were only a few areas where the president's image appeared less than glorious. Among them was the environment. Despite his popularity, a majority of Americans still felt (incorrectly as it turned out) that Reagan was a poor environmental steward. George Bush, his heir apparent, foolishly bought into the fallacy when he pledged to be the "Environmental President."

The plain truth is that increased living standard correspond directly to a cleaner, healthier environment. Economists call it "the wealth effect." Increased wealth leads to increased spending. That applies as much to environmental protection as to anything else. Watching their assets and incomes rise leads people to feel more confident to spend more. Wealthier societies spend more to protect their environments than poor societies. They protect more because they have more. In the last third of the twentieth century, the United States spent more than one trillion dollars protecting its environment—far more than any other country. If the U.S. were not creating more wealth, it could not spend more wealth to protect the environment. The same process that drives economic growth is the same process that results in less pollution. Pollution is inefficient. It is what happens when something isn't done efficiently. Becoming more efficient means getting more out of what we have; wasting less, polluting less, and protecting more—a cleaner, safer environment.

In presiding over the greatest economic boom in U.S. history, Ronald Reagan did more to protect the U.S. environment than many other president. Besides, he loved whales, too. If President Reagan helped the whale rescue, his handlers thought, maybe he could burnish his environmental image. But anyone who thought that was why Reagan got involved in the whale rescue to burnish his image didn't know Ronald Reagan. The key to Reagan's image was that he didn't care about his image. He cared about his policies.

Duberstein assigned a little-known but critical White House department to take charge of the rescue. The Office of Cabinet Affairs (OCA) worked to iron out policy differences on issues ranging from acid rain to three whales trapped at the edge of the American dominion. The OCA tried to get all cabinet officers to arrive at a consensus before offering the president an option. Sometimes a consensus was impossible to reach. Not so with the whales. Everyone agreed: save them.

Bonnie Mersinger first heard about the whales at 7 A.M., Friday, October 14. She was sitting in her small cubicle in the West Wing of the White House sipping on a thin straw pierced through the side of a cardboard apple juice container. A few stolen minutes with Jane Pauley and Willard Scott were the only contact the attractive woman had with the outside world. Rarely did attractive thirty-one-year-old women become executive assistants to the president of the United States by pursuing interests other than work.

Mersinger swung around when she heard the word "whales" mentioned on her small Sony Watchman television. Her colleagues referred to Bonnie as the "resident White House environmentalist." Like millions of others, the instant Mersinger saw Oran Caudle's footage of the trapped whales, she wanted to see more. She didn't know why exactly, but there was something about whales that unleashed her empathy. Maybe it was her background. Before changing professions in the early 1980s, Bonnie had worked with animals, big graceful animals. She made her living breaking race horses, including Genuine Risk, the 1980 Kentucky Derby winner. Until Mersinger was given the chance to work for Ronald Reagan, she loved more than anything else to train thoroughbreds.

Mersinger knew Reagan would want to help the whales. Their plight played to two of his most profound emotions: his love of animals and his soft spot for hard-luck tales. She wrote him a memo about the stranding on Friday, October 14, but it was too late in the day. President and Mrs. Reagan had already ascended Marine One, parked on the White House South Lawn, to spend the weekend at Camp David.

By 10 A.M. Monday the 17th, ten days after the stranded whales were first discovered, the president of the United States was officially involved in the rescue and Bonnie Mersinger became his personal representative. She knew that protocol limited the president's direct authority to federal agencies. Since two of the rescue's four independent factions, the NOAA and the National Guard, answered directly to him, Operation Breakout presented the president with a rare choice. Everyone in the White House knew that when such an opportunity offered itself, President Reagan always liked to exercise his authority as commander in chief. Mersinger advised Ken Duberstein's office to route the White House involvement through the Alaska National Guard.

She collected newspaper articles about the whales on her computer. Skimming through them, Mersinger jotted down the names of key players: Cindy Lowry of Greenpeace, Ron Morris of NOAA, the oilmen, the Eskimos, and a National Guard colonel named Tom Carroll. A guardsman herself, Bonnie called Frank O'Connor, an old friend in the Alaska National Guard, to see what he could tell her about Operation Breakout. O'Connor said that until the National Guard entered the picture, there was no one in charge with the authority to set priorities. Now, maybe a sensible command structure could emerge. O'Connor assured her that in Alaska, Tom Carroll was the most qualified person to deal with the problem.

Colonel Carroll was the man Bonnie needed. Through him she could convey the president's interest in the rescue and relay his offer of help. Together, she and Carroll could keep the Chief Executive completely informed on the well-being of the whales. Around noon, Washington time, Bonnie called the National Guard's mobile command headquarters at Prudhoe Bay. Although it was still an hour and a half before first light on Monday morning in Alaska, Colonel Carroll had already stepped outside into the bitter cold to cross off checklists so the Skycrane could start towing the barge. A civilian on loan from ARCO answered Bonnie's first call, who informed her the colonel would soon be back. With the windchill, it was close to 100 degrees below zero on the frozen tundra.

If Tom Carroll had been like other men, he would have returned in a few minutes. But Colonel Carroll was obsessed with the problem. The colonel stayed outside, exposed to the life-threatening cold for nearly twelve hours. He relentlessly barked orders over his walkie-talkie to the helicopter pilots and the crew on the barge. The men from ARCO and VECO who just met the colonel thought he was out of his mind. Before the towing began, Carroll solved the key logistical problem: fuel. He estimated the helicopters would need at least 20,000 gallons of high-octane Arctic aviation gasoline to pull the barge 270 miles from Prudhoe to Barrow. The colonel devised a self-contained operation to load the barge with enough fuel for itself and the helicopters. He sent for special refueling pumps from Anchorage. He also ordered his men to work with the VECO crews to load all 20,000 gallons aboard the hoverbarge in customized storage tanks.

Every item on Carroll's checklist was crossed off and ready by 11 A.M., two hours earlier than he hoped. However, when he gave the order to begin and the powerful helicopter started to pull, the barge did not move. The downward thrust of air that lifted the 185-ton hovercraft broke the thick layer of ice that covered the shore. Carroll watched helplessly as his pilot, Chief Warrant Officer Gary Quarles, valiantly kept the Skycrane from spinning wildly out of control and crashing into the frozen bay. After Quarles safely landed his craft, Carroll went over to investigate. The barge was mired deep in the mud.

A thick coat encrusted the rubber skirt needed to trap air in order for the barge to hover. Carroll had no choice but to call on the VECO crews, still recovering from the previous two days of backbreaking work, to don their Arctic gear, grab their pick axes and shovels, and get back to work. They chipped off as much of the frozen mud as they could before collapsing in exhaustion. Gary Quarles tried again. He pulled his chopper with 22,500 pounds of thrust. After failing a second time, Carroll knew it was no use: the barge was just too heavy. He ordered the 20,000 gallons of fuel stored on the deck of the barge unloaded before trying yet again. Carroll arranged for the helicopter fuel to be repositioned on the ice. Special Arctic tanker trucks drove all night, traveling hundreds of miles across the surface of a frozen sea to place 600-gallon refueling tanks every two miles along the route to Barrow.

The colonel pondered the latest setback while supervising the shutdown of the hoverbarge. His press aide, Lieutenant Mike Haller, handed him a message. The colonel wiped frozen mud from his numb face as he clumsily tried to unfold the note in a howling wind. It was from a woman in the White House named Bonnie Mersinger. Carroll didn't have time to be bothered. He told Haller to take care of it.

"But, sir," Haller gently protested, raising his voice loud enough to be heard over the wind and engine noise, "she said she wanted to talk with you."

"All right," the colonel relented. "Tell her I'll get back to her as soon as I finish out here."

Finally, around 10 P.M., Alaska time, Carroll picked up the phone and dialed the number written on the message. He registered no surprise when Bonnie Mersinger answered. There were too many thoughts swirling through his restless mind for Carroll to realize that it was 2 A.M., Washington time. He politely but professionally introduced himself to the female voice on the other end of the remarkably clear line. Bonnie told the colonel that the president wanted to schedule a phone call to Prudhoe sometime on Tuesday afternoon. At first, Carroll thought it was a joke. He figured the whole thing was perpetrated by one of his buddies back east in retaliation for one of Carroll's infamous pranks. He decided to play it cool. When she didn't seem amused, Carroll figured he should take her seriously.

He told her he would love to talk with the president but he just couldn't commit to a time. The president of the United States, his commander in chief, wanted to talk to him and he wasn't sure he could take the call? What kind of a guy was this, Mersinger asked herself. Instead of becoming angry, she was intrigued and wanted to find out more. Bonnie asked the colonel what the Arctic was like. His answer sounded like a formal press statement. Bonnie thanked the colonel for his time and told him she would speak to him in the morning.

Her hand hadn't let go of the phone when something came over her. She had to call him back. At first no one answered. Without knowing why, she let the phone ring over a dozen times until someone finally picked up: "Guard-Prudhoe." She immediately recognized the voice. It was Tom Carroll.

"Are you always so formal?" she boldly asked, which startled the colonel. It was the first time anyone had spoken to him like a human being since he left Anchorage. Colonel Carroll was constantly under stress, but he never acknowledged it. When he heard Bonnie's friendly tone, he succumbed to an overwhelming wave of relief and collapsed into his chair. Suddenly the weight of all his worries vanished. He found himself opening up to a woman he barely knew, uncharacteristically confiding that so far at least, the operation was a disaster.

This frank admission broke down the barriers between them. Ignoring the fact that she called him, she jokingly asked permission to go home and get some sleep. After all, she reminded him, it was almost 2:30 in the morning and she had to be back in the White House in four and a half hours.

Carroll couldn't believe how open he was with a woman he had met over the telephone just a few hours before.

It had been almost three days since Tom Carroll last slept. Yet the high-strung colonel seemed immune to exhaustion. At 10:30, the night before another grueling day, the colonel looked around for someone to "spot" him while he worked out with free weights in the ARCO gym. Normally, to the dismay of the detail officer assigned to him, Carroll took his own weights with him wherever he went, but to everyone's relief, Carroll learned before leaving Anchorage that the ARCO exercise facility had their own. After working up a heavy sweat by pumping iron, Carroll wrapped a white towel around his broad shoulders and walked back to his office through the heated hallways of ARCO's $300-million self-contained living complex. He wanted to talk to Ron Morris, the NOAA coordinator, to close the books on Monday, October 17, day two of Operation Breakout.

Carroll was certain that a phone call from Prudhoe to Barrow, 270 miles away across the frozen tundra, would be expensive. But he didn't even have to dial the number one to reach it; it was a local call, cheaper than a crosstown call in Manhattan. He called the Airport Inn and asked to be connected to Ron Morris's room. Ed Benson, the owner of the hotel, told Carroll that Morris was up on the Top of the World, drinking with his new friends.

Throughout the day, Carroll checked on the whales and their rescuers by radio phone. By Monday afternoon, October 17, several Eskimos with their own chain saws were on the ice, helping Arnold Brower Jr. keep the lone hole big enough for the whales to breathe. But the shifting winds and dropping temperatures iced it over almost as fast as the Eskimos could open it. The day's worst news came not from the failed helicopter tow in Prudhoe. Instead, it originated with the whales themselves. Their condition appeared to be rapidly deteriorating.

The night before, Sunday, October 16, Cindy Lowry lay awake in her tiny Barrow hotel room, worrying about her first day on the ice and anticipating what the whales would look like. She wanted to see them that very minute. But the pitch-black darkness made doing so an impossibly dangerous risk. Anyone foolish enough to venture out on the ice became easy prey for hungry polar bears looking for their next meal.

Cindy resolved to wait for daybreak. When she did fall asleep, it wasn't long before her phone rang unexpectedly. It was 5:30 A.M. and her initiation into a most unwelcome daily ritual. Instead of a standard wake-up call, the hotel operator just let an outside call through at around the time Cindy wanted to get up. Since she got so many phone calls, there was bound to be one at right about the time she wanted to be awakened. Whenever she picked up the phone, it was invariably a reporter from the Lower 48 asking about the whales.

Ron Morris wanted to meet everyone before the day got started; perhaps over breakfast at Pepe's. Over gigantic six-egg omelets, greasy home fries, and butter-soaked Wonder bread, the assembled rescue crew listened as Morris chaired the morning meetings. The biologists noticed Morris glance around the dining room to see if nearby reporters could eavesdrop. Then, in a whisper, Morris told them he was carrying an official document issued by the United States government. Tapping his left index finger against the right breast pocket of his faded red-checked flannel shirt, Morris said the piece of paper gave him full and final authority over the whales. "I can kill them whenever and however I want," he joked. Cindy was appalled. Geoff and Craig laughed nervously. Who was this man? they thought. The nearby reporters who, in fact, could hear everything, eagerly scribbled down the quote their editors would never use.

"Who is this bloke?" inquired Charles Laurence, a photographer from England's influential *Daily Telegraph*. "He must be out of his bloody mind."

Other reporters sitting near looked Laurence's way and nodded their silent approval. But that was all they could do. Unlike other stories where they thrived on the imperfections of their subjects, the reporters assigned to cover the whales were met with a most unusual reality. It was the whales people cared about, not the bizarre idiosyncrasies of their rescuers. Like him or not, Ron Morris was the only official source of rescue information. If we reporters wanted access to Morris (which, of course, we all did), we had to stay on good terms with him. We laughed at his jokes— some of which were actually quite funny—while no one reported on his drinking, because he did not visibly drink anymore more than anyone else. Many invited him for meals, drinks, and late-night bull sessions—all of which he was happy enough to oblige. Morris enjoyed visiting the television edit suites where he could watch footage of himself and the rescue on fascinating equipment. It was fun and he had the chance. Who wouldn't have?

Whatever we thought about the biologist-turned-rescuer, none of us thought Ron Morris a fool. He possessed a remarkable sense of how the media worked and how to use that knowledge to maximize his own personal prominence. Just a day after his arrival, Morris cornered Geoff and Craig and told them not to talk with any members of the press unless he approved their doing so in advance. By blocking the press's access to rescuers other than himself, Morris felt his own stature would be enhanced.

He was quoted in every story and appeared on every newscast. He created his own image of a gentle, tireless rescuer that the obsequious media passed on in his stories.

For all of the private confessions of people who claim to dislike Ron Morris, how would any of us had behaved if thrust unprepared into a similar situation? We were the ones who rewrote the rules of journalism, allowing Morris to run the operation free of the scrutiny or criticism we applied to everyone else examined under the microscope of American journalism. We risked starting to forget that the story was not about Ron Morris, it was and should have been about the whales. Morris became a convenient and unfortunate fall guy for too many of us, myself included.

11

The President Watches TV, Too

It was Monday morning, October 17. The three trapped whales had already survived ten long days in a shrinking Arctic Ocean ice hole. What would have marked the end of a fatal ordeal for any other creature was, for this lucky trio, only the beginning.

Meanwhile, Cindy Lowry was on the scene. The woman whose efforts to aid the helpless animals turned their plight into a national obsession was on her way to see them for the first time. Before driving out onto the ice with Geoff, Craig, and Ron Morris at about 11 A.M., Cindy checked with the hotel desk clerk for messages. She had no idea what to expect. It was her first morning in town. She thought maybe Kevin might have called to say hello.

As she walked toward the desk, she saw a frazzled bleached-blond receptionist frantically trying to write messages while hunching her shoulders to hold a telephone to each ear. In one of the two-second intervals when the hotel phone stopped ringing, Cindy meekly tried to sneak in a request for her own messages.

"My name is Cindy Lowry," said the pretty, smiling whale saver. "Do I have any messages?"

"Do you have any messages?" the receptionist asked, accusatorily, in her thick Colombian accent. "You must be kidding." She then shoved a stack of fifty coffee-stained messages directly into Cindy's startled face. Nervously thumbing through them, Cindy was amazed at how quickly all these people found out who she was, and where she was staying. She counted about thirty reporters from newspapers, and radio and television stations across the country who wanted to schedule interviews.

But what really struck Cindy were the other non-reporter messages. Like the one addressed to "the Greenpeace Lady" from a woman in Columbia, South Carolina: "Why don't you use dynamite to blast away the ice?" the message read. Another woman from Louisiana had a similar idea: "Why not drop napalm from helicopters to melt the ice around the whales?" A man from California asked Cindy: "Why they didn't drop some bait into the water and pull them out like fish on a hook."

People were spending their own money and time to track her down at the top of the world to offer their advice on how to save the three trapped whales. Cindy always knew whales were special, and now Middle America did, too.

Cindy didn't know until she read the paper the next day that even more calls were coming into Tom Carroll's command center in Prudhoe Bay. Hundreds of them came from the same kinds of people with similar ideas. The suggestions ranged from the impractical to the downright ludicrous. Nonetheless, Cindy could not help but be touched by the concerns of people so far away.

One person who called was a young businessman from Minneapolis named Greg Ferrian. On Monday, October 17, he heard Peter Jennings on ABC's *World News Tonight* describe the Eskimos' losing battle to keep open the lone breathing hole. ABC correspondent Gary Shepard reported that, despite the Eskimos who worked around the clock, the falling temperatures made it almost impossible for them to keep sections of the hole from freezing over.

Greg Ferrian was familiar with the problem. His father-in-law owned a company called Kasco Marine that manufactured small water circulating pumps designed to keep ice from forming around boats in the winter. Kasco sold most of their five-hundred-dollar "deicers" to marinas and duck-pond owners throughout the Great Lakes region. Alaska was a vast new sales territory. Greg figured the deicers would work just as well for whales as they did for ducks. The deicers worked just fine in the dead of a Minnesota winter when temperatures regularly dropped below the readings presently being recording in Barrow of minus thirty degrees.

True, Greg thought, the machines might not work well in the coldest Arctic weather, but this was only October. Barrow was still several months from becoming that cold. Ferrian convinced himself the deicers could do the job. They could help the three whales buy the time they needed to survive until the hoverbarge arrived from Prudhoe Bay. And the deicers could do so better and cheaper than anything else.

Greg wanted to help but he wasn't sure where to start. Finally, he decided to call a local television station, KSTP-TV, ABC's Minneapolis affiliate. The KSTP newsroom told him to call ABC News in New York. After speaking with seemingly everyone else in the 212 area code, Ferrian finally reached someone nice enough to help him. She was a desk producer who was helping the ABC crew in Barrow cover the story. Although she had taken dozens of other calls from like-minded people trying to help, the woman was good enough to pass on Colonel Carroll's National Guard phone number.

Ferrian was surprised that the connection to a place three hundred miles above the Arctic Circle sounded so clear. Greg tried to describe the deicers to Colonel Carroll's press aide, Mike Haller, who told Ferrian that the colonel would have to approve the plan, but, of course, he was out on the ice. Haller suggested if Greg really was serious, he should call back after dark, around 4:30 P.M., Alaska time. By then, the colonel might be back at the ARCO/VECO command center.

When Greg Ferrian finally reached Colonel Carroll, his warm and personable manner seemed a welcome relief from much of the rude treatment he encountered en route to the top. The colonel listened patiently as Greg repeated his confident claims about the deicers. Carroll told Greg the deicers sounded like a great idea. They might be just the thing to keep the holes open and the whales alive, Carroll said. If it were up to him, he'd use them in a minute. But it wasn't. Ron Morris had to approve.

Ferrian cleared the line for a new dial tone to call Ron Morris. Remarkably, he got through on his first try. But Morris abruptly cut him off before he could explain his device.

"I've got to go," Morris barked. "I've got a helicopter waiting to take me to a press conference."

Ferrian plaintively appealed one more time. "All I need is one word, a yes or a no. Can't we at least try?" he begged.

"One word?" Morris teasingly asked. "No," he snapped. Ferrian heard the click as Morris hung up.

But Greg didn't give up. Morris's response only further emboldened him. He called his brother-in-law, Rick Skluzacek, who ran Kasco Marine in his father's absence. Greg felt Rick should know something about his scheme to drag his company's deicers all the way to the Arctic. Turning truth on its head, Greg told him that Operation Breakout wanted to use deicers to help save the three stranded whales. Rick knew Greg had a penchant for crazy ideas, but this was definitely the craziest he ever heard. Experience taught him to beware. But Rick's initial suspicion gave way to the opportunity and challenge of demonstrating the deicing machines to hundreds of millions of people around the world.

Now Greg had a real problem. Rick was actually interested. What would happen if Rick really did want to go to Barrow? How could Greg tell him the truth? That he lied to his own brother-in-law? Instead, Greg opted against panic and decided to worry about minor technicalities later. Greg Ferrian called Carroll back and lied again. This time he told him that he and Rick had already decided to help. They were booked on the next flight to Barrow with six deicers.

Undaunted by the colonel's repeated reminder that their machines' use was not his decision to make, Greg asked the colonel if there were gas-powered electric generators they could use in Barrow. The colonel said he thought there were, but he wasn't sure. Before he could say that only Ron Morris could authorize their use, Greg had hung up.

"Damn," Carroll said, impressed at the Minnesotan's tenacity. "This guy doesn't fool around."

Ferrian called his brother-in-law and lied again. It got easier each time. He told him that everything in Barrow was set. All they had to do was pack their deicers and go. After a sleepless Sunday night, Rick called 3M, Control Data Corporation, and other Minneapolis Fortune 500 companies. He tried to convince them to donate their private jets to fly the equipment to Barrow. The whales were such a great story and Ferrian such a great salesman, that three of the companies actually said yes. Each one had to back down, however, when they learned that none of their planes were available.

When Greg priced commercial flights to Barrow, he had a new reason to worry. There was no way he could lie about that. He knew Rick wasn't 100 percent sold on leaving merely chilly Minnesota for the already bitter cold Arctic. The $2,600 round-trip airfare to Barrow might end the charade once and for all. Even Greg wondered whether the whole plan was too farfetched.

Greg knew the more time Rick was given to think about going to Barrow, the chances increased he would have to rule against it. Greg decided to give his brother-in-law no choice. He not only booked the seats, but he called KSTP-TV in Minneapolis and told them that he and Rick were going to Barrow to help the whales. Now, there was nothing Greg's brother-in-law could do. It was on the record. Jews called it chutzpah. Minnesotans called it guts. Whatever it was, Greg Ferrian displayed it in abundance. He and Rick Skluzacek were on their way to Barrow.

Greg Ferrian hoped that KSTP-TV might mention the duo's trip to Barrow on the six o'clock news. The second KSTP news director Mendes Napoli heard about the call, he threw down his red pencil and dashed out the door to find his reporters. Napoli instantly knew he was onto the hottest story in the Twin Cities. The trapped whales, now leading all the network newscasts, had a local angle and KSTP was the only station that knew about it. Coming right before a critical ratings period, the news was almost too good to be true.

Napoli ran to the other side of the newsroom to use the radio phone. He desperately tried to reach Jason Davis, one of his top reporters who had left with a crew to prepare to do a live report for the upcoming six o'clock news. When Napoli found him in the microwave truck, he informed Davis there would be no live shot. He told him to go home and pack lots of warm clothing. Davis had a new story that would take him to Barrow, Alaska, with two local men who thought they could help free the three trapped whales.

Napoli read Greg Ferrian's home number to Davis over the cluttered radio. Davis pulled a portable cellular phone out of his nylon day pack and called Ferrian to introduce himself. "I'm Jason Davis, from *Eyewitness*

News," the reporter said in his unmistakable Australian accent. Ferrian didn't need any introductions, he was a local-news junkie and instantly recognized the voice of Jason Davis. Ferrian's gamble paid off more than he hoped let alone expected.

He thought getting a mention on the news was a long shot. A crew was assigned to go with them to Alaska? He was ecstatic. Now there was finally something he could tell his brother-in-law that was true. There was no way Rick could back out. Hours later, Rick and Greg were standing in line at the Delta Airlines ticket counter for their flight to Fairbanks. The agents checking them in were so excited to hear they were going to help the whales, they shipped the six compact deicers at no extra charge.

KSTP called the contractors remodeling their recently purchased corporate jet and told them the plane would be needed the next day to fly an *Eyewitness News* crew to Alaska. The contractors worked all night to get the Gulfstream ready for its new owners. They removed a gaudy double brass bed and ceiling mirrors from the plane and replaced it with a modest bar. The plane's previous owner, bankrupt television evangelist Jimmy Swaggart, thought drinking a sin.

Colonel Carroll didn't know what to make of the calls from Minnesota. He called Cindy in Barrow to ask her what she thought, but she had just left the hotel. Cindy was finally on her way to see the whales.

Geoff and Craig tried to prepare Cindy for the whales' worsening condition. Temperatures in Barrow were dropping by the day. The chain-saw crews could barely keep up with the new ice. The holes were freezing fast, and the barge was still at least three days away. As they drove their Chevy Suburban across the glassy smooth ice of Elson Lagoon, Cindy couldn't believe how isolated the three of them were. With all the reporters, whirling helicopters, and Eskimos with chain saws, she expected a hubbub of activity.

Instead, she encountered an overwhelming, almost deafening solitude. From the time they crossed onto the frozen lagoon for the seven-mile drive along the Point Barrow sandspit to the whales, she saw nothing but a barely discernible ski machine whining past far off in the distance. Even with the unblinking gaze of the world fixed upon it, the North Slope appeared no less hostile, no less alien, and no less inimical to life than at any other moment in its timeless existence.

They crossed over the sandbar that separated past from present. Their isolated world vanished in a sea of attention. The closer they got to the holes, the more people and activity they saw: ski "taxis" ferrying reporters to and from the whales, reporters conducting interviews at the water's edge. The contrast with the barren scenery on the ride out was surreal.

Eskimos could instantly tell who belonged on the ice and who did not. Cindy did not. Those who did belong wore blood-stained walrus and seal-skin parkas and carried high-powered rifles slung over their shoulders to guard against polar bears. Those who didn't, like Cindy, stood shivering in brightly colored ski clothes, fashions better suited to alpine resorts than Arctic expeditions.

Geoff took Cindy to meet Arnold Brower Jr., who had been out all night with his team of Eskimos cutting open several new holes in the ice. She was amazed that he showed no signs of fatigue. An Inuit hunter often spent days on end exposed to the harsh elements searching for game to feed and clothe his family. Millennia in the Arctic enabled the Eskimo to withstand conditions that the hardiest white man could not. No one doubted the ruggedness of the VECO crews who broke the hoverbarge free of ice. But by watching them work, the white man soon learned that the Eskimos could have freed the barge faster with half the men and none of the suffering. They were a different kind of men. The Eskimos were built for the Arctic. It was their home.

The Eskimos cut ice at a feverish pace, oblivious to the temperature of minus thirty-five degrees. With no gloves or hats, and their coats unbuttoned, the Eskimos joked, laughed, and even performed traditional dances on floating slabs of ice. Cindy and her bundled but shivering fellow whites stood nearby, prime candidates for frostbite.

"Why would you come out to work in such cold?" this reporter naïvely asked a busy Eskimo.

"Cold?" the Eskimo responded with equal naïveté. "We're just out here enjoying the weather."

Arnold knew of Cindy and Greenpeace long before she set foot in Barrow. For years, her organization fought against subsistence whaling. Under any other circumstance, these two people were enemies. To Arnold, Cindy was bent on the ruination of his people and their ancient way of life. To Cindy, Arnold and his people continued to senselessly slaughter an endangered and magnificent creature with increasingly modern tools. Brower realized this was a rare chance in the history of the Inupiat Eskimos. If he could win Cindy's friendship, maybe some way could be found to lessen the tensions dividing subsistence whaling villages and their environmentalist opponents. He eagerly extended a gloveless hand in a genuine desire to get things off to a good start.

Standing between them, Geoff could feel the tension and the opportunity. If Cindy accepted his hand warmly, great strides could be made. If she did so grudgingly, the damage might never heal. Cindy's pretty face instantly broke into a warm, radiant smile as she eagerly reached to grab Brower's hand for an emotional shake of friendship.

Brower looked at the woman and told her what she already knew. She needed warmer clothing. When Barrow saw a stranger freezing, they didn't ask whether they want to borrow clothing, they just put it on them. Seeing that she was on the verge of frostbite, he grabbed the fur ruff dangling unused around his neck and leaned over to wrap it around her brightly reddened cheeks. When she saw the fur, Cindy instinctively backed away.

Brower did not understand. Did she want to be his friend or not? He didn't know why Cindy declined his hospitality. Was she recoiling under the touch of a blood-stained whale killer or was there another, less offensive reason? Realizing her actions were being viewed as an affront, she profusely thanked Brower for his concern but told him she couldn't wear fur.

"Why not?" Arnold asked. "Are you allergic?"

"No, no," Cindy said, laughing. "I just don't wear animal fur."

Brower never would understand these crazy whites from the Outside. He told her the ruff was hers when and if she changed her mind. Cindy waited anxiously for one of the whales to surface. She still had not seen them. Two television cameramen jostled for position to get "good video" of the environmentalist's first day on the ice. The strong-willed Lowry was still a bit too unsure of her surroundings to tell the cameramen to back off. As Cindy walked toward the empty holes with Arnold, the cameramen were too busy arguing with each other about who stepped into whose shot to notice Cindy's discomfort. They probably wouldn't have listened to her anyway. Their job was to get the best video, not to win popularity contests. If that meant hurt or angry feelings, so be it. After the story ended and they were reprieved from this Arctic hell, they would never again see any of the people they were offending anyway.

Cindy could tell the whales apart before she even saw them. She absorbed every bit of information about the whales Geoff, Craig, or Arnold could give her. The pictures in the paper and on the news gave Cindy as much perspective as anyone. Now, it was her turn to wait those first long minutes until the whales finally surfaced. When Geoff and Craig initially observed them five days earlier, the whales held their breath for six minutes at a time. But in the last few days, the two biologists noticed a change. With the dropping temperatures, increased human activity, and ice closing in overhead, the whales started surfacing more frequently. Instead of every six minutes, the whales popped up every three or four minutes. Geoff and Craig guessed that this was a sign of increased stress. The more strain the whales felt, the less time they would spend below the surface. The baby whale surfaced much more frequently than the other two, a further sign of its frailty.

Malik noticed the new behavior first, but he kept it to himself. He didn't want to upset the people working hard to save the three whales. Perhaps the whales would resume a more normal diving pattern before anyone noticed anything was wrong. But after another day without improvement, Malik was no longer the only one who knew the whales were in trouble. On Monday morning, the baby whale could barely lift its head out of the water to breathe. It was bloodied and battered from repeatedly banging against the razor sharp edges of the hole. Cindy leaned over to gently comfort the sickly whale with the touch of her hand. She murmured encouragement as it heaved ragged breaths. Her heart ached for the little whale she called Bone because all the skin had rubbed away from the whale's snout. The name immediately caught on.

The Eskimos used their own Inupiat language to name the baby Kannick, or Snowflake. The two other whales would have their choice of several names, but none would stick. The Eskimos called the largest whale Siku, one of the hundreds of words in the Inupiat language for ice. The rescuers from the Outside called it Crossbeak, for its crooked jaw that never allowed the whale to properly close its mouth. The smaller of the two adolescent whales was given the Eskimo name Poutu, a uniquely Inupiat word referring to a specific type of ice hole. Those English speakers who called it anything at all, called it Bonnet.

Late Monday afternoon, word got to Arnold Brower that Colonel Carroll was making little progress with the hoverbarge in Prudhoe Bay. Brower and Malik urged Morris to start thinking of alternatives in the event the barge did not work. Up to that point, there were no other options. It was the hoverbarge or bust. Morris said waiting was the only thing they could do. Morris's lack of Arctic experience limited his ability to think of new ways to help the whales. Instead, he continued to insist that Colonel Carroll would soon free the barge.

"But what if it doesn't come?" Arnold Brower asked impatiently. "Then what do we do?"

"You guys are the experts," Morris said defensively. "You tell me."

Malik suggested cutting new holes. Maybe the extra room at the surface would ease the whales' distress. Brower thought it was worth a try. He gathered three men with chain saws and instructed them to cut open a new hole twenty-five feet by twenty-five feet, about a hundred feet west of the existing hole.

When they first expanded the original hole, Arnold and his men cut huge blocks of ice that they hitched to the back of a truck to pull them out of the water. Each new block they moved convinced them that they had created a most inefficient system. When Geoff nearly fell into the icy waters while trying to lasso a rope around an ice block, Malik and Arnold realized they had seen enough. Malik started cutting much smaller chunks of ice, pushing them under the frozen ledge with the long aluminum shaft of a light harpoon used for seal hunting. Now, it took just minutes to open up a new hole. There were no trucks and no ropes, just a few Eskimos with chain saws and poles.

The Eskimos walked a hundred feet farther, ready to do it again. Malik paced off the dimensions of the new hole. He and Arnold sawed through the perimeter of the rectangle Malik had marked with the sole of his sealskin mukluks. Then they cut the floating island of ice into pieces small enough for one man to easily shove under the edge of the surrounding rim. The Eskimos improved with practice. Each new hole took less time to cut than the one before.

But the whales would not move. They stayed in the first hole, the one they knew. Malik thought the activity at the original hole kept them from moving on. He asked people to move away from the old holes to see what the whales would do without any humans to lure them. None of the media moved. Like others, CBS cameraman Bob Dunn nodded his head agreeably and said, "Sure," but he didn't budge. Malik did not understand. Why did he say he would leave and then not move?

Even though each of the networks had hours of whale footage by Monday, October 17, the video of the whales was just too compelling. Reporters always had to chase their subjects. Now, their cameras, microphones, and pens could take all the time in the world recording the magnificent, if not tragic images of three glorious whales trapped in tiny holes. After traveling so far to see them, it was impossible to get up and leave.

Everyone's footage was so equally spectacular, the cameraman joked they were on the fast track to the first collective Emmy Award for television news photography. The conditions were so perfect, nobody could lose. Even I took great pictures. As with the fully automatic 35-millimeter cameras sold since the start of the decade, all you had to do was "focus and shoot."

The pictures transmitted back to the Lower 48 were so consistently stunning, the networks kept wanting more. The better the video, the more of it the networks aired. The more they aired, the more enthralled the public became. The more enthralled the public became, the more pressure was put on the rescuers to save the whales. Almost as fast as the story broke, the rescue was controlled by a force beyond anyone's control, the force of collective human fascination. Operation Breakout was on autopilot, the first "focus and shoot" story of the television era.

When the biggest event in Barrow's history broke, the town's top leader was nowhere to be found. The North Slope Mayor, George Ahmaogak, left town a week earlier, before the whales were national news, to attend an Alaska Federation of Natives meeting. But when the meeting ended and Barrow was the center of the world, the mayor didn't come back. For days, no one knew where he was or when he would return.

All the attention must have frightened the beleaguered mayor. George Ahmaogak was embroiled in controversy over more than the allegations of drinking and domestic violence. Not only was the coverage of the whale story on autopilot during the rescue's early days, so was Barrow. It might not have had an official leader during those critical early days, but it still had its continued responsibilities. Arnold Brower called Dan Fauske, the North Slope director of finance. In the mayor's absence, Fauske was the only person authorized to tap the borough's treasury. He asked Fauske for money to feed his hungry men. Fauske planned the borough's $200-million annual budget. Surely the borough could afford a few hundred dollars for doughnuts and coffee. Fauske agreed.

Soon all the town's unexpected burdens fell into Fauske's shoulders. Randy Crosby called from Search and Rescue wanting more fuel for his helicopters. Since Saturday, October 15, the two SAR helicopters had been providing the media with nonstop shuttle service to and from the whale sight. Crosby had no idea what he was getting his department into when he agreed to give the NBC crew a free flight out to the whales. All the other reporters asked for equal treatment.

In 1975, Fauske traded in the fertile rolling hills of western Iowa for the bleak white tundra of Barrow. He thought it would be a neat way to spend his summer before college. It was an exciting time. The Prudhoe Bay oil fields were starting to boom and so was Barrow. Fauske earned thirty dollars an hour delivering water he drilled through ten feet of ice in one of the thousands of frozen lakes on the tundra just outside Barrow. Things were so good, Fauske never showed up for freshman orientation.

The Inuits saw Fauske as the one man who could help them make sense of their immense new oil wealth. He was white and smart, and he loved Barrow. In one of the best bargains they would ever strike, the Eskimos agreed to pay for Fauske's college degree in exchange for his promise to come back and run the borough's finances. When he returned from Gonzaga University, Fauske quickly whipped the North Slope Borough into financial shape. He not only raised more than a billion dollars to finance Barrow's massive capital improvements program, his strict management also earned Barrow the highest bond rating in the country.

Fauske agreed to reimburse Randy Crosby's excess fuel costs but saw a financial nightmare on the horizon if he failed to crack down right away. Unable to reach him any other way, Fauske showed up at Ron Morris's Tuesday morning meeting to tell him he did not have the authority to spend Barrow money without his approval. Morris told him all his costs would be reimbursed.

"By who?" Fauske demanded.

"The U.S. government," Morris unconvincingly answered. Fauske knew a vague answer when he heard one, and he knew of nothing more vague than the "U.S. government."

Randy Crosby almost wished Fauske refused him more fuel. Maybe then he could get his hangar back from the television cameramen and technicians who had taken it over. While waiting for free flights out to the whales, the dozens of reporters and technicians lounging around drank his free coffee and ate his free doughnuts. They looked like raffish students at a sit-in.

One of them spotted a basketball rim behind one of the parked helicopters. They started playing pick-up games using a dirty mechanics rag in place of a ball. Randy was glad to see them occupied.

"Just be careful," Randy pleaded, knowing he was at their mercy.

"Watch that rag," he told people who obviously weren't listening. "Unless you all got four hundred thousand dollars for a new engine, don't let it fall into the intake vent."

"Sure," they said. "We're always careful."

Colonel Carroll thought he was being careful, too. He tried to keep the media as far away from his Prudhoe Bay operation as he could. The hoverbarge operation was going poorly, and he did not want the hole rescue to bog down because of a few problems. He knew that the media could kill the story just as quickly as they created it. By Monday night, the 17th, the hoverbarge was only three hundred yards further from where it started the day. What should he tell the President the next day? Should he say that the operation was a disaster? He needed someone to talk to.

At 5 A.M., Tuesday morning, Bonnie Mersinger phoned from the White House to start making arrangements for the president's call. She was surprised to find the colonel wide awake. They had spoken just a few hours earlier and she was exhausted. What could possibly give the intriguing colonel so much energy, she asked herself. The slight breakthrough she thought she made with him the night seemed gone. Colonel Carroll was back to his formal self. He wanted to continue their conversation but he was too busy. Either it would happen some other time, or it wouldn't happen at all.

In just a few minutes, Bonnie told Carroll, Marlin Fitzwater would announce the president's schedule for the day. She asked him for four to six minutes around 3 P.M., Washington time. As the hour for the talk with his commander-in-chief drew near, the colonel displayed considerably less bravado than he had the night before. He was a nervous wreck and Bonnie loved it.

"Whenever you want me, why you just say so," he said, trying to draw on sapped confidence. She told him to stay in close touch. He would speak with several layers of White House bureaucracy before actually talking to "The Gipper." The first layer, the White House Communication Agency, was responsible for providing all the president's communication needs. The secretive office was manned by elite, highly trained Army, Navy, and Marine officers of the White House Signal Corps. A Signal Corps officer asked the colonel whether the National Guard would need the phone line they were using. For every presidential call, the Signal Corps wanted to establish control over a line several hours in advance. The colonel checked with Mike Haller, his press officer, who jokingly offered his gracious assent to the commander-in-chief's use of it until lunch.

After "Signal" secured the line, Bonnie called back to verify information for a fact sheet the president would use during his conversation with the colonel. Bonnie asked Colonel Carroll what kinds of questions the president should ask him. It was important the president sound up-to-date since the press office would release an audiotape and transcript of the call.

At first, the fuss over a simple phone call seemed absurd to Carroll. But respect soon took the place of amusement. He learned that when it comes to the president's communications, no detail was too small. Besides, as long as the endless preparations gave him an excuse to talk to Bonnie, he had no objections. Bonnie asked the colonel about the principal characters in the rescue. She went through her list of people and organizations.

"What about the environmentalists?" she asked.

"It's Greenpeace," Carroll said.

When he didn't add anything disparaging, Bonnie sighed in relief. The last thing she wanted was to hear the colonel start shooting off his mouth against environmentalists when the president was finally starting to care about them. Bonnie had purposely designed this phone call not to appear overtly political. She didn't say anything directly. She just prayed the colonel would not make President Reagan look foolish. Bonnie had completed her advance work. She told Carroll that the next time they spoke would be after the president's call. Once the White House Signal Corps tapped into the phone line, they took control.

Colonel Carroll was in the cafeteria drinking coffee when the call came in from Washington. An ARCO secretary shouted his name.

"Colonel Carroll," she cried. "The White House is on the line!"

"I'll be right back, the president wants to have a word with me," the colonel deadpanned to the nonplussed guardsman sitting next to him. He picked up the receiver in his cubicle and said, "This is Colonel Tom Carroll speaking."

"This is White House Signal. Please hold for the president."

A few moments later, at 3:03 P.M. Washington time, an unmistakable voice came on the line. "Colonel Carroll?"

For a brief second, the colonel froze. His heart stopped beating and his mouth turned cotton dry. Could it really be Ronald Reagan—the president of the United States—who just asked for him by name?

"Yes, sir," said the colonel, now sitting straight and nervous in his chair.

"This is Ronald Reagan."

"It's a pleasure, sir."

"Well, I'm just calling to tell you how much I'm impressed by all that you are doing up there in this effort on the whales and to get an on-site report on the rescue effort."

"Very good, sir," the colonel responded. "There are a tremendous amount of people up here who appreciate the fact that you've taken time from your schedule to call." The president politely asked Carroll to dispense with the obsequious supplications and get to the whales. The colonel told the president about the bitter cold, but spared him the details of his problems with the barge. Carroll recited the names of everybody involved and their organizations, just as he had rehearsed with Bonnie.

Bonnie, listening in on a White House speaker phone, laughed when the president deftly tried to cut short the nervous colonel. "Sir," the colonel continued, unmoved by the president's appeal for brevity. "I think this phone call will make a substantial difference in the morale of everyone involved. From the crews out there right now with the barge to the people working in Barrow. This is the kind of thing that makes it all worthwhile."

"Well," came the president's trademark utterance. "You can tell them all we're very proud of you and what you've done up there. And I'll let you get back to your rescue mission now. But just know that a great many people are praying for all of you."

Before he hung up, the president wished the colonel good luck.

But even Ronald Reagan's legendary luck wouldn't be enough to get the mired hoverbarge across 270 miles of frozen Arctic Ocean to Barrow.

12

G'day, Australia

To journalists, the "story" of the three trapped whales showed more than just the miracle of modern telecommunications. It demonstrated just how powerful they had become. Never before had they propelled so many important people to act so quickly and decisively to affect an event of such questionable significance. In the hands of just a few people, a tiny hole in the middle of the Arctic Ocean was transformed into a place of global importance, at least for a few cold October weeks in 1988.

For one of the first times in the rapidly changing world of television news, a story of marginal significance was turned into one with major significance based solely on the uninformed judgment of people distant from the event. People in the know knew there was nothing newsworthy about the trapped whales; while people who knew nothing about whales had no idea how little they did know.

The real story was that great wisdom was not required for people in the media to obtain great power. The nonstory became a big story not in the minds of those who knew the most, but in those who knew the least. It was a story less about the whales than it was about how the whales became a story.

The transformation from nonevent to big event happened in three clearly defined stages. First, the whales were talked about as possible fodder for harvest. Then biologists Geoff Carroll and Craig George heard about them. They called the Coast Guard who told the *Anchorage Daily News.* Within twenty-four hours, the story became the "kicker" for Tom Brokaw's October 13, 1988, broadcast on the *NBC Nightly News.* Six days after Roy Ahmaogak found them floundering in slushy arctic waters, the three whales were national news. Stage one.

The second stage lasted three days. From Thursday, October 13, through Sunday, October 16, the whales as news item rose steadily through the then-important half-hour network newscasts. In just seventy-two hours, the stranded whales went from "kickers" to "leads." It took that long only because the networks needed a few days to get their equipment and personnel to the top of the world. When they first appeared on network television, the whales ended newscasts. By Sunday night, October 16, 1988, they started them. Stage two.

But it was stage three that set the stage for the whales' release. Once they led network newscasts, the world's attention gave the rescuers added impetus to draw on the superhuman effort and extravagant resources they would need to save the grays. Early questions about how seriously the United States government took Operation Breakout were answered when President Reagan made his October 18 phone call to Tom Carroll. The President's six-minute telephone chat with the Alaska National Guard colonel had some wondering what in the world was going on. Now, even the president of the United States was hypnotized by the plight of three marooned mammals on the North Slope of Alaska. With the imprimatur of a popular president, we could save our beloved whales in good conscience.

Soon, the American whale mania had gone global. Foreign television crews began arriving on set further crowding a town already about to burst. Shortly after news of the president's phone call ran on the wires, Ken Burslem answered a ringing phone in his Los Angeles office. Burslem was the Eastern Pacific bureau chief for Network Ten, one of Australia's three commercial television networks. His assignment editor in Melbourne wanted to know more about the whales. Burslem told him that the whales were fast becoming the biggest story in America, bigger even than the presidential sweepstakes looming just three weeks away. He thought their plight would grip animal-loving Australians the same way it was mesmerizing the

Americans. The Australian-based assignment editor gave Burslem the okay. Burslem booked himself and his crew on the next flight to Alaska. He wanted to be the first Australian to broadcast images of the whales to the folks Down Under.

It took a few seconds for Burslem to recall what little he knew about the frozen north. He confessed to his editors back home that his six years as Network Ten's U.S. correspondent did not begin to prepare him for an adventure on Alaska's North Slope. If Barrow seemed remote to a Yank, it seemed downright intergalactic to an Aussie.

Like most other globetrotting correspondents, Ken Burslem lived his life like a doctor on call. He kept two suitcases permanently packed for last-minute story assignments. He kept one at his office and the other at home. When he got the call to Barrow, he figured his regular gear wouldn't be enough to keep him warm in the Arctic. It didn't take a genius to figure out it was cold in Barrow, but as an Australian journalist assigned to cover America from sunny Southern California, he was utterly unprepared for the bone-chilling experience that lay ahead. It would be one of the most unforgettable of his twenty-five-year career.

He grabbed a lightweight ski parka in the mistaken belief that it would keep him warm during his short stay just 1,700 miles south of the North Pole. After all, he thought, how cold could it be? It was the second week of October. The temperature was in the mid-eighties in Los Angeles, and back home the mild winter was stepping aside for another glorious Aussie spring. The three-man crew from Network Ten boarded their flight at LAX with the infectious smiles and pleasant demeanors native to mates from Down Under. When they stepped off the plane in Fairbanks, their jovial good humor was swept away in the subarctic wind. It was already minus ten degrees there—the coldest temperature any of them had ever experienced. Burslem didn't know whether to panic or buy himself a case of beer.

They checked into their hotel on the banks of the Chena River in downtown Fairbanks and called Melbourne to check for any new details. The news desk told him they were scheduled to do a "live cross" back to Australia in just over an hour. Burslem wished he'd opted for the case of beer. Instead, he panicked.

"I'm glad I called," Burslem said. "Would have been a pretty boring live cross without me, huh?" He laughed.

They gave him the number for KTVF-TV, the local television station in Fairbanks. They were arranging live interviews between the anchors of Network Ten News in Melbourne and Sydney and the exhausted but still witty Burslem, who called KTVF and asked for the person in charge of live crosses.

"Live what?" came the unsure response.

"Aw, hell," Burslem chided himself. He couldn't count how many times he had made that mistake. The rattled Aussie hardly needed reminding that Americans used the term "live shot" when referring to live satellite television interviews. How long had he been in America? he asked himself out loud.

"I'm so sorry, mate," he said to the confused man in the newsroom. "I mean the 'live shot' to Australia—do you know anything about it?" His eardrum nearly burst when the receiver at the other end of the line clattered to the floor.

"It's the Australian," screamed the excited KTVF employee. He asked Burslem where he was. When Burslem gave the man the name of his downtown motel, he was told that someone from the station would meet him in the lobby in five minutes. Burslem and his crew of three arrived at the KTVF studio dressed for a cool night at a Queensland "beach barbee." The folks at the station couldn't help but cackle. One of the men pulled Burslem aside and apologized for the laughter. Suppressing his own giggles, he told Burslem that if he went to Barrow dressed like that, he would die. Burslem stopped laughing himself when the man's friendly warning finally registered.

Burslem resolved to worry about the problem once the live interview was out of the way. Unlike American television, Australian television had few of the pretensions and none of the exaggerated self-importance so often associated with the American networks. Mistakes weren't ignored, they were often played up. Australian television reporters were allowed to show much more human emotion, particularly the light kind, than their American colleagues. For Ken Burslem, it would prove a good thing.

His instructions from Sydney were to stand outside in the frigid Alaska night so Australia's summer viewers could get a sense of how cold it really was. "Act cold," came the last word from Sydney. If there was one thing Burslem didn't need it was someone telling him to shiver while standing outside in temperatures of minus ten degrees. What he didn't know, his flimsy red ski jacket would soon teach him. The folks at KTVF were delighted to help this cheerful Aussie make television history. If it worked, it would be the most remote "live cross" ever broadcast in Australia, and the underdressed crew had not even reached Barrow. The Australians did not realize that Fairbanks, Alaska's second city, was a cosmopolitan mecca compared with the tiny Eskimo village. One of the studio cameras was rolled out the big back doors and onto the snow-covered parking lot to prepare for the outside shot. Burslem stood between the camera and a large drift of plowed snow dwarfing him in the background. When someone from KTVF asked if that snowdrift was all right, Burslem howled loudly.

"Hell, we're Aussies," he said to the overattentive staff. "Most of those lucky bastards we'll be talking to don't even know what this stuff is. They sure as hell are not going to know one heap of it from the next," he said, reassuring his nervous helpers. If everything went off properly, the shot would work just like Oran Caudle's from Barrow. But instead of playing back prerecorded tape, Burslem stood in front of a camera responding to live questions coming in over a phone line from Australia. The picture ran from the camera to a satellite dish in KTVF's parking lot. The dish would beam the video signal to the same satellite Oran used from Barrow, Aurora I, the geostationary orbiter parked 22,500 miles in space above Alaska. In Seattle, three thousand miles to the south, the signal would be "looped" or relayed onto another satellite.

From there, the Network Ten crew in Los Angeles watched Burslem make his trademark funny faces on their test monitors. In Los Angeles, the signal was looped to its third satellite before being picked up simultaneously in Melbourne, Sydney, and Canberra. In less than a second, the image of a Ken Burslem sticking out his frozen tongue started at the top of the world and traveled more than 125,000 miles before it ended up near the bottom of the world. Moments before Burslem was scheduled to go live he pulled his favorite earpiece out of his pocket. It was the same one he took with him on all his stories. As he lifted it to his ear, the KTVF technician told him not to use it.

"Use one of ours," he said confidently. They were rubber and wouldn't freeze to his ear. His helpful protestations went unheeded. Burslem thanked the man and told him not to worry. How, he wondered, could an earpiece freeze? The interview would last only two minutes. The stations in Australia communicated with Burslem over a regular telephone line. He plugged one end of the earpiece into a phone and stuck the other in his ear. He couldn't watch it, but he listened to the program broadcast live in Australia like any viewer back home. When he heard the anchor announce his name and location, Burslem knew it was time to stop making the funny faces. He was on the air.

But as he got his cue, he felt a sharp sting in his left ear and tried inconspicuously to lift the hand not holding the microphone to fiddle with the sharp, unexplained pain. When he did, he was horrified. It wouldn't move. The man was right, the damned thing had frozen to his ear. Here was Ken Burslem, the American-based correspondent, reporting live in an historical broadcast to his native Australia with a tiny earpiece frozen to the side of his head. He just wanted it to end and when it did, he thanked God. Wrapping things up, he realized he couldn't quite remember what he had said.

But the people who saw it will remember it for a long time. Burslem knew something about his voice seemed funny, but he was too new to Alaska to realize what it was. He tried to coil one of his crew's rubber cords only to find it stiff as uncooked pasta. When he reached his gloved hand to rub his itching chin, he could not feel a thing. The itch was nature's warning. His lower jaw was frozen. When he tried to speak his words came out slurred. Back home they thought he was drunk.

His producers thought so, too. They just assumed their man got caught with his pants down. They knew he had just an hour warning before the live interview, not enough time to burn off the fire in his blood. If the same had happened to an American correspondent, warning or not, he would have been fired immediately. Luckily, Ken Burslem was an Aussie. But in Barrow, Burslem's problem only got worse. As interest in the whales spread across Australia, Burslem was forced to stand outside Oran Caudle's frozen studio for longer and longer stretches in the middle of the bitter Arctic night. After just a few days in Barrow, Burslem actually found himself pining for balmy Fairbanks.

By popular demand, Oran Caudle broadcast all the television transmissions from Barrow over the local cable channel. If the Nielsen company had bothered to monitor the North Slope, Oran's ratings would have shot through the roof. Ken Burslem was an instant Arctic celebrity. Spontaneous crowds gathered around to watch their new hero do his nightly live broadcasts to Australia. As a joke, the Eskimos presented him a symbolic key to Barrow's new alcohol treatment center. Burslem loved it. He swore to his producers that he was stone sober, but they didn't believe him. His slur was too real. Only a drunk could sound like that, they were convinced. "For Christ's sake," he exclaimed. "I wish there was liquor here to drink!"

It was impossible for Burslem's producers Down Under to realize just how cold it was. With the wind chill the temperature difference between Barrow and Brisbane amounted to one hundred forty degrees. When their own ratings started shooting through the roof, the Australian producers' dropped their concern. Their viewers couldn't get enough of Network Ten's man in Barrow. Soon, Ken Burslem was an Aussie legend. The whole nation tuned in each day to watch their heretofore-temperate U.S. correspondent report live from outside the North Slope Borough television studio in what looked to be a drunken stupor. Life played an ironic trick on Ken Burslem. He was one of the only reporters in Barrow who didn't drink.

It was a vicious circle for Burslem that ended only when the whales were free. The drunker his frozen jaw made him sound, the more people Down Under wanted to hear him.

More stations across Australia tried to schedule their own live crosses with the jolly man at the top of the world. By the end of one of these long nights of chatter, Burslem could barely speak, almost unable to manage even the inebriated slur for which he had become so famous. Not to be outdone, Ken Burslem's Australian rival, Network Nine beat its own path to Barrow. With Burslem's celebrity, Nine's mission was to stay close. They did an admirable job in the Australian whale sweepstakes. Their big coup came on one of the last nights of the saga when they put the staggering mayor of Barrow on live television. George Ahmaogak didn't need a frozen jaw to sound drunk, he was already. The folks Down Under fell instantly in love with their Inuit soul mate.

13

The Arctic and the White House
Joined by Love

The whales stranded 10,000 miles away became big news in Australia. While the American networks, caught up in their own self-importance, lost perspective of the relative insignificance of the story, the Australian reporters assigned to Barrow determined to let their viewers have fun. Measured against the scale of their own expectations, the Aussies came away clear winners. Ken Burslem would later win the Thorn Award, Australia's most prestigious television journalism award, for his distinguished reporting from the top of the world.

For those involved with the rescue, in the days immediately following the president's call there was little fun to be had. For National Guard colonel Tom Carroll, the euphoria of the president's call did not last long. He sobered up the instant he looked out his window. He clung to a plan whose problems grew more pronounced by the hour. Tuesday night, the second full day of the pull and the eleventh since the whales were first discovered, the barge that justified the rescue and was supposed to free the whales had become Operation Breakout's Achilles' heel. It was no closer to Barrow. Each time one problem seemed solved, another appeared.

The Skycrane helicopters Colonel Carroll designated to transport the recommissioned barge quickly showed their limits. The barge's massive tonnage combined with the brutal Arctic conditions proved more than the Skycranes could handle. After the helicopters finally ripped the barge free from its four-year frozen dry dock, its vast weight kept breaking through the newly formed shore ice. Each time the giant praying mantis machine pulled the barge out, it fell through the ice again after traveling only a few hundred yards. At this pace, it would have taken a week just to get out of the harbor.

By the night of Wednesday, October 19, Tom Carroll's operation found itself in deep trouble. The barge was barely five miles from where it started. The rotors of the expensive helicopters were cracking under the strain, threatening the safety of their crews. The press caught quick scent of the rescuers diminished faith in Colonel Carroll's faltering battle plan. Ron Morris's amusement at Tom Carroll's battering was a badly kept secret. The two didn't think much of each other.

People assumed he was jealous of the presidential call. Morris felt stifled by Carroll's refusal to return his phone calls. Morris wasn't alone in that criticism. By the middle of Operation Breakout's first week, some of the media thought Colonel Carroll was dodging them. Now that things started to falter, Carroll was accused of trying to shield himself from unpleasant questions. By that Wednesday night, October 19, Tom Carroll was at the end of his rope. The press started turning against him. ABC-TV producer Harry Chittick called him the "Keystone Colonel" for his inability to move the barge.

A growing contingent of Eskimos tirelessly cut hole after hole while the barge lay listless just an hour's walk from its original berth. Why, if this wasn't a race, did the media make the colonel feel that he was falling behind? He gathered his helicopter pilots to discuss plans for one last attempt to move the barge. If it didn't work, they would have to think of other options. If none were feasible, the colonel and his men would be forced to face the unfathomable prospect of returning to Anchorage in failure. The indignity of accepting his career's first operational defeat was bad enough. But being run out of his own state by a carpetbagging media was more than the hardened colonel could stand.

By Wednesday, October 19, the whales had been sloshing in the ice holes around Barrow for twelve days. The entire rescue mission, now five days old, was built around VECO's ability to use its hoverbarge. Tom Carroll faced a crisis of his own. His training told him to separate heart from mind. His job was to do, not to feel. But he couldn't help it. He felt plenty.

Colonel Carroll spent years carefully constructing sturdy walls of dispassion. Now, a woman five thousand miles away, a woman he had never even met before, was the force that unleashed pent-up emotion. She was the only one he could turn to for comfort.

Bonnie and Tom talked constantly throughout Operation Breakout. In the first few days after the president's call, neither had yet mustered the courage to explore the other's marital status, but the game went on. The two grew remarkably close. After the disastrous Wednesday, the colonel and Bonnie spoke half a dozen times. The day's final call lasted four hours. He didn't know why, but Carroll felt safe talking to Bonnie. Maybe it was because she was a National Guardsman herself, or because she worked for the president he so adored. Maybe she just evoked something that he suppressed far too long.

As much as Carroll was drawn to her, Bonnie was pulled even more toward him. But she had one critical advantage. For days, the colonel could only wonder what the woman he was quickly falling for looked like. Bonnie didn't have that problem. Every time she turned on a television, there he was. She saw an attractive, confident leader of men. Wednesday night, Tom Carroll dropped his guard. He confessed that things weren't going well. He and his men just spent hours devising a last-ditch plan to get the barge on its way. While she needed to know the operation's progress so she could report to the president, she found herself interested for Tom's sake. She desperately wanted the new plan to succeed, not so much for the whales, but for the colonel she knew only via the telephone.

Ever since they first tried freeing the barge, the National Guard rescue command used each of the helicopters to take turns pulling it across the ice-covered harbor. Carroll wondered what would happen if both helicopters pulled the barge at once. Would the effect of a double pull be twice as powerful? Would it be enough to get the barge out of its doldrums and on the way to Barrow? Working with slide rules and pocket calculators, Carroll and his pilots stayed up until the early hours of Thursday, October 20, working through formulas and equations to determine whether the double pull was even a theoretical possibility. They put their mathematical skills to the test for hours until they finally got some answers. The helicopters would have to pull from a much lower altitude and with less than full power. The eight-hundred-foot tow lines had to be doubled in length. Too much pressure applied to either of the thick steel cables could send both helicopters spiraling to the ground in stereophonic explosions. If the colonel decided to try it, he would be the first. No one had ever attempted a double pull before. Regardless of the effect on the whales, Carroll figured the exercise would provide valuable lessons for more important missions in the future.

Carroll was worried about the media. He knew they had to be invited to cover the attempt, but he didn't want to make too much of the event because of the risk. If they sensed a hint of danger, they would be all over him, shaking the confidence of his men, increasing the chance of fulfilling their own nay saying prophecies. The kid gloves used to cover Ron Morris were thrown off in the media's treatment of Colonel Carroll. With Ron Morris off-limits, Carroll was the only game the media could train their sights on. At first light the next morning, the colonel and his men, putting up an optimistic front, walked out onto the Prudhoe Bay ice for one last try. The helicopters were gassed up and ready to go. The lengthened tow cables coupled their underbellies with the stagnant barge. Succeed or fail, military transport history was about to be made. The press pool circled overhead in a National Guard helicopter flown in from Barrow. Carroll double-checked that he could reach the pilots by radio. Before they took off, he gave them their final instructions.

"You're the pilots," he assured them. "It's your call. Any time you feel it's too dangerous, drop the cable and come on down." His pilots knew the risks. They performed the calculations together the night before and reached the same conclusion. It was dangerous, but it just might work. The press hounded the colonel to do something. But if he wouldn't jeopardize the lives of his men for the sake of three stranded whales, he certainly wasn't about to do it for a press corps that had all but offered to make him their lynching party's guest of honor.

The choppers lifted off the ground at the same time and hovered a few hundred feet apart in front of the lopsided barge. The pilots went through their checklists and waited for the barge captain to signal that he was ready. When both helicopters and the barge were set, the Skycranes gradually eased forward in unison until the taut tow cables stopped them.

The helicopters increased power until, straining against the cables, the barge crept out of its last hole and started slowly sliding across the jumbled ice. The colonel and his men felt a brief flicker of hope. Maybe this would work. Their raised expectations were quickly dashed. No sooner had the barge started on its hopeful journey before it crashed back through the ice. It was the same old story, smooth sailing for five hundred yards followed by another setback.

"It's no use," radioed pilot Gary Quarles. "I'm begging off this one. It's just not going to work."

The colonel was disappointed but not surprised. In fact, he felt a certain relief. The heavy burden placed on his shoulders five days earlier was finally lifted. His men and the crews from VECO had done everything they could to move the barge. Nothing would work. The task was too daunting. General Schaeffer couldn't ask any more. No one could. He took risks, but limited them so that none of his men or equipment would be exposed to any unnecessary danger. Sure the media would point their fingers his way. But as the commanding officer, he was prepared to take the heat. It was his job. He had no problem taking all the credit a few days earlier. Now the tables had turned.

When Ron Morris got word that the barge was a lost cause, he ordered Arnold Brower Jr. and his Inuit crews to cut as many of their new holes as they could. It was too late to call off the rescue now. The whole world was watching. The whales had to be saved.

Cindy Lowry couldn't hold back her tears when she heard the double pull had failed. She watched Bone grow weaker with each passing breath. The new holes were wide enough and long enough for the three whales, but for a reason no one understood, they would not use them.

By noon on Wednesday, October 19, day four of Operation Breakout, the Eskimos had cut a chain of fifteen holes stretching a quarter mile toward the open water lead five miles away. The thirty-foot-high pressure ridge separating the whales from the open water that meant freedom still loomed on the horizon. But for now, the rescuers concentrated on getting the whales moving in the right direction. They would worry about the pressure ridge when and if the whales ever got there. The difference between the high-tech means used to move the barge and the low-tech means the Eskimos used to cut through the ice wasn't lost on Colonel Carroll. The barge was a failure while the chain-sawed holes seemed promising though still untested.

Cindy called Campbell Plowden at the Greenpeace office in Washington to discuss alternatives to the hoverbarge. Plowden was one of the foremost whale advocates in the world; surely he would have a suggestion or two. At the beginning of the conversation Plowden apologized for the difficulty she had reaching him. Greenpeace had to hire eight temporary employees at the height of the Barrow rescue just to answer telephone calls from thousands of people around the world.

Plowden suggested Cindy get in touch with a person who had been calling the Greenpeace office for days with an unusual offer of help. He was a man named Jim Nollman and he called himself an "interspecies communicator." Nollman said he could coax the whales out of the original holes by playing back recordings of other whales with special underwater sound equipment. Cindy had heard plenty about Jim Nollman and not much of it was good, but she figured she didn't have a choice. As far as she knew, Nollman was the only person in North America who had sound equipment capable of functioning in the Arctic. She accepted his offer of help and asked him to come to Barrow, promising to pay his expenses.

Thin-blooded to begin with, Cindy couldn't stay out on the ice for more than a few minutes before she started shivering uncontrollably. It took weeks for her teeth to stop aching from all the chattering. Her poor footwear held up so poorly she spent half her time lifting a leg off the bone-chilling ice and shaking it to circulate the blood in her numbed feet. Had she not refused to wear animal fur, most of Cindy's physical suffering could have been avoided. She could freeze to death with a clean conscience.

She and Craig walked back to the meager warmth of a small portable hunting shack constructed at the tip of the sandbar to give the Barrow whale rescuers a respite from the inescapable cold of the windswept ice. The tiny hut stood like a beacon at the edge of North America, a hundred feet from where the continent slipped beneath the frozen Arctic Ocean.

When they pushed open the hut's flimsy door, Cindy and Craig were welcomed by several friendly Eskimos taking a break in the cramped but relatively warm quarters. They offered the two visitors Styrofoam cups of piping hot coffee which they both gladly accepted. Cindy noticed the uncut chunks of muktuk that the resting crew chewed on as high-energy snacks.

She wanted to ask them how they could eat whale meat at the same time they were working so hard to save the three whales stranded just a few hundred feet away.

For the Eskimos, the answer was simple. The creatures they were working so hard to save were not whales they depended on. The Inupiat Eskimos in Barrow ate bowhead, not gray whales. It was their very dependence on the whale that led Malik, Arnold Jr., and now dozens of other Inuit volunteers to come out and help the troubled grays. Inuit tradition revered whales.

Before heading back to the ice, they asked Cindy if she wanted something to eat. In addition to whale meat, the shack was stocked with walrus, seal, even some polar bear meat. When she said she didn't eat meat, they offered her raw fish instead. After having stood out in the freezing cold all morning, she was so hungry that it sounded tempting. As long as it wasn't meat, Cindy would gladly eat it.

"Here, dip it in some Eskimo butter," said the Inupiat worker who handed her a piece of frozen fish on a toothpick. She quickly plunked the fish into the yellow odorless liquid and popped it into her mouth. The instant her taste buds registered the unusually pungent flavor, she gagged and wretched uncontrollably. Cindy's unprepared palate was in violent revolt. When she regained control, she lamely looked up at the concerned workers and asked exactly what it was that stopped just short of making her vomit.

"Probably the butter," came one guess.

"What's wrong with butter?" Cindy asked to a chorus of laughs.

"You see," said one Eskimo, "it's not your kind of butter."

"Well, then, what kind is it?" Cindy asked impatiently.

"It's from seals," the man answered quietly. "It is seal oil. We call it Eskimo butter."

That was all the explanation Cindy needed. She shuddered in disgust and walked back out into the cold.

In the twelve days since the three gray whales were first discovered, the scene on the ice changed dramatically. It was almost unrecognizable from the time Craig, Geoff, and Billy Adams, their Inuit guide, first went to verify the reports that three whales were stranded off the end of the Point Barrow sandspit. That cold October Tuesday, the three men saw three whales struggling aimlessly against the uncaring force of Arctic nature. The landscape was bleak and gray. There wasn't a soul within ten miles of the six creatures. The three men never dreamed they could save the whales. The most they hoped to accomplish was to study them until they died. Maybe they could publish a study in a marine biology journal.

Now, the most distant edge of North America had become the center of the media world. Heavy traffic traveled on the glassy smooth ice of the frozen lagoon whose western boundary was marked by the sandbar. A tiny corner of an endless, silent and motionless universe suddenly became an oasis of noise and activity. Speeding helicopters broke the hush by buzzing continuously over the increasingly crowded whale site. What started as three men visiting a like number of whales clinging to a lone hole, became hundreds of people surrounding dozens, and soon hundreds of freshly cut holes that would eventually stretch seven miles toward the western horizon.

Until the *Exxon Valdez* spill six months later, the October whale rescue was the single biggest media event in the history of the state. The hundred and fifty journalists assigned to Barrow formed the largest press contingent ever to invade any part of Alaska for any reason. But of all the places in the Last Frontier, reporters chose to gather themselves and their expensive technology around a few tiny man-made ice holes at the top of the world, the most remote edge of America's most remote state. At the rescue's height, there was one reporter for every seventeen residents of Barrow.

14

Barrow:
Frostbite for the Big Time

Within a few days of the president's call to Colonel Tom Carroll, at least twenty-six broadcasting companies from four continents were transmitting their version of events from the overworked control room in Oran Caudle's studio. Less than a week earlier, the facility had never before been used to transmit. Its huge white satellite dishes stood as a powerful testament to money many Alaskans thought poorly spent.

Now Oran's facility transmitted footage of the whales almost twenty-four hours a day, to every corner of the globe. Suddenly, Barrow was the most glamorous byline in all the world. Vendors from across the state flew into Barrow to start hawking their wares. T-shirts of many different designs each proclaimed their own version of the same theme: I'M SAVING THE WHALES.

Pepe's Mexican restaurant had to open earlier in the morning and close later at night to accommodate the several hundred Outsiders with no place else to eat. Fran Tate, the owner, was no stranger to national media exposure. She courted it at every opportunity. The mere fact that she owned a Mexican restaurant within striking distance of the North Pole landed her on the set of *The Tonight Show* with Johnny Carson and on the front page of the *Wall Street Journal* long before any reporters bothered to come to Barrow.

Fran Tate insisted the increased hours were for the convenience of the press, but the skeptical media suspected that she would stay open as long as she could to charge her customers what they considered outrageous prices.

Harry Chittick thought the fact that Pepe's could charge twenty dollars for their greasy version of a hamburger and get away with it was as newsworthy as anything happening out on the ice. He was right. The ABC News producer wanted to get a sound-bite from one of the out-of-town media while he was paying his oversized bill. Chittick's cameraman readied himself right by the cashier. When CBS cameraman Pete Dunnegan paid his bill at the cash register, Chittick's videographer recorded Dunnegan turning to the camera, sticking a toothpick in his mouth, and shrugging. "Twenty-one bucks for a cup of coffee, hmphhh," he said, scratching his head. "Must have been the extra sugar." That humorous sound-bite closed that night's ABC's *World News Tonight* broadcast.

It was also the perfect close to Pepe's culinary career for Pete Dunnegan. Fran Tate was livid when she saw his quip on her TV. At dinnertime, she cut Dunnegan off at the door. In front of his colleagues, she told him never to set foot in her restaurant again. Dunnegan happily obliged. He was the envy of the press corps. The rest of us had no choice but to suffer Pepe's gastrointestinal consequences. The more Barrow and the three whales made news in the United States, the more interest foreign broadcasters showed in reporting the story themselves. In the two days following the president's call to Colonel Carroll, British, Australian, and Canadian television crews arrived in Barrow, adding further bait to the fever-pitched frenzy at the top of the world.

But most intrigued by the whale story were the Japanese. By the time the rescue reached its crescendo, three of the four national networks had crews in Barrow. They marveled at America's latest bizarre obsession. They were less interested in Bone and its skinless nose than they were in people like Cindy Lowry, who cared so much about the tasty creatures. They wanted to explore what it was about three whales that could so completely unite almost everyone in a nation as huge and diverse as the United States.

Takao Sumii, the president of the Japanese NTV network phoned me the evening following President Reagan's call. It was Wednesday, October

19, day twelve for the stuck whales, and day five for Operation Breakout. He tried to explain what it was about the American media his network was seeking to cover. I may have been a journalist, but I was also a TV viewer. I could see the emotional pull of the story although I couldn't figure out the dynamics of its rise in prominence or urgency. To me, it seemed like the story from Barrow started out about whales but evolved into one about the media. Only after I arrived in Barrow did I begin to understand how true that was.

On the MarkAir flight from Anchorage to Barrow, Masu Kawamura, the NTV correspondent, told me my job was to report on the media's coverage of the event, to give the Japanese viewer a sense of the episode's absurdity. Like other Americans, I guess I wanted the whales saved but didn't lose too much sleep about it. Not knowing any of the background or complexities that led up to the rescue, I was no more or less interested than the next person. It was that widespread attachment and fondness for the endangered animal that created the story in the first place. I watched anxiously as the whales slipped closer toward what looked to be an inevitable, pathetic death. Knowing nothing about the Arctic and its conditions, I cursed that damned colonel who the networks said was the one who couldn't get the barge to Barrow. I was exactly what the Japanese assigned me to analyze.

In Japan, whale meat was an age-old delicacy. The Japanese wondered what it was about the tasty mammals that seemed to so strongly touch the hearts of Westerners. They resented the international pressure that forced them to pretend to have ceased commercial whaling. Far from stopping their slaughter of the great creatures, the Japanese just put a new, benign name on it and went right on whaling.

The 1986 International Whaling Commission convention banned what was left of commercial whaling for five years. As signatories, the Japanese faced economic sanctions if they didn't comply. The Japanese proposed a compromise. Norway, Iceland, Japan, and the Soviet Union would agree to give up commercial whaling if they could continue to hunt whales for "scientific purposes." Fearing no accord at all, other IWC agreed.

Before the ink had even dried, the demand for whales within the Japanese "scientific community" skyrocketed. Japanese "scientists" discovered they needed 1,100 "samples." But no one knew what it was these "scientists" wanted to "study." Roughly the same number of whales could now be killed for scientific purposes after the moratorium as were killed for culinary purposes before the moratorium. Call it "culinary science," perhaps?

Japanese "scientists" bought whale carcasses from domestic sources as well as Norwegian and Icelandic whalers. When the scientists completed their "research," they sold the carcasses back to the whalers who then resold them to Japanese food wholesalers. To the Japanese and other clear thinkers, this whale rescue made little sense. How were these three stuck whales different than three stuck Texas shorthorns? Why not just sell the whales to Japan and make some money rather than spending money to save livestock that were meant to be harvested in the first place?

When we arrived and were met by Rod Benson, he tossed our bags into the snow-filled bed of his natural gas-powered Chevy pickup, and drove us straight out to the whales. We were several hundred yards out to sea before I even realized we were driving on the ocean. That's right. Driving a Chevy on the Arctic Ocean.

After traveling from New York, Toronto and Tokyo, the first thing any of us saw at the top of the world was a strange smiling man sitting in a canvas director's chair at the edge of an ice hole in the middle of the frozen Arctic Ocean. He was singing a strange chant he said was destined for the whales that were nowhere to be seen, deep underwater. Trying to escape his rhapsody, I started thinking maybe Masu Kawamura, our Tokyo correspondent, was right. Was Lewis Carroll's rabbit hole really that far-fetched?

We were then introduced to Geoff and Craig, who were busy calming Cindy after an unexplained altercation with Jim Nollman, the interspecies communicator. What I didn't know at the time was that Cindy was arguing with Nollman about his insistence on playing South African guitar music instead of the whale sounds he promised her from Seattle.

Then, standing on the edge of the ice hole, I was struck with an unexplained, stinging pain, first in my left eye, and then, seconds later, in my right. It felt like a sharp object was cutting through my closed eyes. I knew it must have had something to do with my contact lenses but I couldn't get at them. My eyelids were frozen. In the instant it took to blink, the tiny droplets of condensation at the edge of my lashes froze my eyelids together, closing my eyes. My contact lenses had frozen to my eyes and my eyelids were stuck together. I hadn't even been out on the ice for five minutes. Sensing my disorientation, an Eskimo walked over and helped me to his idling car. My eyes quickly defrosted. I thanked him profusely and wore my glasses for the rest of the trip. Acts of extraordinary kindness were the rule, not the exception, in Barrow.

Rod Benson dropped us off at the Top of the World Hotel so we could check in with our NBC associates. They were NTV's American network partner. I introduced myself to NBC producer Jerry Hansen. With a smile, he assured me our trip to Barrow would be a memorable one. Delighted to get it off his hands, he playfully tossed me the keys to a battered old Chevy Suburban NBC rented earlier in the week. "It's all yours," he said with obvious relief. No matter how bad it might have been, I said to myself, it certainly seemed more inviting than spending several hours a day hanging onto the back of a speeding dogsled in windchill temperatures dipping to minus one hundred fifty degrees.

Jerry gave me the standard instructions. "Never turn it off, and fill it up every night." There was only one gas station within 100,000 square miles. That, combined with the Suburban's poor gas mileage made it a good bet I would remember where it was. What Jerry neglected to tell me was never to put the automatic transmission into "park." On only our third day in Barrow, the truck's frozen transmission died halfway between town and the whales. Only after we collectively cursed the damned garage that charged us two hundred dollars a day for a truck that didn't work did we realize that the Chevy broke down because no one taught us how to operate it.

Left in park, transmission fluid doesn't warm up with the rest of the car. Throwing the truck into gear with all the lubricants frozen destroyed our vehicle in less than fifty miles. With a watchful eye out for polar bears, we removed our gear from the truck and lamely hitchhiked back to town. I reported the truck abandoned and passed by it for the next ten days on the way to and from the whales, wondering whether it would ever be claimed or just join other abandoned vehicles and garbage that clutter the sides of Barrow's few roads and alleyways.

By Thursday, October 20—day thirteen—Oran Caudle's studio was on the verge of a meltdown. The night before, despite the chaos that threatened to engulf him, Oran managed to pull off a live broadcast of the ABC News late-night program, *Nightline*. Never before had *Nightline* broadcast from a more remote location. In New York, Ted Koppel wondered whether it was worth the risk to go live to Barrow. Only after Harry Chittick, the ABC producer on the scene, assured New York that they could pull it off did Koppel and his staff agree to give it a try.

Dressed in parkas and sweatshirts, Ron Morris and Arnold Brower Jr. sat in aluminum folding chairs in the sparse setting of Oran Caudle's studio. The backdrop was cluttered with empty equipment boxes. The picture captured by the studio's one camera looked like it was shot by a tenth grader at a wealthy suburban high school somewhere in the Lower 48. Brower and Morris answered Ted Koppel's questions about the whales that were piped in over a conventional phone line from New York. Like millions of others, Koppel wanted to find out what it was about these three whales that turned whale hunters like Arnold Brower Jr. into tireless whale savers. When Arnold's answers fell short of what Koppel was looking for, Morris jumped to the aid of his Inuit colleague.

"They responded like any other community would," Morris said. "This is a humane effort. They were chagrined and felt sorry for these critters. It was the same kind of outpouring I see when other animals are trapped in Alaska." Brower breathed a sigh of relief. ABC News correspondent, naturalist, and resident whale expert Roger Caras guaranteed Ted Koppel and his millions of viewers that the whales would never survive their ordeal.

"I hate to be a wet blanket..." Caras said from the comfort of the ABC Manhattan studio. "They are exhausted, they are stressed, and they've got a gamut to run. There will be polar bears on the lookout for any animal that's stressed or weak. Southeast Alaska, then British Columbia has many pods of killer whales, and the way these whales will be pumping with their flukes, will be very slow and will be detected as vibrations in the water by the killer whales who will close in. Then along the coast of Oregon, they'll pick up the white sharks. Then, if they have any energy left at all after running this gamut of teeth, they've got to move all the way down to central Mexico. All without eating.

"I don't think they will ever get to Mexico. They'll be lost from sight once they've cleared the ice and no one will ever know what happened to them. As much as I hate to say it, I don't think they are going to get there."

The once underused facility was now a madhouse. More than twenty domestic and international networks and local television stations, jostled, argued, and threatened each other and a frazzled Oran Caudle for access to his studio and its transmission equipment. Oran didn't know where to turn. It got so bad that by midweek, reporters just barged into the studio and without pause abruptly threw Oran out of his own office. His adulation of the network "big boys" quickly turned to scorn. They were turning his fantasy into a nightmare. They were rude, drunk, and had egos too huge to measure.

One night, a technician from one of the other Japanese networks scheduled a feed to Tokyo but never bothered to tell Oran. When the technician's time was approaching, he waltzed into the control room and, ignoring the crew using the room, turned on all his switches. But when he reached to adjust the audio level, he cranked it up so high that he blew out the fuses on the soundboard. Fortunately, it was one of the last feeds of the day and the only one left to transmit was Ken Burslem, the cheerful Australian. Had the wayward technician fouled up an American network's transmission, they would have erected Barrow's first lamp post from which to hang him. Oran was up all night repairing the damage and getting ready for the next day's madness. The technician never apologized.

The producers from the three networks came to Oran and suggested he give them control of his studio until the story was over. They knew what they were doing, they assured him. Among them, the three producers had been in the business for more than seventy-five years. At what should have been the moment of his greatest professional triumph, Oran Caudle was being eased out of his own job.

Oran asked ABC's Harry Chittick why he and Jerry Hansen were so concerned about a meltdown. Chittick explained that like any major story from a remote or foreign location, their number one worry was access to the satellite. In the news business, Chittick said, competitors have two objectives. The first is dramatic footage and sound-bites. The second is to deny the same to their competitors.

As Oran knew, Aurora I was the only satellite that could "see" a signal from Barrow, and Oran's studio was the only facility that could access it in that remote part of the world. A single broadcaster could easily gain a monopoly on the story by buying all the available time segments on Aurora I, a technique known as "bird-jamming." If one company could book all the time for itself, no one else could use the satellite. The bird jammer would face a pleasant dilemma. He could shut out all his competitors and keep the story for himself, making it an exclusive, or he could make a killing by selling segments of the time back to his competitors at enormous markup.

A meltdown was the last thing Caudle wanted. He checked with Alascom, the company that owned the Aurora I satellite, to see if anyone was trying to jam it. They told him that the rush of last-minute orders enabled Alascom to raise its prices past the point where even the networks could afford to corner the market. Adam Smith's invisible hand was so powerful it could even stretch to the heavens.

Still, the American networks ended up with most of the time. After all, it was their story. Lucky foreign broadcasters like NTV and BBC had international affiliation agreements with American networks. Their footage was transmitted at times when their U.S. partners had excess inventory. The others scrambled for a few extra minutes here and there and paid exorbitantly for the privilege.

Caudle was not just frustrated, he was getting frazzled. After all, it was his video that launched the story in the first place, and now he was being discarded like yesterday's garbage. Worse still, he heard rumors that some of the Outside media were making fun of him and the frontier town he came to help settle.

Suddenly, Oran had an unglossed look at the inner workings of network news. By comparison, the North Slope Borough television studio did not seem so bad after all. What struck Caudle were the endless arguments. ABC's Harry Chittick yelling at NBC's Don Oliver, the Japanese yelling at each other, and everybody yelling at CBS. For two straight weeks, Caudle and his assistants worked from four in the morning until well past midnight. The day began with live shots for the American morning-news programs. A steady stream of correspondents and camera crews pushed through his studio's revolving door for the next twenty hours. Finally, and fittingly, each day would end with the media's one true, unadulterated pleasure: Ken Burslem and his post-midnight "live cross" antics to Australia.

Caudle and his North Slope television studio staff were reduced to walking zombies. His apple juice and granola breakfasts were replaced by coffee, coffee and more coffee. Colonel Carroll would have been proud. Out on the ice, coffee was served by the barrelful. Cutting new holes while keeping the existing ones open was now a round the clock effort. The initial few hundred dollars authorized by North Slope budget director Dan

Fauske to feed a half-dozen Eskimos grew at the same exponential rate as the rescue itself.

By the middle of Operation Breakout's first week, Fauske's costs had already ran into tens of thousands of dollars. It was turning into one of the coldest Octobers in Alaskan history. Temperatures were already reaching minus forty degrees. Just a few months later, in January 1989, North America would record its coldest-ever reading of eight-two degrees below zero just a few hundred miles south of Barrow. It was so cold, dozens more Barrowans were needed to keep the holes open.

With the mayor out of town and out of touch, Fauske knew it was his call. Like never before, and almost certainly never again, the eyes of the world were on his tiny hamlet. Fauske knew that if the whales died, and he hadn't done all he could on his town's behalf, the world might blame him. The conservative Fauske was faced with the risk of his life.

He knew that if there was anyone who could save those whales it was Arnold Brower Jr. and the Eskimos of Barrow. Brower knew it too. Just as soon as Fauske gave Arnold the okay for new expenses, Brower was back asking for more. He got it every time.

Except during whaling season, more than 70 percent of Barrow's workforce was unemployed. To help alleviate one of the modern era's most chronic by-products, Barrow created a local employment service called the Mayor's Jobs Program in the mid-1980s. To Fauske, helping the whales seemed like the perfect chance to put both the under-used program and Barrow's unemployed people to work. Brower posted a sign on the job board in the main hallway of the borough government building. Hundreds of out of work Barrowans, some more sober than others, and a surprising number of whites stood in line for a chance to earn twenty-one dollars an hour cutting holes out on the ice. It would cost the borough more than $100,000.

The small rescue Cindy Lowry organized just five days earlier was now a massive, professional operation. It employed hundreds of highly paid laborers from the Mayor's Jobs Program, VECO, ARCO and the National Guard. But for all the added reinforcements, the whales wouldn't swim beyond their original hole. Ron Morris needed help. He summoned two top whale biologists from the National Marine Mammal Laboratory in Seattle. Maybe they knew a way to lure the whales away from the icy death that awaited them in the first hole.

That first hole was now one of many in a sea of ice stretching out to the open lead. But it was the only hole the whales would trust. They couldn't bring themselves to leave it. During the day, they could surely see the light from dozens of other new holes cut in front of them. No one, not even Malik, could figure out why the whales would not move. He thought that if they let the first hole freeze over, the whales would have no choice but to swim into the new ones. Cindy said it was just too risky. Malik wasn't convinced enough to argue.

The longer the whales lingered around their first hold, the less strong Bone became. The baby whale was so weak, Cindy wondered how long it could hold on. What would happen, she thought, if the other whales moved? Would Bone have the strength to move with them? Watching Bone suffer tested Cindy, but she found a reserve of strength. Everyone on the ice admired Cindy's compassion. It was genuine, no doubt about that. If the whales belonged to anyone, they belonged to Cindy.

Although she had no official role in the operation, she was the most important person on the ice. She was beyond question and above reproach. No one, not even Ron Morris, dared take any action without first winning Cindy's consent. People watched with fascination as Cindy stroked each of the tired whales with her soft, caring hands. And with Bone, it was special. Because it was the most vulnerable and least likely to survive, Cindy grew particularly close to it, and to everyone's amazement, Bone seemed to grow. The baby whale seemed to respond to her encouragements. Remarkably, Bone always surfaced near Cindy no matter where she stood around the hole, like an infant instinctively able to locate its mother. Somehow the baby seemed to know that the tiny maternal presence on top of the ice was the key to its redemption.

But as close as the two appeared to grow, Bone drifted closer to death. As it slipped away from Cindy's hand, her once-buoyant spirit started to sink along with it. Nothing seemed to work, not the barge, not the president's phone call, not the new Eskimo holes, and certainly not the interspecies communicator. While the other two whales looked weak and unresponsive, the baby was downright listless. Cindy and Ron were fighting despondency. By the night of Wednesday the 19th, twelve days after they were first discovered, the whales seemed doomed. No matter how precise the Eskimos' hole-cutting technique had become, it seemed that as soon as they could open up a new one, it would start to freeze over. Drifting snow blown by thirty-mile-an-hour winds quickly turned the open holes to slush, threatening to entomb the whales before morning.

15

Minneapolis Comes to the Rescue

Just as hope was fading, help was on its way. After flying all night, Greg Ferrian and Rick Skluzacek, the Minnesotans bearing deicers, finally arrived in Barrow. Throughout the trip from Minneapolis, Greg never told the truth to his brother-in-law Rick or Jason Davis from *Eyewitness News*. He did not inform them that Ron Morris refused to authorize the use of their deicers. Greg told Rick that everything was set for their arrival at the top of the world.

When he first heard about it, KSTP's Jason Davis thought the idea of following two local boys trying to save three whales up near the North Pole sounded like a great adventure. But the instant he deplaned, Davis' enthusiasm evaporated. They were nearly blown over by a thirty-mile-an-hour wind that made January in Minnesota seem balmy. Rick's first hint that things weren't going quite as smoothly as predicted came when Greg admitted the two had nowhere to stay. A minor detail, Ferrian promised.

They called the Top of the World Hotel from the airport. "Booked" said the receptionist. It was the same story at the Airport Inn. Greg stood in line waiting to ask the Eskimo woman behind the MarkAir ticket counter if she knew of a place they could stay. He noticed a large cardboard sign written in Magic Marker and hung by a string at the head of the line.

"All raw whale, seal, walrus, and polar bear meat must be stored in leakproof packages for shipment on MarkAir." When he turned around to point out the odd sign, Rick was already focusing his pocket camera to take his own shot. When Greg reached the head of the line, he asked the overworked agent if she knew of any accommodations. He tried to joke that the trip from Minneapolis was a bit too arduous for a commute. Nonplussed by his poor attempt at humor, the agent suggested he call the Naval Arctic Research Laboratory (NARL) north of town.

"North of town?" asked a befuddled Greg Ferrian. "I thought this was as far north as it gets?"

"NARL is as far north as it gets," came the response. They loaded their six deicers into the back of an Isuzu I-Mark taxi and climbed aboard for the five mile ride out to the northern tip of the continent. When the driver told them the fare for the short ride was fifty dollars, they realized they had not only reached the edge of their continent but the edge of their means. They arrived at NARL just in time to claim two of the last guest rooms in the remarkably tidy facility. The sterile smell of a hospital hung heavily in the air. In case either of them was burned with chemicals or acids while conducting one of their Arctic experiments, there was a red emergency shower nozzle in the hallway outside their room.

From the television reports he had been watching before leaving Minneapolis, Greg immediately recognized the North Slope biologists Geoff Carroll and Craig George as they dragged their weary feet and aching bodies into their office across the hall. Ebulliently, he introduced himself to the exhausted duo, who had returned to their office to escape the whales, if only for a few minutes. Greg asked for just a moment of their time to explain the deicers they had brought all the way from Minnesota at their own expense.

"These machines can keep your ice holes open," Greg assured Geoff. "That's our business." Geoff thought it was worth trying the machines but he dreaded the idea of yet another sleepless night on the bitterly cold ice worrying about polar bears mauling him. He knew though that the whales needed help. The remarkable string of luck that had brought the whales this far seemed at an end. The dropping temperatures only deepened the whales' dire straits. Craig told Greg and Rick they had to find Ron Morris. The biologists promised help, but they had to get away from Morris first, if only for a few hours. The coordinator had turned the whole rescue into a media circus and he was its ringmaster. For their own sanity, they needed a break.

Geoff told the two Minnesotans that the best way to catch Morris would be to wait for him at the Search and Rescue hangar. Craig drove them to the hangar at the end of the runway and introduced them to Randy Crosby. They waited two and a half hours before Morris landed in one of Crosby's helicopters. With a slight wave of his hand, Morris tried to brush off Greg's insistent appeals. "All I'm asking is that you let us tell you about our machines." Greg pleaded. "You have to at least give us that much. After all, we just spent thousands of our own dollars to try and help."

"All right," Morris relented, "I'll give you a minute and a half to explain them." He listened to Rick's short but plaintive explanation while carefully examining his fingernails in a conspicuous attempt to show his disinterest. Standing up to walk out of Crosby's office, Morris doubted the deicers would work. Even if they did, he added, he thought they would make too much noise. Rick pleaded with Morris to at least let them try the deicers. After all, the Coast Guard successfully used them to keep open a fifty-square-yard hole in the middle of a frozen Lake Superior. Unimpressed, Morris told them to go back to NARL to await his decision. He said he would call them with a definitive answer.

Rick and Greg returned to their tiny room now cluttered with ice melting machines, and waited for Morris to call. After more than two anxious hours, they could wait no longer. Rick had to know whether his trip was a total waste of time and money and exactly how to kill his brother-in-law who dragged him into it. Around 6:30 that evening, they called Morris at the Airport Inn. His wife told them he could not be disturbed. He was preparing for his *Nightline* appearance.

A minute later, there was a commotion in the hallway. When Rick peered out the door he saw Geoff and Craig hurriedly knocking on every closed door in the building. Craig spotted Rick and cried, "There you are. We've been looking all over for you."

The biologists just returned from the ice. Conditions were deteriorating. The holes were freezing again. "The whales are losing it," Geoff told them. "I don't think they're going to make it through the night."

"Screw Morris," Craig barked when Rick muttered something about waiting for the coordinator's call. "We've got to get those things on the ice." They loaded two of the deicers into the ice and snow covered bed of Craig's pick-up truck. They drove back to Search and Rescue to try and find a portable electric generator to power the deicers. Randy Crosby told them the heavy crosswinds made the already risky proposition of flying at night too dangerous. As they waited for conditions to improve, Rick and Greg passed out sales brochures to the dozen or so nightshift journalists waiting for any news to report. Among those handed a brochure was Geoff and Craig's boss, Dr. Tom Albert, the director of the North Slope Borough's Wildlife Management office.

After his appearance on *Nightline*, Ron Morris went back to the hangar. It was 10 P.M., Wednesday, October 19, and Tom Albert was waiting for him. He angrily shoved the brochure in Morris's startled face. "Either we harvest those whales or you give these guys a chance." Albert stormed off before Morris could answer. At around 11 P.M., Randy finally found a portable Honda generator in the back of his hangar. After he replaced the spark plugs and cleaned the carburetor, the small Japanese generator smoothly purred to life. It was loaded, along with the deicer, onto a SAR helicopter and flown off into the pitch-black Arctic night. Hovering above the black void, Randy searched for the lone light of the hunting shed erected on the edge of the sandspit. When he was directly over it, he switched on his landing lights to look for a safe place to set his chopper down.

Cindy and Arnold Jr. had just about given up hope. That night was the worst weather yet. They were thinking about heading back to town for some sleep. All that kept them alone with the whales on this minus forty degrees night was their unspoken fear that the next time they returned, the holes, like the whales that depended on them, would have vanished without a trace beneath firmly frozen ice and windblown snow. The arrival of the Minnesota brothers-in-law brought Cindy and Arnold back from the edge of despair. They expectantly gathered around the small silver and red generator while Randy tried to start it. But it was so cold, its components had frozen solid during the twelve-minute flight from the hangar.

Craig suggested they try again with his own portable generator. That would require another trip back to town. As they all flew back to the hangar, Cindy knew they were leaving the vulnerable whales to their fate, if only for an hour. She wondered if they would survive. She wanted to stay out on the ice with them, but Arnold Brower Jr. wouldn't let her. There were polar bears everywhere. If she stayed alone, the whales would have a better chance of surviving than she would.

Greg was exhausted. He pushed his tired body as far as it would go. He had to get some sleep. It was after midnight and he hadn't slept since before leaving Minneapolis thirty-six hours earlier. Since Rick was the expert on the deicers, Greg was free to fall comatose on his cot at NARL. Rick stood shivering aimlessly in the dark Arctic night as Craig rummaged through his cluttered tool shed for the generator. How could he have lost it, he asked himself. He used it just a week earlier on his hunting trip with Geoff. When he found the generator, it started on the first pull. Treating it just like his truck, he left its engine running for the ride back to the SAR hangar where Randy and Cindy were waiting.

Randy was not thrilled with the idea of flying his helicopter with a gas powered combustion motor running inside his cabin. Crosby prayed that the FAA never found out what he was about to do. Not only was flying a helicopter with a flammable engine running incredibly dangerous, it would also be incredibly cold. It was minus sixty degrees just a few hundred feet off the ground and the onboard heater barely worked with all the windows shut. But with a running engine emitting deadly carbon monoxide fumes, they would have to fly with the windows open.

The trip out was the worst experience anyone of them could ever remember. Randy's arms were so numb from the cold, he could barely fly his aircraft. His left eye froze shut. Cindy broke down in tears that instantly froze to her stinging red cheeks. Rick wished he were dead, and Craig tried to take his mind off the excruciating cold by concentrating on a tune he was trying to hum. Finally, the chopper touched down. Randy lowered his head onto the frozen vinyl dashboard, relieved that his dangerous mission was over. Craig and Geoff cradled the still purring generator like a fragile infant as they walked it out to the slush covered first hole.

Like panting dogs, the panicked whales were surfacing every few seconds. Craig figured the whales had reached the end. At any minute, the mammals could drown. Rick frantically plugged the power cord into the end of one of the compact deicers and dropped it into the corner of the rapidly freezing hole. After bobbing up and down a few times, the buoyed device bounced into position. It was ready to be turned on. At the flick of a switch, it started to work. The slightly warmer water pulled up from a few feet below the waterline bubbled up at the surface. Instantly, the slush and ice around the buoy began to melt. The deicers worked.

In its first ten minutes, the deicer melted the slush and ice in half of the first hole. Almost as quickly, the whales started to calm down. Cindy, Randy, Craig, and Greg were exuberant. Finally, they found a way to help the whales. In his euphoria, Rick discovered a renewed source of energy that propelled him onward to the next hole. He set up his second deicer and dropped it in the hole. Within seconds, it too worked. Soon, the next hole was ice free. Drunk with delirium, four lone souls danced on the surface of a frozen sea in the bitter cold black of an Arctic night.

They knew not to trust everything they felt and saw. Their exhausted consciousnesses crossed into a new realm. They stammered in disbelief. The next sight their eyes beheld was more than their weary minds could compute. The whales were in the second hole. Just a few minutes after it cleared of ice, the whales gave the first sign that they were interested in being rescued. The whales had moved.

The next move was man's.

16

Saving Whales
the Old–fashioned Way

Colonel Tom Carroll was frazzled. He tapped the sharpened tip of his pencil on the Formica conference table provided for him by ARCO, his Prudhoe Bay hosts. His glazed eyes peered aimlessly through the frosted glass window and out to sea. In front of him lay a field of dirty Styrofoam coffee cups that had accumulated since his National Guard unit hastily set up shop there five days earlier. All his mind could focus on was the prostrate, abandoned barge which lay listless on the ice.

The operation to save the three whales proved to be the strangest mission of his life. Called from his Anchorage home on a Saturday afternoon, Colonel Carroll was initially put in charge of a logistical aspect of a burgeoning whale rescue. His commanding officer, General John Schaeffer, assigned him a single straightforward task. General Schaeffer ordered him to move a 185-ton hoverbarge from its frozen dry dock at Prudhoe Bay to Barrow, 270 miles across the ice-covered surface of the Arctic Ocean.

Just seventy-two hours after arriving in the Arctic netherworld, Tom Carroll was briefing the president of the United States. If that wasn't enough, he was also falling in love with one of the president's assistants whom he had never seen. But just as the colonel's star began to rise, it fell back to earth with the force of a falling meteor. The colonel was back on the ground facing the bitter reality of Arctic logistics. His fifteen minutes of fame were drawing to a close, at least for now.

By the night of Thursday, October 20, day five of Operation Breakout and day thirteen for the stranded whales, Colonel Tom Carroll found little comfort in the thought that his mission seemed a failure. He told his men they performed their duties with honor and distinction. They were assigned a difficult task with no more than an even chance of success. Despite mounting press recriminations, the colonel told his men they could hold their heads high.

Just as the colonel's emotional cycle entered the acceptance stage and his natural healing process began, General Schaeffer called and asked him what he was planning to do for an encore. Carroll thought Schaeffer was poking fun at him. After all, he thought, any more performances like the one he just directed and the entire Alaska National Guard might be the next endangered species.

General Schaeffer told Colonel Carroll if it were not for the National Guard, the whales would have long since perished. Carroll had much to be proud of. The general insisted that the Guard's participation and the colonel's command would continue as long as the rescue did. The Guard had invested too much time and money to back out now. If they did, the general said, the press would interpret it as a sign of weakness, a blow from which the Guard might not quickly recover.

It would also send the wrong signal to the rescue itself. If the Guard, with all its resources, gave up on the three whales, how would that play with the chain-saw-wielding Eskimos? Schaeffer ordered Carroll to devise alternate plans to assist in the whale rescue. If no further logistics were available in Prudhoe, he wanted Colonel Carroll to redeploy most of his men and equipment to Barrow. That was where the action was. There was plenty the Guard could do there. Randy Crosby and his Barrow Search and Rescue helicopters were overworked. The Guard could help SAR run helicopter press tours of the whale site, and if necessary, they could coordinate press access to the rescue. Tom Carroll was back in business, though on a smaller scale. But as far as the press knew, he had never missed a beat.

Just a few hours earlier, the whales recorded their first hint of progress since the rescue began. At last they started to explore the new holes the Eskimos had cut for them on Wednesday. The Minnesota deicers couldn't possibly have arrived at a more dramatic moment. They saved the whales when they were literally on their last breaths. Wednesday night's brittle cold completely sealed nearly every hole except the two kept open by the deicers.

The colonel thought quietly for a moment about ways to help. His brief experience with the barge taught him many valuable lessons. Chief among them was the difficulty of performing even the Arctic's simplest jobs. Unlocking the barge from its four-year frozen berth was a feat in itself. Herculean efforts were required just to move it, some of which had never been tried before. While creative ingenuity was the only option available to many Arctic expeditions, the colonel's detailed post mortem determined that an operation so fraught with unconquered obstacles could not depend entirely upon improvised solutions.

Carroll decided that Arctic innovations were better left to the innovators. If the National Guard was going to play a role of any significance in the whale rescue, the colonel resolved, it could only be done through tested, proven means.

Carroll called Ben Odom, the head of ARCO Alaska, and the rescue's chief financier. The two men had been in daily contact ever since the colonel and his unit arrived at Odom's expansive North Slope facility five days earlier. The barge failure didn't change Odom's mind. He wanted those whales freed and his checkbook would stay open until they were.

Ben Odom's enthusiasm for the project was shared by nearly everyone at Atlantic Richfield. From the executive dining room to the canteens, the rescue was a big topic of conversation throughout the ARCO Alaska tower. It united the company's 25,000 employees like no other event Ben Odom could remember.

No oil company in Alaska ever got more favorable press coverage than ARCO did during Operation Breakout. Normally the whipping boy of oil dependent environmentalists, ARCO now worked side by side with Cindy Lowry and Greenpeace. ARCO swallowed any hint of criticism by pouring resources into a rescue destined to save three animals endangered by nature, not man. Of course, the green's later sniffed that ARCO's work freeing the whales did nothing to clean up the 11,000 acres of North Slope Arctic tundra they claimed were "ruined" by oil drilling.

Standard Oil Company was one of ARCO's global competitors as well as a partner in the gigantic consortium of oil companies working the North Slope fields. Standard Oil donated three chain saws to the rescue. No good deed, no matter how small ever goes unpunished, particularly when committed by an oil company. When Standard confirmed their donation, the media immediately howled that the company spent more money announcing their contribution than their contribution was even worth.

Odom couldn't have been more encouraging to the colonel and his National Guard guests. The barge setback notwithstanding, the longer the rescue went on, the more ARCO could benefit from the goodwill generated by their efforts. Besides, Ben Odom wanted the whales freed for the same reasons everyone else did. They were innocent victims whose plight couldn't help but stir human compassion. He told Carroll that he and ARCO were at his service. Whatever the colonel wanted or needed, Odom would do his best to provide. Carroll contacted Ron Morris in Barrow to find out what options, if any, the NOAA coordinator was considering. The colonel informed him the Guard had the mandate to help in whatever manner Morris saw appropriate. Morris told Carroll that he and Cindy had called upon experts at NOAA and Greenpeace to draw up a comprehensive list describing every plausible technique for breaking the ice or moving the whales.

Cindy Lowry was amazed by the extensive research her colleague, Campbell Plowden, had conducted from the besieged Greenpeace headquarters in Washington. Between asking and being asked questions of and by nearly everyone professing to be an ice or whale expert, Plowden had been on the phone for four days straight. He sent nightly faxes to Cindy in Barrow outlining what he had learned that day. She reviewed and edited the reports before passing them on to Morris.

The most promising alternative to the abandoned barge seemed to be "portable" water jet pumps. Originally designed to dislodge minerals imbedded in granite, they proved more than capable of blasting through thick Arctic ice deposits. The powerful pumps shot water pressurized at 35,000 pounds per square inch. Manufacturers assured Plowden they could blast through an eight foot wall of solid ice. But there were no pumps to be found in Alaska. Private contractors only brought them up to the North Slope on a per job basis. Like the Boeing Vertol helicopters Bill Allen wanted to use to tow the barge, the independent water jet operators fled the slim pickings of the North Slope in search of more promising pastures.

Every other option had too many drawbacks. Phosphorus burning powders were ruled out because of the potential destruction to other marine life, including free-swimming whales, that were in the area. The steel and glass cutting particle steam erosion laser was too heavy to transport from the Lower 48, and the mini icebreaker owned by the Amoco oil company was busy protecting a drill ship in the Arctic Ocean two hundred miles north of Prudhoe.

Earlier in the week when the barge was still expected, Cindy heard a rumor there was an icebreaker docked in Prudhoe Bay. The owners of the ship, the *Arctic Challenger,* turned down Plowden's request for help. It would be suicide, they argued, for their small ship to fight the Arctic ice so late in the year. The last time they tried to sail from Prudhoe to Barrow the voyage took three weeks, the ship was severely damaged, and that was in September. Luckily, no lives were lost, but this year the ice was even thicker and the owners were not about to risk their ship again for the sake of three whales. Plowden couldn't blame them.

About the only idea that seemed even remotely feasible, if comparatively lame, came from the suddenly resurrected Tom Carroll. After hearing about the Eskimos cutting manual ice holes, Carroll asked Marvin King, VECO's top man in Prudhoe, if he knew of any readily available device that might cut holes even faster.

"Well, there's that ARCO ice bullet," he said in a tone lacking confidence.

"The what bullet?" asked Carroll.

King gently rubbed his tired face, sat down and let out a sigh. Their efforts to free the barge could have killed him and his men. It was one of the most difficult tasks any of them had ever performed. Remembering all the frostbite, singed lungs, painful coughs, and frozen eyelids, the last thing King wanted was to get out there and start all over again with another one of the gung-ho colonel's crazy ideas. Known by several other names, the "bullet" had one simple function. "Smasher," "ice crusher," "ice bomb," each described a late-twentieth-century Arctic technology at its simplest. The five-ton concrete spike emblazoned with the light blue ARCO corporate logo looked like a giant toy spin-top. The bullet dangled on a steel cable beneath a helicopter. It was winched a hundred feet up in the air and, in a reaffirmation of the laws of gravity, dropped to smash through the ice below. Sophisticated? No. Effective? Always.

The colonel wanted to know more about the bullet, but there wasn't much more King could tell him other than ARCO owned it and lent it regularly to VECO. Based on his incomplete understanding of ice conditions in Barrow, it didn't take much for Carroll to determine that the force of a five-ton shaft of concrete dropped from one hundred feet would obliterate whatever lay beneath it. Colonel Carroll wanted to test it. Late Thursday evening, he called Bill Allen at his Anchorage home to see if he could smooth the way to getting ARCO's permission to use the bullet.

Ever since he touched the whales with his bare hands five days earlier, Bill Allen seemed a changed man. His employees at VECO noticed it the morning after his trip to Barrow. He was more at ease, more attentive. Before his encounter with the giant whales, Allen could not fathom an animal as large and as graceful as the one he gently petted at the top of the world. Unlike ARCO, his colleague Ben Odom's company, VECO had almost no contact with the general public. It sold its products within the oil industry. Except during a 1984 political scandal that rocked the state legislature, hardly anyone outside the "industry" had ever even heard of VECO. Its role in saving the whales could only detract from VECO's bottom line. Bill Allen contributed his company's time, energy and money for one reason. He wanted to save the whales.

Allen's secretary, Pearl Crouse, flung open the door to her boss's office, on Wednesday, October 19, sporting a bright grandmotherly smile. As she ushered in a bundle-laden postman, Crouse nearly burst with pride in the boss she adored. The mailman was carrying a canvas mailbag stuffed full of handwritten letters for the VECO chairman.

Children from schools across the United States and Canada drafted letters to Bill Allen with salutations such as "Dear Mr. Oilman," and "Dear Whalesaver." Many of the letters had no address, just "Whale Rescuers, Alaska." Within seventy-two hours of Operation Breakout's birth, the letters had found their way to VECO's Anchorage headquarters on Fairbanks Street.

Reading the heartwarmingly scribbled notes, Allen's mood improved. Carroll could not have picked a better time to ask him for his help in getting the bullet. In his ebullience, Allen would likely have agreed to almost any suggestion. The entire operation started when he authorized the use of the hoverbarge. But in the time it took for the barge to be rendered impotent, Operation Breakout had taken on a full-fledged life of its own, no longer dependent on any one man. Allen knew there was no stopping the rescue's momentum. Realizing it would proceed with or without him, he was determined to see it through, helping in any way he could.

The colonel had one more solo act to perform. If the bullet passed its test in Prudhoe, the National Guard would start punching its own path of holes out to the open lead, picking up where the Eskimos left off. Carroll briefed his Skycrane pilots about the new plan. They were to test the concrete block to see if it worked. Waiting near the silent Skycranes for the test to begin, Chief Warrant Officer Gary Quarles and his crew stared across the burnt orange horizon, mouths agape as they watched what looked like an extraterrestrial vehicle with six-foot-wide treads slowly crunching its way across the barren landscape.

Arctic men called the odd truck carrying the heavy concrete bullet a "Rolligon." The oil industry spent millions of dollars to design a machine that could carry heavy loads in the Arctic without damaging the sensitive environment. Since the wide treads dispersed the truck's massive weight over a broader surface area, it could cross fragile tundra and ocean ice without breaking through.

The bullet was attached to a recoilable high-tension cable and hung from the middle of the Skycrane's slender fuselage. Unlike the strain of towing the barge, this test was virtually risk-free. The high powered helicopter would have no trouble lifting the block and dropping it into the ice below. For once during their North Slope assignment, the pilots had it easy. No late-night mathematical computations, no two-way radios, no pep talks. Either the block would break the ice or it wouldn't. Sitting next to his copilot, Gary Quarles powered up the Skycrane, locked in the bullet and prepared to head out to an open area of ice in the middle of Prudhoe Bay. At the last second, Colonel Carroll hopped on board for the ride. The pilots lowered the aircraft to just one hundred feet above the surface of the ice. When it was properly positioned, Quarles firmly gripped the joystick, anticipating the sudden upward thrust when the bullet was released. With a nod from Quarles, the copilot released the winch holding the bullet in the chopper's cargo bay.

Like bomber pilots on a sortie, they pressed their helmets against the side windows for a better view. They peered down to see the effect of their nonexplosive concrete bomb. They looked for the identifying buoy which was supposed to float in the newly opened water. When they spotted the bright orange buoy, it was bobbing up and down among the shattered shards of ice. The bullet worked. It broke clean through the two-foot-thick harbor ice. If the bullet could penetrate through that, it could easily smash the ice half as thick off the tip of Point Barrow. Jabbing vigorously into the air, Colonel Carroll landed an animated smack of congratulations onto Gary Quarles's flight helmet. The copilot pushed the recoil button to raise the bullet back to its resting place under the fuselage. Maybe he wasn't dead weight after all, thought Carroll. Maybe his latest idea would help the Barrow rescue in its quest to free the whales. When they returned to base, Carroll called Morris and Bill Allen to tell them the bullet was on the way.

On Friday morning, October 21, the Skycranes were outfitted for the 270-mile flight to Barrow. The National Guard asked Randy Crosby and his Search and Rescue team to help them look for a local place to set up shop. There was only one place that could accommodate the National Guard and Randy Crosby's hangar was it. Not having much choice, Crosby reluctantly offered to house the Guardsmen and their workaholic colonel in his own facility. He sent one of his workers to restock the hangar with plenty of coffee. Carroll and his men arrived in Barrow exactly two weeks after the whales were first discovered and six days after making his first exploratory trip. Somehow, the whales had survived. Despite unimaginable stress, the whales managed to outmaneuver their own seemingly sealed fate for a fortnight.

With the exception of the still weak baby whale Bone, the mammals seemed as fit as at any time during their 350-hour ordeal. The middle-sized whale had been given the name Poutu, an Inupiat word roughly describing the icy hole it was trapped in. Poutu was breathing normally once again, its pneumonia overcome. The whale biologists Ron Morris summoned from the National Marine Mammal Laboratory in Seattle arrived to pronounce the animals in remarkably good condition.

Several of the reporters, including me, asked why the whales weren't being fed during their confinement. The biologists told us that they wouldn't have eaten anyway. Like all other California grays, these three came to Alaska to take advantage of the rich deposits of amphipods that line hundreds of thousands of square miles of the Arctic Ocean's shallow seabed. They just finished spending the last five months fattening themselves up. Each put on several tons of extra blubber during the summer. Once they left on their 4,500-mile journey from the frozen Arctic to balmy Mexico, the whales wouldn't eat again until they returned in the spring.

Craig and Geoff were convinced that a marine miracle kept the whales alive in their tiny hole for two long weeks. The whales managed to balance their survival against a formidable assortment of obstacles. Each of the five thousand breaths each whale had taken required a tricky maneuver against strong ocean currents through a small opening in the ice while fighting exhaustion and mental fatigue. Malik didn't think it was a miracle. He knew it was the whales' inner strength that compelled them to survive. If the bowhead whale could sustain his people for so many years, Malik knew the three grays could surely find a way to save themselves, if one was available. Cindy didn't know what it was that pushed the whales onward in the face of certain death, but she thanked God for it.

During the two weeks of Operation Breakout, the Top of the World lobby was transformed from a modest hotel lounge into an international marketplace whose item of commerce was information about the whales and the effort to rescue them. The hotel was more than just the broadcast and print nucleus for media trying to cover the story. It also became Barrow's social hub. Self-proclaimed experts on just about everything from the Arctic to the whales purveyed their various theories to hordes of anxious newsmen clambering for any unreported angle. Here, rescuer and reporter commingled and cohabitated.

The smell of scotch cut through the smoke-filled lobby. Reporters and technicians clutched their overused and underwashed glasses. When glasses broke, the more determined connoisseurs had to make do with Styrofoam cups, a tradition NBC producer Jerry Hansen started that was soon mimicked by others. Climbing the sharp-edged iron steps of the world's northernmost hotel was an ascent into a rarefied atmosphere in American journalism. Nowhere else could the coordinator of a United States government rescue constantly be seen drinking liquor in front of a passive, mesmerized press corps.

Affected by the cold and the lengthening darkness, the mood in the lobby of the Top of the World Hotel changed noticeably on the morning of

Thursday, October 20. News of the deicers' success spread. Reporters hustled to phone in the report to their bureaus. Hours earlier, before going to sleep, their final prognosis could not have been worse. The bitter weather and howling winds threatened to entomb the whales before daybreak. A few reports predicted that the last person to leave the whales would be the last one to see them alive. Ironically, there were no television cameras on the ice with Randy, Cindy, Craig, and the Minnesotan Rick Skluzacek to record the whales' first move toward freedom. An unprecedented international obsession born out of the ability to capture the whales every move on film and video missed the first and only time when something specifically significant happened.

Not every reporter missed Wednesday night's miracle on ice. There were two lucky ones. As they arrived in Barrow on the same flight as Greg and Rick, *People* magazine's Maria Wilhelm and Taro Yamasaki knew they were far behind in their effort to cover the rescue. Most other reporters arrived in Barrow days earlier. Maria figured they already knew where everything and who everyone was. Boarding the plane in Anchorage, she realized she desperately needed an edge to get back in the race. That edge was sitting right across the aisle in the form of two collapsed Minnesotans.

Aside from Jason Davis's *Eyewitness News* team that wouldn't arrive in Barrow until a day later, Maria Wilhelm was the only reporter who could report Greg Ferrian and Rick Skluzacek's story. Maria was ecstatic. Someone answered her prayers. Just hours after stepping off their MarkAir flight, Taro and Maria had the only pictures of the deicers thawing the hole and the whales moving into the new hole. As if to make up for the previous night's blunder, reporters lined up early Thursday morning to get their first shots of the whales since they moved into the new hole. Each morning found ABC's Harry Chittick to be the first network man able to pull himself out of an irresistible Arctic slumber—4:30 A.M. came early enough in the Lower 48, but after a day in the strength-sapping cold of the Arctic, it was more than most people could bear. Throughout their millennia, the Eskimos always thought of themselves as hibernators. The only respite from the endless frigid night of winter was long, deep sleep. In sleep, a body unprepared to function in the Arctic could slow its rapid-fire metabolism to a more normal rate.

Like the Eskimos themselves, reporters were overcome by the same indescribable exhaustion. No amount of sleep seemed enough. Traditionally light sleepers fell into unwakable comas. The lobby of the Top of the World Hotel was filled with people claiming they were sober when they fell asleep fully clothed, not to stir until ten hours later. After eight hours on the ice with the whales, it was all I could do to stay awake past 9 P.M. Not everyone responded in the same way. Our cameraman, Steve Mongeau, stayed up drinking and laughing until all hours with our host Rod Benson. After just a few hours of sleep, Mongeau was always the first to get up. Not only that, he worked harder and longer than anyone I saw in Barrow. I couldn't get enough sleep and still was always exhausted.

But interestingly the mononucleosis, which limited me to no more than a few hours of daily activity back in New York, seemed to disappear. Maybe it froze to death. To the marvel of his colleagues, Harry Chittick managed to be not only awake but coherent for his 5:00 A.M. network conference call. The Vietnam vet and National Guard member claimed his secret came tumbling out of an eight-dollar box of cereal he bought at Barrow's only supermarket. Only the clattering radiator and the rhythmic crunching of Chittick's chewing broke the dark Arctic stillness. Pouring a measured portion from his seven-dollar gallon of milk, he gazed wondrously at the surreal jagged ice mounds of the Chukchi Sea. They reminded him of the unforgettable images transmitted from the surface of Mars during the mission of the Viking space probe, stunning photos zapped across the forty-million-mile void of space. He marveled at the sea's curious and enduring luminance. There was no moon on those particular days to light up the blackest of nights, yet the sculpted surface of the sea was limited only by the bounds of Chittick's imagination.

Comfortably wrapped in a tattered Army-issue green wool blanket, Chittick calmly waited for his phone to ring. Intermittently wiping drops of milk from his gray-flecked beard, he savored the solitude of the still, pre-morning Arctic. When his phone did ring, it would signal the beginning of yet another frantic, brutal day on the ice. At first his superiors in New York tried talking him out of going to Barrow. It would look bad, they argued, for him to run off to the top of the world in an obvious attempt to play catch up with NBC, which broke the story. They soon changed their minds. Even though it took ABC seventy-two hours to transmit its first self-shot story from Barrow, they felt fortunate that Chittick was there to cover what had mushroomed into one of the biggest media events of the decade.

The indefatigable Chittick told his superiors that he ran into an exhausted but elated Cindy Lowry just a few hours earlier.

"The deicers worked, the whales moved into the next hole!" she exclaimed.

During his five days in Barrow, he had never seen Cindy so ebullient. He had watched her growing despair as she stood by helplessly as the whales' conditions rapidly deteriorated. He had seen no hint of the euphoric emotion she now displayed. Unable to imagine the agony of a single hour on the bone chilling ice, still less an entire day, ABC News executives could not understand why Chittick and his crew missed the whales' first big move.

Chittick tried to explain that, except for a lone light stationed to ward off curious polar bears, the whale site was pitch-black. Besides, he could hardly order his videographers to drop their $100,000 cameras under water to film the whales swimming to the new hole. For that moment to be perfectly timed, the whales would have had to stick their heads out into the cold air long enough and speak English well enough to announce their impending move.

The misconceptions Chittick had to overcome were mild compared with the tales of other pressmen. British photographer Charles Laurence, shooting for London's *Daily Telegraph,* was so hastily dispatched to Barrow he didn't have time to obtain American money. The first in a series of costly misjudgments the Briton made concerned his assumption that since Barrow was in the United States, its few commercial establishments would accept credit cards. When he wasn't dangling perilously from the back of a speeding dogsled hired by a more fortunate crew nice enough to let him hang on, he was screaming at his editors back in London to wire him the money he needed so he could properly cover the story.

His predicament grew worse when he discovered that no way existed to wire any kind of money to the tiny Eskimo hamlet. The nearest modern bank was in Fairbanks, seven hundred miles away. After enduring the humiliation of begging for cash, he eventually persuaded his office to authorize a paltry $500 wire transfer to Fairbanks. Even if Laurence could figure out how to get his hands on the money, five hundred dollars would barely last him two days in Barrow. He was livid, but desperate. Laurence spent most of his first few days in Barrow frantically trying to get the money tantalizing him from Fairbanks. Dozens of calls later, he found a courier willing to deliver the small sum to Barrow. After he paid the courier, the cash was half gone.

Moreover, the frustrated photographer had to put up with the incessant stream of absurd instructions he received from his desk in London. With no money, woefully inadequate clothing, and nearly frostbitten appendages, Laurence was lambasted whenever one of his well-financed competitors managed to get a picture he didn't.

"Whatever you do," came the order from his superiors in London, "make sure you get great pictures of the whales as they escape." Up to now, his English refinement had kept him in check. But no more.

"Ah, bloody hell. You've got to be joking," he shouted incredulously. "Do you think the whales are actually going to flap their flukes and wave good-bye as they swim away?" he mockingly asked.

Laurence was so enraged at the request he stopped people passing by the wall phone at the Naval Arctic Research Laboratory. "Excuse me," he implored of a perfect stranger. Loud enough for London to hear, Laurence asked of the passerby, "Can you believe this? These idiots want me to get pictures of the whales as they escape. I'm too upset to tell them. Can you please try and explain to them that we are talking about whales, not a trio of happy campers who wave good-bye at the end of their summer holidays?"

His editors got the message and backed off. Their man resented being overworked, underpaid, and totally unappreciated. What he didn't get from London he more than got from those he entertained with his uproarious tales. In analyzing our coverage, none of the estimated one hundred and fifty reporters who flocked to the top of the world would have argued with one universal observation: No war, revolution, or political campaign that any of us had ever observed proved any more physically demanding as the Barrow whale rescue. To some, like Charles Laurence, it was a sign from heaven telling them to explore other lines of work. To others, like Harry Chittick and yours truly, it was the story of a lifetime, and of television journalism at its apex. There was no room for the usual hangers-on to interfere with coverage. We enjoyed unlimited access to all the key players in the drama without the retinue of press aides that attended most government operations.

After the whales made their first tentative move toward freedom, the rescue took on a new urgency. The whales had given new hope to an anxious world. An instinctive death wish was no longer a valid explanation for their poorly understood behavior. They had demonstrated the will to live and proved that they could and would work with their rescuers. Now that the whales were cooperating, there really was no turning back.

17

Polar Bears Threaten
to Steal the Show

The rescue's command looked inward to the one group who had kept the whales alive since they were first discovered: the Eskimos. By Wednesday night, October 19, Arnold Brower's holes finally started to pay off. At the Thursday morning meeting with Ron Morris and Cindy, Brower offered to try to cut breathing holes clear out to the pressure ridge five or six miles away.

In the meantime, village elders thoroughly versed in the ways of their native habitat would search for a way through it. At Brower's suggestion, Morris tersely ordered Dan Fauske, Barrow's budget director, to authorize Eskimo search teams to target by land and air weak spots in the massive ice wall. Fauske was not accustomed to being treated like a supplicant. Morris's request sparked his ire. *Who did this guy think he was?* Fauske wondered. Only after Arnold Brower interceded, saying it was his idea, did Fauske relent. Eskimo hunters directed their helicopter pilots to promising routes through the ice ridge where they marked potential pathways by dropping plastic bags filled with red Kool Aid crystals. The red markings stood out clearly against the universal white backdrop.

The ways of the Inupiat Eskimos were new to Morris. Not surprisingly, his relationship with Brower and the Eskimos was quick to unravel.

Not without reason, he felt the Eskimos and their supporters were anxious to show him up. In an effort to shore up support for his leadership, Morris hired two of his own ice experts to help him out. As a coordinator from NOAA, he was in a position to tap resources like few others. NOAA ran the National Weather Service, which employed many of the world's leading hydrometeorologists, specialists on ocean ice. He called Gary Hufford, perhaps the foremost ice expert in the world. Morris ordered him and his associate, Bob Lewellen, to come immediately to Barrow. But much to Morris's chagrin, Hufford was the first to admit that, despite all his professional training and international reputation, Arnold Brower Jr. knew far more about the local native ice conditions than he did.

Brower's promise to cut holes all the way to the pressure ridge pitted the intrepid Eskimos against the one force that even they could not master: the encroaching darkness. Resting near the top of the planet, Barrow experienced the most dramatic variances of daylight of any permanent human settlement on the globe. Between August 2 and November 17, Barrow goes from eighty-four days of total daylight to sixty-seven days of total darkness. The four months in between are a headlong race toward endless night. In this four month period, Barrow loses up to twenty minutes of light every day. In the first five days of Operation Breakout alone, rescuers lost more than an hour of useable daylight.

The increased darkness brought not only Arctic depression, but rapidly plummeting temperatures. Thanks to the Minnesota deicers, the Eskimos didn't have to worry about keeping the existing holes from freezing. Instead, they could concentrate on cutting new ones. The small pumps the press started calling "Arctic Jacuzzis" did that job for them.

By 9 A.M. Wednesday, Greg Ferrian and Rick Skluzacek were back on the ice. They were too busy to notice that every television and still camera north of the Arctic Circle was pointed right at them.

At that stage, they were still only heroes in the making. Because New York time is four hours ahead of Alaska, news of the late-night miracle on ice came too late for the network morning shows. But word of the Minnesotans' triumph dominated Thursday afternoon's satellite transmissions. By night time, their lionization was complete. Rick Skluzacek and Greg Ferrian were instant, if short-lived, American heroes. Remarkably, the same

Peter Jennings broadcast that propelled Skluzacek and Ferrian to Barrow caught the attention of another Samaritan businessman. This one manufactured chain-saw components in Portland, Oregon. Dudley Hollis of Omark Industries saw the Eskimos struggling to cut holes in the ice, and knew he had a product that could help. Less impetuous than the in-laws from Minneapolis, Dudley Hollis, a former logger from Australia, carefully assessed whether his product could actually help the Eskimos. His company made and sold chain for power saws to manufacturers around the world. At first, Hollis wanted to send a hundred-foot reel of extra chain. Hollis thought the Eskimos might need it to replace their chains when they snapped under the immense strain of sawing thick ice.

Just when they were about to send the reel of chain to Barrow, Hollis remembered the eleven Husqvarna chain saws in Omark's test laboratory. He called Dan Fauske at the North Slope Borough to see if he wanted them. "How much is this going to cost?" asked Fauske warily. His ears pricked up and his eyes opened wide when Hollis told him Omark would donate them. "Well, then," said Fauske jovially, "get your ass on up here."

Hollis's first day on the ice was almost his last. He fitted the adaptable saw with extra long blades enabling the operator to more easily cut through the ice. He explained the safety procedures as clearly as he could. But just in case, he snapped on a pair of thick steel mesh safety trousers. Sure enough, the first Eskimo to fire up a Husqvarna carelessly spun around without looking, whacking Hollis's leg with the saw. If it weren't for the safety trousers, the chain, spinning at fifty miles an hour, would have sawed his leg right off, leaving him to bleed to death on the ice. For the rest of the day, even in this godforsaken place, Hollis couldn't believe how happy two legs could make a person.

That same morning, Harry Chittick convinced Randy Crosby of North Slope Search and Rescue to take an ABC camera crew on a polar bear hunt. After all, Chittick thought, when you covered any kind of a story from the Arctic, you had to show polar bears. All Crosby had done for the past five days was fly press missions to and from the whale site. As long as he wasn't needed for medical evacuations, he didn't object. In fact, he loved it. It was the most exciting thing he had ever done. Crosby relished the opportunity to take Chittick, a fellow pilot, on an aerial tour of his adopted Arctic home. Crosby knew where to look for the bears he and his Eskimo neighbors

called Nanooks. He told Chittick that at twelve feet tall, they would be almost impossible to miss. Several Eskimos on hunting expeditions near the
whale site saw bears as close as a thousand yards from all the human activity.

Polar bears are fearless. They hadn't yet bothered the whales or their
rescuers only because they didn't want to. If they weren't frightened by
Barrow, where they regularly roam the streets, they would not be too worried about a few buzzing chain saws and ski machines far out on the ice,
the bears' home turf. Chittick was surprised to learn that the polar bear
was not a land animal. Since it lived primarily on ice and ate from the sea,
the polar bear was classified a marine mammal, just like the trapped whales.
The bears only ventured onto land when migrating caribou were visible
from the ice pack or when no food could be found in their normal habitat.

Polar bears were protected by the federal government although they
weren't formally put on an endangered species list until 2008, when there
were 25 percent more polar bears roaming the Arctic. While non-natives
faced strict penalties including long jail sentences for killing a polar bear,
Eskimos were allowed a limited hunt under Alaskan subsistence laws. The
five or six times each year when an Eskimo was lucky enough to shoot a
polar bear occasioned a local feast. Just as when a whale was killed, the
news was broadcast on KBRW, Barrow's radio station.

The announcement on the radio made clear that only native Inupiat Eskimos were invited to take part. Non-Inuits—even non-Eskimo spouses,
children, and parents—were not permitted to participate. The absurd "race
and blood" provisions of federal and state law adopted to protect Inupiat culture only served to divide by race everyone else living in native communities. Not to mention, with an intermarriage rate exceeding 80 percent, who
was an Eskimo anyway? In their quest to do good, federal rule makers weren't
as thorough as their German predecessors at Nuremberg in precisely clarify-
ing what "percent" of non-Inuit "blood" would be enough to expel a wife, a
daughter, or a brother from the family dinner table.

Besides, at the rate the polar bear population was expanding, there
were probably more polar bears roaming Barrow than there were "racially
pure" Inuits to hunt them. Polar bears are difficult species to count because they constantly roam and live in hard to access places. But a 2005
study by the Polar Bear Specialist Group of the International Union for
Conservation of Nature estimated the global population at 25,000. If true,

it means there are likely more polar bears alive today than ever before; a quarter more than there were thirty years before. But baby polar bears sure do make good mascots for environmentalists on parade.

Sliding open the huge hangar bays, Randy Crosby hooked the tow tractor to the front end of the new Bell Long Ranger 214 whirlybird. According to Crosby's own regulations, one helicopter always had to be ready for an emergency. Since it was just over an hour before the first scheduled media flight out to the whales, they had less than that time in the air to spot a bear. He lifted off the Search and Rescue helipad dimly outlined by faint yellow lines obscured by the windswept snow. He swung the aircraft to the southeast and out to sea five miles due west of Barrow. The pressure ridge that Morris and the Eskimos were looking to cleave was the natural home to one of the world's most ferocious land animals.

As Crosby flew overhead hoping to find bears, Arnold Brower and his Eskimo scouts were down below armed with high-powered rifles to protect them from the deadly and unpredictable animal. In the most dangerous areas, people knew to walk back to back. They did this on the ice. They walked with guns drawn and elbows locked as they scouted the towering ice walls of the pressure ridge looking for a place to cut a path for the whales. They hoped to avoid a confrontation with one of the huge and remarkably agile giants, but if they could not, they were ready to win it.

Crosby flew northeasterly toward the whale site from the open water side of the pressure ridge. He kept the helicopter less than 100 feet from the surface of the gray-black depths of the ice cold water. He told Chittick and his cameraman to keep their eyes intently focused out the right side of the aircraft. Polar bears liked to hunt along the edge of the ice pack where they could easily slip in and out of the food-rich sea. Just as Crosby was about to lift his Long Ranger to a higher altitude to head for another spot where he had seen polar bears, a mass of white fur leapt out from behind a slab of ice and bounded angrily toward the helicopter. Crosby swept the aircraft sharply around at a hard angle and dropped to just ten feet off the water to let the ABC cameraman get the best possible shot of the bear.

Exposing its teeth and swiping its deadly claws, the massive bear started to rise on its hind legs. Chittick was baffled. Did this bear really think it could attack a swirling helicopter flying ten feet off the ground? But as his mind was framing an image of perplexity, Chittick's puzzled face fell expressionless. The bear stood fully erect. Chittick thought his eyes had finally betrayed him. He felt them tilting up to stare the bear in the eye. He was flying in an airborne helicopter and looking up to see the head of a land animal standing on its hind legs. Just how tall was the damned thing? The bear's angry growl was easily audible over the din of the chopper's spinning blades.

Unbelievably, the bear flailed its paws in an attempt to swat down a hovering helicopter. Unbelievable. The ABC cameraman captured the entire dramatic sequence on video. It was not only the most remarkable sight in Harry Chittick's career, it was also some of the best video to come out of the rescue. Because "pure" Eskimos were the only people allowed to kill a polar bear under state and federal law, they were the only armed scouts the networks could hire. (Whether the scouts assented to have their blood tested to verify their "Eskimo purity" no one rightly bothered to ask.) Reporters covering the whales were told never to go more than a few hundred yards away from the whale site without an escort, except on the now heavily traveled ice paths.

On the way back from our first day covering the whales, Masu Kawamura and I parked our balky truck on the side of the road and strolled onto the ice pack. We just couldn't get over that we could drive, walk, and play on top of the Arctic Ocean. Our otherwise fearless cameraman, Steve Mongeau decided to stay in truck. Mongeau had reported from the Arctic before and knew plenty about polar bears. There was no way he was walking "out there" without a gun.

Masu and I marveled at the fact we could probably walk clear across the top of the world and way down the other, all the way to Norway, across a frozen ocean. Suddenly we got hit with a bout of whiteout—a blinding condition caused when swirling snow wipes out visibility. We both dropped to the ground to regain our balance and escape the biting wind. When I looked around for Masu I could see nothing. I knew he couldn't be more than five or six feet from me. We knew we weren't far from the whales because we easily heard the helicopters and the saws. But neither of us could see anything.

As the wind howled, I first wondered what I was looking at below me. Were they Masu's footprints? They couldn't be more than a few seconds old. But they appeared much bigger, if they were footprints at all. I couldn't be sure. Maybe, perhaps probably it was just my imagination. But as the wind died and the whiteout faded, I convinced myself I could see the outline of a massive polar bear that seemed to be staring right at us.

In the shortest instant, it had to have been frightened by the helicopter hovering overhead. Or maybe it wasn't anything at all. Neither of us was prepared to swear we saw anything—certainly to members of our own fraternity who would only laugh at us. That night, our host Rod Benson did exactly that. There was no way, he howled, we were that close to a bear, and besides no one else saw him and if he were that close to shore he would have wandered onto shore where he would have been soon. Masu and I were told that a favorite strategy of the Nanook is to wait for its victims to be blinded by whiteout. It was a good fantasy to engage in: (a) Had there actually been a bear and (b) had it decided to come for us, we wouldn't have had much of a chance and he wouldn't have had much of a meal—so we were even.

Arnold Brower and his scouts came back from their pressure ridge expedition with bad news. They told Morris that while there were certain weak spots, none were shallow enough to be tackled by chain saws. They could not be sure, but it seemed as though most of the ridge was grounded. That meant the huge ice towers reaching thirty feet in the air also reached more than thirty feet below the surface, firmly anchoring the ice to the ocean floor.

By Friday morning, October 21, Operation Breakout needed a breakout of its own. Although the whales had started to use the holes cut for them by the Eskimos, there still seemed no way through the pressure ridge. What could break the ridge? The question asked since day one had only one answer: an icebreaker. The rescue was right back to where it started a week earlier with Cindy Lowry back on the phone making calls to faraway places. Many of them went to Campbell Plowden, her colleague in Washington. Before the first Outside reporter arrived in Barrow to cover the fledgling whale rescue, Plowden was already working behind the scenes to find a ship that could save the whales. Friday morning, October 14, the day after the first news of the stranded whales appeared on *NBC Nightly News*, Plowden called his contacts in the U.S. Coast Guard, which operated two world-class icebreakers.

The flagship icebreaker, the *Polar Sea*, was herself making news. She was mired in the ice-bound Northwest Passage on the way back from a ship rescue. A Canadian vessel was stuck near the western end of the Passage just a few hundred miles east of Barrow. The *Polar Sea* was trying to guide it to safety. Under normal conditions, Plowden was told, the ship would have sailed right past Barrow. But because of the unusually bad weather in the Arctic, the ice at the Northwest Passage's western end was frozen too thick, even for the *Polar Sea*. Instead, both the icebreaker and the ship she came to save had to sail the other way, 1,500 miles across the top of the world and out into north Atlantic waters just a few hundred miles from Iceland. From there it was 12,000 miles back to Barrow through the Panama Canal. Plowden didn't need to ask any more questions. The *Polar Sea* was not an option.

"What about the other icebreaker?" he asked, knowing that the Coast Guard operated a second such vessel. The newer and sleeker *Polar Star* was in drydock at Seattle, undergoing extensive repairs. Neither American icebreaker could help in the cause that was uniting the world. How could the United States military have only two icebreakers? Plowden asked himself? Maybe because it was people like him who always found reasons to oppose any defense spending, let alone $300 million for an icebreaker designed to facilitate the transit of "contaminated" commercial ships through "pristine" waters.

Except for Alaska, which consistently argued for more, the Navy had little use for icebreakers; the Coast Guard even less. In the passion of the rescue, few people paused to reflect that, thankfully, until then we simply didn't need them. Unlike the Soviet Union, not a single U.S. seaport was ever closed for winter, even those in Alaska. In fact, some believed we didn't even need the two we had. Most of the time they assisted Canadian vessels in the Northwest Passage: Canadian waters; and Canada had its fleet of ice breakers—newer, faster, and more reliable than America's.

In his conversations about the U.S. icebreakers Plowden heard reports that there was a private 200-foot icebreaker in Juneau. His calls revealed she would be no use. At less than half the size of the *Polar Sea,* she was much too small to do the job. Designed to break the relatively thin ice in southeast Alaska, she would have enough trouble just getting to Barrow, let alone contending with the huge ice blocks of the pressure ridge. Plowden got the name of a marine services company in Seattle that reportedly worked closely with all the world's big icebreakers. The man at Crowley Maritime Corporation asked Plowden if he had spoken with anyone from the Soviet Merchant Marine office in New York. The Soviet Union operated the world's largest and most powerful fleet of icebreakers. With few warm water ports, they desperately needed them to assure passage of Soviet merchant and military vessels.

Right after he spoke with Crowley Maritime, the same anonymous woman who called Cindy Lowry in Anchorage earlier that morning with word of the VECO hoverbarge phoned Campbell Plowden in Washington.

"Have you thought about the Soviets?" asked Jane Whale. Jane told Plowden she just spoke to Armand Hammer's Los Angeles office. Hammer was the nonagenarian industrialist who made his first fortune acting as international trading agent for the then embryonic Soviet Union. He later parlayed his business interests into a controlling stake in the giant Occidental Petroleum Company, which he ran until his death in 1990. Hammer commented correctly that he was perhaps the only man alive who was close friends with both Vladimir Lenin and Ronald Reagan.

Jane Whale's initial request for Hammer's help met with an icy response. She told Plowden the woman she spoke to was blunt.

Although Cindy told him not to bother, Plowden called David Ramseur, from Alaska governor Steve Cowper's office. He wanted to see if the governor could authorize the Coast Guard to request assistance from the Soviets. "Are you nuts?" came the rough reply. If the state of Alaska didn't ask the United States government to request Soviet assistance when an American ship got stuck or when seven Eskimo hunters were lost at sea, how would Cowper justify doing so for three lousy whales?

By Monday morning, October 17, the whales were already world news. Plowden woke up at 3 A.M. that day to call David McTaggart, the director of Greenpeace International who was in Rome. McTaggart was sick in bed but his assistant, Brian Fitzgerald, listened as Plowden explained the problem. Plowden wanted McTaggart to persuade his contacts in the USSR Academy of Sciences to send an icebreaker. Fitzgerald promised to convey Plowden's request to his bedridden director. Plowden apologized for being unable to provide more detail. In addition to the expensive international phone rates, he was in a rush. He had to be on the set of ABC's *World News This Morning* for an interview about the rescue. He told them he would be in touch as soon as he was finished with *Good Morning America*, the second

ABC News program on which he was scheduled to appear. Fitzgerald took
Plowden's message directly to McTaggart. If he could send the Soviets a
telegram, that might lubricate the interminably slow-moving machinery
of Soviet bureaucracy.

Before leaving ABC's studios, Plowden called in to check for messages.
Fitzgerald had just called from Rome. McTaggart agreed to send a telegram to the appropriate Soviet authority, Arthur Chilingarov at the State
Committee for Hydrometerology and Control of the Natural Environment, if Plowden would draft the text and find Chilingarov's telex number.
Plowden spent the rest of Monday morning trying to get through on the
constantly busy phone lines at the Soviet Embassy in Washington. When
Plowden finally did get through, the clerk at the embassy gave him the telex
number and address of the Moscow office. The man about to be asked to
help three whales had an office on Pavlik Morozov Street, the USSR's boy-
martyr figure who personified Marxist-Leninist virtue by denouncing his
own father to Stalin's NKVD in 1932. Sergei Eisenstein made the "hero-
ism" of Pavel Morozov into a classic Soviet propaganda film in 1937.

Not ten minutes after Plowden got Chilingarov's number in Moscow, a
reporter from the CNN called about the Greenpeace request. Plowden
was furious. Did someone betray him? How had the news media learned
about his plans so quickly? CNN volunteered that the Soviet Embassy informed them of his call during their regular morning beat checks. Plowden
had denied any knowledge. Now he would look like the one who leaked
the story. If word leaked out before an official request was made, the plan
would die. Plowden drafted and faxed a copy of his proposed telegram to
Greenpeace's Rome office for McTaggert to approve and forward to Moscow.
Less than an hour after he sent the message to Rome, it was in Moscow.
When Comrade Chilingarov arrived at work the following morning, Tuesday, October 18, Moscow time, the message from his old Greenpeace friend,
David McTaggart, was waiting on his desk.

"Greenpeace urgently requests your assistance to help rescue three
California gray whales trapped in ice holes less than a mile off shore from
Point Barrow, Alaska," the message began. The pressure ridge wasn't discovered until several days after that first telex. It continued, "A rescue operation is now underway but it will only succeed if the open lead, now six
miles from the whales, does not freeze over. If this lead were to freeze

over, would you be able to make an icebreaker available to help clear a path for the whales to escape? Please contact our Washington office which is in direct contact with our people in Alaska. Regards, David McTaggart."

As news of the whales spilled over into Europe, Chilingarov could hardly contain his glee. After suffering decades of the Western disdain for its persistent whaling, the Soviet Union was at the receiving end of a golden public relations windfall. Even with the International Whaling Commission's 1986 moratorium on commercial whaling, the Soviet Union was still by far the world's single largest harvester of gray whales. At the very moment that Chilingarov got the request to help save the three grays stranded in Barrow, whalers on board rusty old Soviet whaling vessels were scrubbing their bloodstained decks after another productive season plying the waters of the Chukchi Sea hunting gray whales. The hunt was supposed to be limited to subsistence purposes only, but glasnost had unshackled the Soviet media enough for it to report that most high protein low fat gray whale meat was used as feed for Soviet minks sold for top dollars to the dirty capitalists.

The Soviet Union acknowledged at least 169 gray whale kills in 1988. Now, with no strings attached, the USSR was being handed an opportunity to appear before the world as a saver of whalers. Suddenly, by cutting a path through the ice, the Soviet Union could claim to care for whales with the same love and attention it cared for its people. The Soviet Union was invited to save the same whales its commercial whalers would have wanted to harvest. The Soviet Union would reap a nice little public relations windfall. It would win plaudits from people the world over it otherwise did little to impress. It need not have worried about making a good impression with the environmental left—they long admired the Soviets for their painstaking concern for environmental protection. All's fair in love and whaling.

18

The Whales Nearly Bring a
Government to Its Knees

David McTaggart's telex appealing for help was the first Arthur Chilingarov heard about the three trapped whales. Yet the Soviet minister immediately grasped the event's striking potential. It was a critical time in his leader's tenure. To date, Communist party chief Mikhail Gorbachev's extensive efforts to transform his empire's external image had proven a great success. But his domestic campaign to resuscitate the moribund Soviet economy was not going so well. He had been unable to shed the shattered legacy of the twentieth century's most anachronistic ideology. The only measurable index Gorbachev managed to increase in his brief reign as Soviet premier was the ever rising and unfulfilled level of his people's expectations.

Mikhail Gorbachev had no choice but to give his subjects their first tiny taste of freedom since the Great October Socialist Revolution of 1917. His regime was tottering from decades of stultifying sclerotic top-down central planning. Gorbachev did not rise to power in the Soviet Union promising its denizens to dismantle the empire; he did so based upon the promise of Soviet restoration. To keep the winds of carefully managed cosmetic change from blowing into a full-scale counterrevolution required great skill. Skill, as it turned out, which Gorbachev did not possess. It would take Gorbachev time and good luck to keep his tottering wreck from falling to pieces. Gorbachev had neither the time nor did his reforms have the strength to prevent that heap from imploding.

So far, he had won some time through a series of measures aimed at keeping the lifeline of Western support open. At that point, Mikhail Gorbachev and most people in the West—especially in the media—thought it was he who had managed to get the best of Ronald Reagan and achieve a great Soviet breakthrough.

A seasoned diplomat, Chilingarov knew to avoid rejecting the Greenpeace request out of hand. But he didn't want to commit Soviet resources before his government gave him an okay. He wanted to keep his options open. He immediately drafted a reply to Greenpeace dated October 18, the day after David McTaggart's initial cable.

> Confirm receiving your telex of 17.10.88. We are trying to take measures for clarifying availability of spare icebreaker with Far East Shipping Company. We will inform you. Regards. Chilingarov. Gosgimet, Moscow, USSR...

The Soviet–Greenpeace collaboration was a natural. While they disagreed about some things, the one issue that mattered most to both of them was U.S. power. They both wanted it weakened.

Campbell Plowden read Chilingarov's telex on Wednesday morning, October 19, the day after President Reagan phoned Colonel Carroll in Prudhoe Bay. Plowden's ecstatic response was soon doused by sobering news. The Soviets were interested, but according to Cindy Lowry, the whales' prognosis was deteriorating. If they were to be saved, the Soviets would have to make up their minds to get to Barrow in a hurry.

After a quick call to Rome to verify he had permission to reply, Plowden penned the following appeal:

> Confirm receiving your telex of 18.10.88. A hovercraft barge is being towed to Barrow to attempt a rescue. It has been delayed several days. We don't know when it will arrive or how well it will work. Whales are very stressed. In case this rescue does not work, we urgently need to explore alternatives. Thank you for your efforts to

check availability of spare icebreaker. Regards, Campbell Plowden
Whale Campaign Coordinator; Greenpeace International.

The cable came over Chilingarov's telex machine just past midnight
Moscow time on October 20, day five of Operation Breakout. A few hours
after Chilingarov read Greenpeace's latest communication, the deicers
arrived from Minnesota to relieve the whales' late-night deathwatch. Like
the whales' condition, the chances of Soviet involvement would quickly
improve. By Thursday morning, October 20, news of the stranded whales
had more than crossed the Atlantic, it had already begun to involve Western Europe. With an ear pressed firmly against the Western heart, the
Soviets knew the whales were big news. If they help could save the ice-
bound trio, they could scoop up some of the spoils, if there were any, and
if they mattered. Campbell Plowden and Greenpeace knew this, too, and
used it to great effect.

For years, Greenpeace International lobbied hard against commercial
whaling by Norway and Iceland. With the stranded whales now in the headlines, Plowden saw the same opportunity Chilingarov did: a chance to shape
a small part of history. The phones at every Greenpeace office in Europe
were ringing. People from Italy to Ireland wanted to know how they could
help save the three whales trapped in a place none of them had ever even
heard of. European environmental activists were beating down Greenpeace's
doors, waiting to be organized. Of course, Plowden realized there was no way
they could help the three whales in Barrow—but maybe they could help other
whales by putting pressure on governments doing business with the few
nations that continued to hunt for a few of them.

No matter how you sliced it, the three whales did manage to strand themselves at an opportune moment. If ever there was a time to exert pressure on
whaling countries this was it. One of those countries was Iceland, a tiny island nation in the North Atlantic home to only a quarter million people on a
geologic winter wonderland halfway between Europe and North America.

Iceland's people prided themselves on what they thought was their
model society. They had much to be proud of; a highly industrialized
society with virtually none of the social strains found in other Western
countries. Iceland suffered very little from crime, drugs, or homelessness
and suffered not at all from racial tensions. It sounds impressive until one

learns that Icelandic law at that time barred anyone without non-Icelandic "blood" from either citizenship or long-term residency.

While Icelanders liked to think of themselves as being everyone's superior, their lucky fate and current prosperity was largely dependent on the United States. American involvement started in 1941, five months before the Japanese attack on Pearl Harbor, when a U.S. naval task force was dispatched to the island to protect the critical North Atlantic seaways that then served as the difference between life and death for Great Britain. Iceland, long isolated and neglected now became the epicenter of a titanic struggle for the survival of freedom against Nazi tyranny. If the Germans could cut British lines of communication across the Atlantic, the war would end in a German victory.

Adolf Hitler several times toyed with the idea of a descent upon the island and laid preliminary plans for it; but to forestall such a move British troops, soon joined by a Canadian force, landed in Iceland on May 10, 1940. Icelandic annoyance with the British and Canadian garrison, and British losses in the war, which made a withdrawal of the Iceland garrison seem desirable, plus American concern for the Atlantic sea lanes, all combined to bring Iceland within the American defense orbit.

By early 1941, the British were stretched to the breaking point. Winston Churchill's decision to send 50,000 troops to Greece meant already precarious British positions everywhere else became even more vulnerable. Britain's 20,000-man garrison in Iceland had to be thinned at the very moment German U-boats started attacking the unprotected Canadian shipping lanes west of the island. Desperate for relief, the British agreed to transfer its facilities in Iceland to the United States. It was that presence and the protection the United States provided that husbanded Iceland's peaceful emergence as one of the world's richest countries.

But Iceland was nearing recession in 1988. That year's European economic slowdown was drying up the market for Icelandic seafood that accounted for 80 percent of its exports. To a prosperous nation unaccustomed to sluggish growth, 1988 was a year of crisis, which peaked in September. It was good training for what would befall them two decades later with the banking collapse of 2008. Months of acrimony between the governing coalition's three parties led Prime Minister Thorsteinn Palsson to quit the government and take his twenty-member Independence Party with him.

Iceland's new and weak minority coalition was lead by the socialist Progressive party.

Once he moved into the prime minister's chair, Steingrimur Hermannsson's number one objective was to stay there. Imagine that! Keeping his country out of recession was the best way he knew to do that. But just weeks after taking office, he would be confronted by one of the most bizarre crises ever to rock his country. This crisis was triggered not by man, but by three whales trapped in ice on the other side of the world.

Campbell Plowden closely followed events in each of the few remaining whaling nations of which Iceland was one. He knew their strengths, and more importantly, their weaknesses. Like a bloodhound, Plowden smelled a vulnerable new government borne out of crisis, not popular mandate. The stranded whales gave Plowden more than an idea. They gave him the chance to strike against Icelandic whaling. The Barrow whales had mobilized a continent of activists and tens of millions of their supporters. Now they could join the more important battle to end the commercial pillage that pushed the magnificent creatures to the edge of extinction.

After clearing it with his superiors, Plowden sent a cable to Greenpeace's European offices telling them that the best way they could help save the three Barrow whales was to remind their members that the real threat facing whales were not Arctic ice floes, but rusting whaling vessels loaded with rocket propelled harpoons. It wasn't nature that threatened whales. It was man.

By Wednesday, October 19, West German activists seized on the publicity surrounding the three stranded whales and hoped to use it to strengthen a six-month boycott against German companies that did business with Iceland. With news of the Barrow whale stranding, the boycott took off. Looking for a local angle to a remote story, German media started covering the previously obscure Iceland fish boycott. Pickets and protests that had gone on unnoticed for months were suddenly newsworthy. German fish importers were quickly forced to make a decision: stop buying Icelandic products or wait for consumers to stop buying theirs.

Funny that none of those activists ever did much to protest "unofficial" Soviet whaling. Maybe because they admired the Soviet Union's animosity toward the United States?

What was marginal business to West German companies was critical business to Icelandic companies. Tengelmann, the multibillion-dollar West

German supermarket conglomerate, then owner of the U.S. retailer A&P, was the first to capitulate to the boycotters demands. The negative image conveyed to the world was all too apparent to Tengelmann's directors. The world was banding together to save three whales while Tengelmann continued to conduct business as usual with a country that hunted, processed and sold them.

On Friday afternoon, October 21, Tengelmann announced that it was cancelling a three-million-dollar contract with Icelandic suppliers to protest that country's whaling practices. Plowden's gamble paid off. One of the largest importers of raw Icelandic shrimp, long a target of the Greenpeace boycott, finally relented. The boycott of Iceland bore its first fruit.

News of the canceled contract rocked Iceland and its new, weak governing coalition. Prime Minister Hermannsson's new government was born in crisis. Three whales struggling for their lives in the frozen waters of Alaska's Arctic threatened to plunge a nation half a world away into political and economic chaos. The Tengelmann contract amounted to less than a quarter of a percent of Iceland's $1.1 billion annual fish exports, but that was just the beginning. Fish was to Iceland what oil was to Alaska: more than 80 percent of its commerce. Without a viable commercial fishing industry, Iceland would crumble.

Almost immediately, other West German companies followed suit. Aldi Supermarkets (they soon after bought A&P themselves) imposed its own boycott. So did NordSea. Adding the new cancellations to the cost of the ongoing American boycotts, Iceland's $7 million commercial whaling industry had already cost the tiny country $50 million, 4 percent of its 1988 gross national product. Hundreds of people lost their jobs within hours of the new cancellations. Prime Minister Hermannsson's new government had to act on a single, well-defined question. Was the revenue from its own small whaling industry worth this price of domestic economic discontent?

To Arni Gunnarsson, a member of Iceland's parliament, the answer was a resounding no. Gunnarsson was a member of the ruling coalition's Social Democratic party. He came from a district in northern Iceland wholly dependent upon fishing. The canceled contract had already put many of his constituents out of work and shuttered many facilities. Gunnarsson announced he would introduce a bill to disband Iceland's commercial whaling industry on Monday morning, October 24, seventeen days after Roy Ahmaogak first discovered the Barrow whales and ten days after the U.S.

government authorized their rescue. Word of Gunnarsson's plans shocked Iceland's new coalition government. Frantic cables were sent to two of the country's most important politicians, both of whom were out of the country trying to drum up international support for the new government.

The prime minister offered Gunnarsson a deal. If Gunnarsson could hold off until Thursday, the prime minister would announce a permanent ban on commercial whaling. The six-month-old boycott was on the verge of success. On Sunday, October 23, it looked as though one of the four remaining whaling nations was about to stop whaling permanently.

The news was reported in all the Icelandic media and hailed as a great step forward. Since the International Whaling Commission's 1986 ban on commercial whaling, public opinion polls showed whatever their sponsors wanted them to show. Environmentalists brandished data showing an increasing majority favoring a ban on whaling. But opponents produced their own results showing an equally large number of Icelanders against an end to whaling if it meant capitulating to the "economic terrorism" of the boycotters.

The arms of the whaling lobby reached high into the government.

Next to the prime minister, the most important cabinet post was the minister of Fisheries, a post held by a Halldór Ásgrímsson, Iceland's most ardent whaling advocate. Ásgrímsson was in France when he heard about the prime minister's deal. He was livid. How could the prime minister unilaterally announce a whaling ban? Since when did national policy get determined by the prime minister alone? Ásgrímsson fired off an angry cable to the prime minister and returned immediately to Reykjavik, Iceland's capital. He promised to oppose the proposed ban with all the force he could muster. For Ásgrímsson, the issue wasn't Iceland's economy, it was his nation's sovereignty.

Ásgrímsson had powerful allies. Chief among them was Foreign Minister Jón Baldvin Hannibalsson. He was in the United States introducing Iceland's new government to American officials. Planned just days in advance, Hannibalsson's visit coincided with the height of the whale rescue. The foreign minister of a country that slaughtered whales for commercial gain was on a state visit to a nation spending millions of dollars to free them. Surveying the American political landscape the week of October 21 to 28, all he could do was lament the abysmal timing of his trip.

Foreign Minister Hannibalsson's most important meeting was with

Secretary of State George P. Shultz. As his nation's top spokesman, the foreign minister was exposed to the concerns of allies like the United States. Whaling was invariably at the top of the list. With or without the Barrow stranding, he was sure to hear Secretary Shultz's appeal for Iceland to stop it. But now, it was likely to be the only item discussed during the thirty-minute session.

Hannibalsson was acutely conscious of his uncomfortable situation, even before he was handed a telex from the Reykjavik Foreign Ministry. In it was the startling news of German boycotts and the prime minister's announcement that Iceland would halt whaling.

He knew the fisheries minister, Halldór Ásgrímsson, must be furious. Ásgrímsson said he would fight the decision and hoped Hannibalsson would join him. Just as the State Department was preparing a statement to laud Iceland's decision, the embassy of Iceland urged State to delay congratulations until the reports could be confirmed. Hannibalsson met Shultz in his Foggy Bottom office and in no uncertain terms told him that the prime minister's announcement, precipitated by the German boycotts, had pitched his new government into a crisis the degree of which could not yet be determined. By Thursday, October 27, Operation Breakout's second-to-last day, it seemed another government collapse was imminent.

The ferocious reaction of his two top ministers presented Prime Minister Steingrimur Hermannsson with an unwinnable situation. If he dug in his heels for a fight, his government would almost certainly topple. If he backed down, he could retain his post but would be left even weaker than before. To save his own neck, the prime minister backed down. The October 27 deadline came and went, his promise to Gunnarsson unfulfilled. Iceland may have been back in the whaling business, but only at great cost. For Campbell Plowden and the cause he fought for, it was a huge victory. A government was forced to abandon what it thought a great national enterprise; not to mention some sovereignty—all because of three whales in Alaska.

This element of the whale rescue went virtually unreported in the U.S. press. Americans were so obsessed by their own interest in the whales, they did not even notice their resounding impact on real people's lives halfway around the world.

19

Desperate:
Nothing Seems to Work

That the Icelandic crisis escaped notice in the country that touched it off was a remarkable and unreported story in and of itself. While Iceland's turmoil went largely unnoticed, it *was* Iceland after all. Nobody noticed Iceland anyway. But the Soviets paid close attention. The Kremlin's corridors certainly must have been abuzz with the news from Reykjavik.

As the story of three trapped whales mushroomed into a worldwide media spectacular, so too did the pressure on the one man everyone thought had the power to free them: Soviet Hydrometeorology Minister Arthur Chilingarov. American environmentalists, long his opponents, had urgently requested his country's assistance. By the end of Operation Breakout's first week, Chilingarov didn't know what to do. He had to make a decision. Would he redirect Soviet icebreakers to Barrow or not? For the past three days, he had promised to try. By Friday, October 21, it was time for an answer.

Chilingarov had seventy-two hours to decide if there was any compelling reason for the Soviets to assist in the rescue. In the three days since he first learned of the stranding, the story had taken on prominence far beyond its relative importance. He knew the Western media was unpredictable, but he had never seen anything like this. He was at a loss to explain the Americans' passionate response to the trapped whales.

A fire of interest had consumed the United States at the very crescendo of a presidential election. When this interest also engulfed Europe, Chilingarov realized the risks of not acting now outweighed the risks of acting. On Thursday night, October 20, Moscow time—Operation Breakout's sixth day—Chilingarov instructed his ministry to seriously pursue the request. Within hours, word reached Chilingarov that one of the Soviet Union's largest icebreakers was finishing a six-month assignment deep inside the polar ice cap. It was building Northern Pole 31, a floating polar research station. The ship was only three hundred miles north of Barrow.

Chilingarov's office transmitted new orders to Master Sergei Reshetov, captain of the massive 496-foot *Admiral Makarov*. Reshetov was told that once his float station duties were complete on Saturday, October 22, he must steer his Finnish-built 20,241-ton vessel toward a thick grounded pressure ridge ten kilometers off the coast of Barrow, Alaska, U.S.A.

Reshetov received the news with resigned frustration; there was little he could do but obey. To the diminutive captain with unkempt strawberry blonde hair, service in the Soviet Merchant Marine precluded dissent. An order was an order, glasnost notwithstanding. Master Reshetov's job was to carry out his assignments. Six months at sea made Reshetov and his crew more than anxious to return to their home port of Vladivostok. The *Makarov* left in March 1988 for a six-month tour. Northern Pole 31 took several weeks longer than expected to complete. But instead of heading back to the relative comforts of Siberia, the *Admiral Makarov* now had a new assignment. On Saturday, October 22, she was to begin pulverizing three hundred miles of thick Canadian and American ice, en route to Barrow, Alaska.

At 9:11 P.M. October 21, 1988, Moscow time, Chilingarov sent Campbell Plowden the cable that would confirm Operation Breakout's coup de grace and presage the whales' eventual rescue.

We are taking efforts on assisting in whale rescue operations. We are supposed to send for this purpose the icebreaker *Admiral Makarov*. Hope to receive your assistance for our icebreaker to enter U.S. territorial waters and ice reconnaissance for its optimal routing in economic side of U.S. waters.... We have sent required official note to U.S. State Department. We do not have complete assurance in this venture because of shallow waters for icebreaker in the area of the rescue.... We are also in doubt about whales' ability to pass through channel made by icebreakers. Regards, Cmde Arthur Chilingarov.

Anxious to get U.S. clearance for the Soviet vessels, Campbell Plowden called the Soviet embassy's Merchant Marine office in New York. Surely, they know the procedures, Plowden thought. They must process requests like this all the time. The Soviet attache told him that two environmental groups Plowden never heard of had already asked for help. Something about it reminded him of previously unknown Arab guerrilla groups tripping over themselves to claim responsibility for the most recent terrorist atrocity: the World Society for the Protection of Animals and the World Whale Federation based in, of all places, Arizona.

Plowden called Ben Miller, the desert whale saver, to inform him that Greenpeace was involved in getting Soviet support for the rescue. Miller told him his interest sprang from the television and newspaper coverage. A few days earlier, he started lobbying his own State Department contact to request Soviet assistance. Miller told Plowden he was dealing with a man in John Negroponte's office. Negroponte was the assistant secretary for Oceans and International Environmental and Scientific Affairs. He was the State Department's highest ranking environmental and scientific foreign service officer.

Friday afternoon, October 21, Campbell Plowden called Negroponte's office himself. He left a message urging someone in charge to get back to him as soon as possible. Propping the phone against his ear with his shoulder, he dialed the number for Jim Brange at the National Marine Fisheries Service. Brange wanted to help but told Plowden that the State Department could not issue the clearance without Pentagon approval. Brange and Plowden agreed to pursue different avenues. Brange would work Defense and Plowden could flex his clout at State.

At the end of the day, Plowden copied the correspondence between Greenpeace and the Soviets and bound them with an oversized paperclip. He asked his secretary to fax the bundle immediately to Cindy Lowry in Barrow. Two reporters were in the manager's office waiting to use the phone when a three-bell signal alerted them to an incoming transmission. The glossy paper slowly emerged from the fax machine at the Top of the World

Hotel. Unable and unwilling to restrain themselves, the unknown moles read the telexes exchanged between Moscow and Washington. Their eyes met in mutual delight. Rumors of Soviet involvement had abounded since early in the week, but the documents transmitted via satellite from seven thousand miles away could confirm it. They shouldn't have been snooping. Indignity of indignities, they would have to sit on their scoop.

Although the faxes went unreported, the Russian rumors spread through the Barrow press corps. The race was on. The first agency to report the Soviet decision would have the biggest exclusive since the story broke. But exclusives were hard to come by during Operation Breakout. Cramped quarters in the tiny town and its overwhelming isolation made the concept of confidentiality implausible. The instant one reporter learned something he or she thought consequential, it seemed like someone else was already reporting it.

Rescue coordinator Ron Morris encountered what he saw as an insurmountable problem the minute he deplaned in Barrow a week earlier. He confronted a growing swarm of media all competing to cover a story that appeared to have only a few exploitable angles. There were only so many ways to photograph the whales. At first, the rescue was simple enough for every reporter to follow.

Colonel Carroll anticipated a media problem before he left Anchorage. Carroll and his press officer, Mike Haller, knew that the only way to bring order to a frenzied press was to restrict them without overtly trying to limit the flow of information. Prove to them it would be useless wasting energy looking for scoops by making information, pictures, and access immediately available to everyone simultaneously.

When Carroll got to Barrow with the five-ton concrete bullet, he saw that Search and Rescue Director Randy Crosby had unwittingly created his own fledgling press pool. It started as just a trip or two a day, flying Barrow TV's Oran Caudle or Russ Weston of KTUU-TV out to the whales. The enterprise grew like the story itself. Crosby's operation swelled with unimagined activity. SAR went from flying three missions on Sunday, October 16, the rescue's second day, to more than just four days later. His hastily filled out log sheets were scribbled with the names of more than one hundred different passengers. His equipment and his men were being overworked. He wondered how long it would be before something gave.

To reporters, his free charter service proved a godsend. Regular and dependable access to the whale site for every reporter averted the battles often associated with heavily saturated media stories. Thanks to Randy Crosby, every media company that came to Barrow could get as close to whales as often as it wanted. Big or small, rich or poor, it made no difference. Operation Breakout was one of television's most successful equal access stories. The only thing that made coverage of the whale stranding possible in the first place was their propitious choice of location.

The whales stranded themselves close to a village modern enough to boast a satellite television transmission facility. But once the story exploded, the value of the location was inverted. It wasn't Barrow's proximity that saved the whales, now, it was its remoteness. Had the stranding occurred in a location Outsiders thought even marginally accessible, a crushing tide of media would have overrun Barrow. Proper coverage of the story would have been all but impossible. Media relations personnel from every federal agency and news service coming to Barrow to help would only have gotten in the way.

Fortunately for the whales, their rescuers and those reporters who did make the long journey northward, Barrow did not have the facilities to support the huge entourage that usually accompanies the networks on megastories. There were only so many hotel beds and only so many airline seats in and out of town each day. There were no alternatives. The instant Barrow hung out its NO VACANCY sign, the influx stopped dead. Barrow was full. By Thursday, October 20, day five of Operation Breakout, not even Colonel Tom Carroll could find a place to stay.

From the jungles of Southeast Asia to the untamed wilds of the Alaskan bush, Colonel Tom Carroll thought he had seen and slept in it all. Then he got to Barrow, a place where he would spend sixteen hours a day but never spend the night. At quitting time, he would hop on an Alaska Air National Guard eight-passenger Otter aircraft and fly 270 miles across the tundra's numbing void to Prudhoe Bay. He slept in a tastefully decorated room in the ARCO compound now littered with empty coffee cups.

Since the day Ron Morris arrived, the rescue was recharged at daily early-morning meetings. As the operation progressed in size and prominence, so too did the meetings' importance. By the end of Operation Breakout's first week, an invitation to attend was a symbol of access to the

man with the operation's ultimate power. What started as an open breakfast at Pepe's became a mark of rank. Network producers assigned television crews to wait for the meeting to adjourn so they could pepper the
departing participants with questions about the proceedings. But the rescuers were under strict instructions from Ron Morris to direct all media
queries to him.

By Thursday night, October 20, six days after his arrival, Ron Morris
wanted changes. He reshuffled his rescue command. Those who didn't
conform to his approach were pushed out. In came the Outsiders, biologists
Dave Withrow and Jim Harvey from Seattle's National Marine Mammal
Laboratory, ice experts Gary Hufford and Bob Lewellen from the National
Weather Service, and on Saturday, October 22, NOAA's Pacific fleet commander, Rear Admiral Sigmund Petersen.

As the Outsiders arrived, the original insiders were left out, Craig George
and Geoff Carroll among them. The North Slope Borough biologists who
helped keep the whales alive for the five days before Operation Breakout
began were no longer invited to the morning meetings, their knowledgeable
counsel ignored, their pride hurt. Eskimo Arnold Brower Jr., the man who
kept open the whales' original holes and had successfully cut more than
fifty others, became no more than a "native" employee. They stored their
resentments for another day.

The coordinator failed to learn the one critical lesson of Operation
Breakout's first week. Simple technology and native knowledge kept the
whales alive; elaborate equipment did not. Even those involved in the ill-
fated tow of the hoverbarge learned that in the Arctic the low-tech approach
is often the best. Taking a cue from Arnold Brower and Malik, Colonel
Carroll fell back on the simplicity of the concrete bullet, the most unadorned
method yet found for.

By Friday morning, October 21, the two larger whales appeared in better
physical shape than since Roy Ahmaogak first discovered them. The deicers
brought from Minneapolis succeeded in keeping half a dozen breathing
holes open during the rescue's most bitter night. The biting winds and encroaching darkness were no match for the compact water circulators. The
more reliable the machines proved, the more calm the whales became.

By Friday morning, the three famous whales began displaying a remarkable attachment to the ever-present massaging jets emitted by the machines.

The two larger whales, Siku and Poutu, surfaced within inches of the deicers, rolling playfully in the seductive flow of the "Arctic Jacuzzis." Blissful, euphoric relaxation quickly replaced their fortnight of stress.

Arnold Brower and his crews tried in vain to get the whales to make significant moves toward the open lead, now almost five miles away. Brower made an observation that quickly spread from rescuer to reporter and back again. Perhaps, he suggested, the deicers were working too well, so well in fact that they had started to domesticate the once leery whales. What if the ultimate obstacle to the whales' freedom became the whales themselves?

That such an unmentionable observation was just now being examined proved that the rescuers had as much to learn as the whales. Of course, the whales' chief obstacle was themselves. If the cetacean trio had properly interpreted the changing climatic conditions, they, like their fellow creatures, would be well on their way south, leaving the media to search for other spectacles.

The time of the morning meeting was moved back to 8:30 to allow the participants more time to prepare their presentations and make early-morning phone calls. Some of the rescuers reported early at the Search and Rescue hangar for the morning briefing. When they arrived, they were met by several cameramen and their reporters desperate for a morsel of substantiation to confirm rumors of imminent Soviet involvement.

They gathered at the conference table in the hangar's L-shaped office area. Not unlike the colonel's command table at Prudhoe, it was strewn with stained plastic coffee mugs and tinfoil ash trays exuding the noxious smell of vaporized carcinogens. Cindy Lowry, Tom Carroll, Randy Crosby, and Arnold Brower Jr. were determined to propel their unprepared leader toward decisive action. The coordinator, who had proven an adept media manipulator, had yet to offer tangible amelioration of the whales' condition. After a week of public relations, substance was long overdue.

Plus, without Morris's attention to media management there may well not have been a coordinated rescue at all. Massaging the press was critical to the rescue's chain of command. Ideas that would have been unthinkable just a week before were now well within the realm of possibility: invoking the mayor's jobs programs, employing hundreds of Eskimos to cut open holes in the ice, the five-ton concrete bullet, and now, perhaps, Soviet icebreakers. They were all made possible by the masterful wooing of the press. But this Friday morning saw an abrupt end to the atmosphere of good feeling.

Morris trudged irascibly up the thick rubber-tipped steps of the SAR hangar and entered the presence of his minions in a foul mood. The initiative and comity Morris brought to Barrow had regressed into bitter recriminations of almost everyone involved in the rescue. They were all exhausted, especially Morris who hadn't slept more than few hours at a time in nearly a week.

If Morris sought to hide his frustration with Arnold Brower Jr. and his Eskimos, he didn't do a good job that morning. The meeting proceeded with an icy chill. Morris reiterated his insistence that he alone deal with the media. His once reassuring control now fell on hostile ears. Cindy Lowry tried to convince others to give the beleaguered man the benefit of the doubt. He had an impossible task. There was no way everyone was going to agree with him. He was the only one empowered to make tough decisions that would inevitably upset those he overruled. Like him or not, Cindy said, Ron Morris kept the operation together and alive through some very trying times. The whales were about to be saved, she pleaded with her colleagues. Couldn't people try to keep their antipathies toward him in check for just a few more days?

After convincing her skeptical colleagues to give Ron Morris another chance, she spoke by phone with a reinvigorated Bill Allen. Allen and VECO still wanted to be part of the rescue. With delight, Cindy accepted help from anyone kind enough to offer it. Like Colonel Carroll, Allen resolved to attempt less herculean methods to free the three trapped whales. Thursday night, the official abandonment of the hoverbarge all but complete, Allen lowered his sights but kept the freeing of the whales firmly in them. In many ways, the voluntary acceptance of the humanitarian mantle was the biggest single boost to company morale that Billy Bob Allen could remember. The unexpected strength of his employees' will to help creatures in trouble filled him with pride. The rescue transcended industry, culture, and language. His VECO laborers worked as hard to free the whales as anyone. They were trained in oil exploration and extraction, not wildlife management; nevertheless, they displayed a remarkable commitment to freeing distressed animals. The stranded whales changed not only Billy Bob Allen but also the empire he created.

Allen ordered his men to use more tested, less-sophisticated equipment.

Over a conference call, the North Slope operations manager, Marvin King, told Allen that another VECO device had been tested during the day and seemed up to the task. It was a custom-made amphibious vehicle built to tow the hoverbarge to and from offshore oil platforms.

To the delight of the humor-starved press in Barrow, VECO was serious when they named their machine the Archimedean Screw Tractor. Smaller than the hoverbarge, it was still too large to transport in one piece, even in the largest cargo aircraft. The tractor cut a fifteen-foot-wide swath of ice, slicing through it with the propellant force of its two long screw-shaped pontoons. Like the hoverbarge, it sat idle since the 1984 failure of the Mukluk Island oil well.

"Hell," Billy Bob exclaimed. "Let's get that son of a bitch on up there." When the euphoria subsided, Allen weighed the screw-tractor option with tempered expectations. Allen was well aware that at best, his device would augment the rescue, not direct it.

Early Friday morning, Bill Allen told Colonel Carroll about the screw tractor. Pete Leathard couldn't get through on Cindy's interminably busy phone line. He left a message with the receptionist at the Top of the World Hotel, asking Cindy to call him or Billy Bob as soon as she had a spare minute. They wanted to talk about the screw tractor. It was one of several calls Cindy would be unable to return.

The meeting on Friday morning, October 21, became a crucible for Operation Breakout. It was the first session without a master plan. The rescuers were on their own. All that carried the rescue forward was the momentum of Arnold Brower Jr., the Minnesota deicers, and rumors of the Russians. Just when the whales' condition appeared stable, the rescue's seemed terminal.

The rumor of Soviet involvement was not the only one bantered about in Barrow. So was word of the collapse of the rescue; at least in its formal manner. If the Russians failed to come, Ron Morris would have little choice but to exercise his recognized authority, quietly put down the whales, and go home. After mobilizing hundreds of people and millions of dollars, the U.S. government would not have any way to save three whales from the Arctic elements.

Unsubstantiated rumors of Soviet involvement abounded. They sent Ron Morris over the edge. If the rumors were true, why hadn't he, as project coordinator, been consulted? He confronted Cindy Lowry, demanding to know whether she knew anything. Since Soviet participation was first discussed, Campbell Plowden had insisted on secrecy. Only if diplomatic channels failed to produce the desired results would going public become an option. At Plowden's insistence, Cindy kept her tongue.

Morris insisted on an answer from his one remaining friend. His mind raced through the possibilities. He couldn't avoid the conclusion that if indeed the Soviets came, he would be swept away in the Arctic wind. But it wasn't as though he truly expected the adrenaline of the past week to continue unabated. In his heart he knew that one way or another the operation would end. The whales would either die or be freed. His fear that Friday morning was perhaps a sharp and welcome reminder that there was only so much any one man could be expected to do.

As Morris's flare-up came to an end, the room filled with silence. He leaned forward and slowly pushed back his chair. He wiped the beads of sweat from his face and uttered a slight harumph, as if to offer an apology. His colleagues were all too glad to accept. It was time to return to the matter at hand. In the first brainstorming session of the operation, Morris encouraged everyone in the room to offer what they thought were feasible recommendations on how to free the whales. After each person listed his or her options, the group evaluated them.

Morris eagerly swept around the conference table collecting the papers. Options ranged from the concrete bullet Colonel Carroll was scheduled to test on the ice later that day, to the Archimedean Screw Tractor. Not surprisingly, the options most mentioned were the only ones that already worked: the Eskimos and the deicers. The rescuers agreed to continue cutting holes toward the pressure ridge in the hope that the whales would use them.

In the week since Operation Breakout began, the average temperature out on the ice had already dropped to twenty-five degrees below zero. The Arctic ice pack moved south nearly twenty miles and the shore ice grew farther out each day. The once fourteen-mile-wide lead had shrunk to barely a mile across at its narrowest point. If the whales could not be freed before the lead closed, no one could save them, not the Eskimo chain-saw gangs, not the National Guard, not the president of the United States, not even the mighty icebreakers from the Soviet Union.

If the Soviets did not offer their assistance, the rescue command would have to think of other alternatives or call it quits and leave the whales to their fate. Suggestions once laughed at were now considered. Colonel Carroll offered to study the effects of detonating bombs of various destructive forces to blast a path through the ridge. Knowing Cindy might object, he promised to clear his plans with her before trying anything on his own. Even if explosives could break the ridge, they might not justify the risks to other Arctic life.

Chastened by their weeklong wait for others, the rescue command went one step further, and began planning beyond the explosives. Assuming that they could never be used, Morris asked Cindy and others for other ideas on getting the whales past the forty-foot wall of ice.

"What about flying them over the ridge in nets?" she asked. Killer whales, though smaller than the grays, had been moved this way before, but the procedure was dangerous. Luring a gray whale safely into a net under thick ice was one thing, lifting it safely out was quite another. Even the Skycrane, the world's most powerful transport helicopter, might not have the power to pull the 50,000-pound whales out of the water and fly them the mile or so to open water. The whales would have to be tranquilized. Since a dose small enough for a man could kill a whale, administering drugs would prove tricky. Then there was the unknown effect of gravity. Would it split their huge girths wide open, splattering their entrails onto the ice below? That would surely make for morbidly fascinating video.

Dr. Tom Albert from the North Slope Borough contacted a friend in Norway who was an expert in drugging whales. He began preparing the serum. Sea World in San Diego, which had successfully airlifted killer whales, began knitting a huge mesh net big enough for the much larger grays. It was an audacious scheme with little chance of success. But if all else failed, they would be ready to try. With great efficiency, Operation Breakout took on a mission all its own. While the upper echelons plotted to assault the pressure ridge, the Eskimos continued with their meticulous ice cutting. Arnold Brower and his crews had opened fifty-five new holes since they started cutting them earlier in the week.

As soon as the deicers arrived two nights earlier, the three whales started using the new holes. But then, they stopped. Geoff, Craig and the National Marine Mammal Laboratory biologists couldn't figure out why.

Maybe they were resting. After two grueling weeks, the whales were finally breathing normally again. They actually seemed to enjoy their bubbly new surroundings. That same Friday morning, Craig George suddenly changed his mind. Standing quietly with Cindy, he noticed Bone, the baby whale, still lagged behind Poutu and Siku, the larger, more robust whales.

"Damn it," Craig blurted out in sudden realization. "They aren't moving because of the baby."

Only when they were absolutely threatened by Wednesday night's freezing holes did the whales move. When they reached the relative security of the new holes, they stopped. It had to be for Bone. Craig's logic held up to Geoff's preliminary analysis. In a remarkable display of bonding, neither of the two adolescent whales would abandon their helpless dependent. The only thing that could compel them to take such a radical step was a clear and present danger to their own well-being. The deicers eliminated that threat.

By noon, the ice surrounding the whales had resumed an eerie silence. As rumors of the Soviet icebreakers spread, most reporters fled back to town to tap their sources on the Outside. They finally had some legitimate reporting to do: real leads to follow, real people to talk to, real news. Best of all, they didn't have to stand outside in the minus-thirty-degree temperatures to do it. Cindy wanted to make her own phone calls. When she last heard from Campbell Plowden, a Soviet decision, contingent upon U.S. approval, seemed imminent. The hundred-man round-the-clock rescue operation never really required Cindy's constant presence on the ice. Still, she felt the whales were her domain. She had to be with them. But like everyone else, she was hungry, cold, and wanted to go back to town.

Cindy ran to the SAR helicopter, gave Randy Crosby a warm pat on the helmet, and climbed aboard. As Crosby gently lifted his aircraft and its human cargo off the surface of the ice, the chain of holes faded from view. The loud hum of the helicopter proved a welcome relief for Cindy. But the peace of the buzzing engines was short-lived. A second string of reporters waited for Cindy and Ron to confirm the reports now being widely reported in the Lower 48: the Soviets had offered an icebreaker and a support ship to help free the whales. The Russians were on the way. Not knowing what to say, Cindy elbowed nervously past the crowd to get to the nearest phone. She professed her ignorance several times before the reporters began to believe her. Later, when Cindy tried to tell the truth, she and Greenpeace would both appear a bit foolish.

When she walked into the lobby of the Top of the World, the press assumed a very different role. It was as though the lobby were a sanctuary where all who entered were "off the record." Once she went inside, the reporters no longer asked her any questions or stuck any microphones or cameras in her face. It was then Cindy realized that reporters not only expected their subjects to act for them, they were actors themselves.

20

The Russians Are Coming

Campbell Plowden, Cindy Lowry's comrade in Washington, plodded nervously ahead. While waiting to hear from the State Department, he followed up on his two whale crises unfolding 15,000 miles apart. Even for a man whose job description included organizing boycotts and managing chaos, these were hectic times.

Lunch was long past when he received a call from Tucker Scully, Assistant Secretary John Negroponte's top deputy at the State Department. Plowden had waited for Scully's call all morning; his frenzied pace had prevented him from taking even three minutes to wolf down the avocado-and-sprout sandwich he had made for himself that morning. Scully told Plowden that before the State could officially authorize the Soviet vessels to enter U.S. waters, he would need answers to several technical questions. Scully wanted more information about the Soviet ships, such as their specifications and capabilities. He told Plowden it was standard State Department liability procedure. If the ships ran aground or a Soviet crewman was injured in U.S. waters, the Americans didn't want to be responsible. Scully didn't know how long it would take for him to get back to Plowden. Counseling patience, he promised to call back as soon as he could, but advised Plowden not to get his hopes up.

Until then, he told Plowden, "Keep a lid on it. We don't want word of this leaking out before its time," he said. When the time was right, the State Department wanted to break the story themselves. Plowden wondered why people at State spent more time worrying about protocol than about policy. Why were they so insistent about "handling" the announcement? It could only make Plowden wonder. Did they want to steal all the credit? Or did they want to create the proper conditions to spurn the Russians' help?

"How can you possibly read something sinister into this?" Plowden asked the bewildered foreign service officer. "The whole world wants action and all you can do is stall!" Plowden had exhausted his patience. "What is it with you people?" he asked, not expecting an answer. During those fateful October days, Plowden was hardly alone in his demand for immediate action. After almost a week of gripping but frustrating drama, the world's passion for the whales' safety was reaching a climax. Everyone longed for a resolution, and Soviet participation seemed certain to lead to one. The sooner their ships were permitted to enter U.S. waters, the sooner the world would know whether the whales could be saved. Unless the icebreakers could crush the pressure ridge, hope was lost.

Plowden called Cindy. Stymied by the State Department's terminal caution, he had nothing new to report. Instead he listened to his near-exhausted colleague. For the past week Cindy had slept only a few hours a day. Between boisterous reporters making noise at all hours and neverending calls from quote-hungry journalists on the Outside, it was all she could manage. All the private-room lines were jammed, so she took Plowden's call on the phone in the lobby. A long line proceeded to form behind her. Cindy was lucky to find the phone free; most reporters had to wait over an hour that confusing Friday for a chance to be filled in on the story's rapidly unfolding developments taking place a world away.

"Is there anyone there who can help us?" Plowden pleaded. "What about the guy the president called, the colonel? Maybe he has some connections."

Cindy didn't know how to react to her desperate coworker. For reasons she was never able to acknowledge, she didn't want to ask Colonel Carroll. She had only met him a few times, and was in no position to complain about his treatment of her. Every time they spoke, he was perfectly pleasant. She just didn't like the idea of getting him involved. Plowden instantly detected her reluctance, but he insisted she approach the colonel anyway.

"You're the one who claims we don't have any time," he reminded her. "Just ask him to help us."

Plowden, Cindy Lowry, and everyone else for that matter, knew that Tom Carroll must have impressive connections. After all, the president had called him, not Ron Morris. For the first time, Cindy let her preconceptions interfere with the rescue. Her reluctance was overcome by her concern for the whales. Besides, she had worked with Bill Allen, Ben Odom, and the other oil people, and the National Guard never drilled oil wells or polluted the oceans. Dismissing her wayward thoughts, she raced to locate the colonel. She found him reviewing flight logs in the Search and Rescue hangar, impervious to the pandemonium all around him. She was taken aback by the warmth of his greeting. Subconsciously she hoped he would show some visible sign of resentment to justify her negative feelings. Without knowing it, the amiable colonel stirred her guilt.

"If there is a way I can help, I'd be delighted," he told her with what sounded like genuine concern.

"In fact, there is," Cindy answered. "We are trying to expedite the State Department clearance of the Soviet icebreakers and we were wondering if you could help us out."

Carroll froze. His eyes darted about the room, looking as if someone just shot him in the larynx. "The Soviets?" he asked, not knowing whether he actually restated the two words. The question took him by surprise. He was stunned and flustered, and could not hide it. Since no one from headquarters in Anchorage mentioned anything about the Russians, he never believed it. He thought it was just another rumor. He wondered what was true and what was not. If Cindy realized the question had shocked him, she might tell the media that he opposed the idea. They would really let him have it.

His mind raced, but it only turned him in circles. He glanced frantically around the room looking for something, anything, to distract him long enough to regain his equilibrium. For once, everyone in the room was occupied and no one was calling his name. He was alone. How could he possibly be expected to help clear the Soviets to sail in American waters? He was a colonel in the National Guard, not a diplomat or a freelance peacenik. Operation Breakout notwithstanding, Tom Carroll's duty was to the Guard, to his country.

"The Soviets," he began. "Well, you see it's just not that…" His confidence soon wavered, however, as he stammered on. "I'm just not sure exactly how to…there are things you probably don't, I mean you can't… The Soviets, huh?" The composure that brought Tom Carroll this far was gone. Vanished in the Arctic chill.

His reaction to the word "Soviet" was as instinctively visceral as Cindy's reaction to the word "military." The only difference was that Carroll's animus was justified while Cindy's was not. "Soviet" was one of the most abhorrent words in an American soldier's vocabulary and with good reason. Gorbachev or not, the Russians still had more than one thousand intercontinental ballistic missiles (ICBMs) aimed at American cities, and three million troops poised to pierce the heart of Europe with garrisons in hostile nations around the world.

Carroll's head throbbed. He had no orders or indications from his superiors on how to handle this one. God forbid he appear to aid and abet America's strategic opponent. He tried to convince himself that he was blowing the whole thing out of proportion. He was getting only an hour of sleep each night, and the coffee he was forced to drink amounted to little more than muddy water. Still, he had his career and the integrity of his superiors to consider.

It was time for a decision. Cindy had pushed his button.

"NO, NO, NO!!" he snapped. "Why on earth would you want the Soviets? There is nothing they can do that we can't. Besides," he insisted, now the center of attention in the stunned silence of the SAR operations room, "the ice is too thick and the water is too shallow."

Cindy's hunch proved right. The colonel's aversion to all things Soviet might have jeopardized the whales had it gone undetected. But now it had been brought to light for all to see. The colonel had been neutralized. His opposition was effectively removed from the icebreaker's path. She showed up the colonel and that was all that mattered—even if his comeuppance came at the price of elevating the Soviet Union. Still, Cindy was too stunned to gloat.

Her restraint further highlighted the colonel's anguish. He showed desperation; she, composure. He wanted to keep the Russians out, yet his irrational reaction only eased their way. Cindy politely asked Randy Crosby if she could borrow his phone to call Plowden in Washington. Out of deference to his new friend, Crosby silently nodded his assent. It was a painful moment for the colonel and he didn't want to make it any worse. She entered Crosby's office, leaving the door open. She didn't want the colonel to think that she would further humiliate him behind closed doors. Her refusal to engage in vengeful behavior only aggravated his defeat.

Surprisingly, she had no trouble getting through to her Washington office. Plowden was awaiting her call. "Tell your people at the State Department that we all want the Soviets to come. We need them here."

Colonel Carroll draped his fatigued frame over a metal folding chair. A pane of glass separated him from Cindy as he lowered his head resignedly into his hands. He would have to cooperate. He would try one contact: Bonnie Mersinger in the White House. Plowden got the details on the two Russian vessels from the Soviet Consulate's merchant marine office in New York and passed them on to Tucker Scully at the State Department. The news was everywhere. Plowden could not possibly contain it. His contacts at the National Marine Fisheries Service appealed to their superiors to expedite State Department authorization. The wheels were well in motion. The stage was set for an official announcement later that afternoon.

Cindy told Randy she wanted to go back to the ice. She wanted to be with the whales. She would leave politics and international negotiations to others. But just in case, she phoned Ron Morris who was making calls from his room at the Airport Inn. His wife had just arrived from Anchorage and not a moment too soon. Her presence had an almost immediate calming effect on the high-strung coordinator. Cindy asked Ron if he knew anything about the pending announcement, and he told her he did not. He promised to tell her when and if he did, a promise he couldn't keep.

Cindy flew out to the whale site on the first press pool flight. At Colonel Carroll's direction, Crosby and SAR were to fly a single crew from each medium: print, radio, and television. There was one flight in the morning and one in the afternoon. Whatever the pools gathered would be made available to everyone so much of the coverage consisted mainly of this footage. Crews wanting their own material—perhaps to supplement a scoop or some kind of exclusive—had to find their own way out to the ice.

Unsure of when she would have another chance to eat anything other than raw fish dipped in seal oil, on the twelve-minute flight out Cindy consumed a cold Pepe's grease burger, which she had saved from the night

before. From the protective cocoon of the cabin, she looked out at an aus-
tere yet magnificent sight. The cloudless skies glowed burnt orange over
the timeless Arctic landscape.

While Cindy spent the late afternoon on the ice, Ron Morris received
an urgent call from the office of William Evans, the undersecretary of the
Department of Commerce in Washington. The faceless State Department
pinstripes had finally decided to permit the Soviets to enter U.S. waters.
Their analysis determined that the cost of rejecting the Soviet offer would
be greater than accepting it. The Russians were coming. But like most
other facets of international diplomacy, the mechanics of making the announcement were far more complicated than the announcement itself.

The State Department called the shots. To deemphasize its importance,
the State Department wanted the lowest-ranking person they could find to
make the announcement. They wanted to build as large a buffer between
the upper echelons of American government and the whale rescue as they
could. State wanted to distance itself from potential failure. Ron Morris
was their man. They told Morris to call a press conference with a strong
Arctic backdrop, a setting no one could possibly confuse with the Doric
columns of Washington. He eagerly agreed. Morris chose the reporters'
favorite spot, across the street from the Top of the World Hotel. He would
stand with his back to the jagged ice of the sea. The very picture of isolation was in fact just a stone's throw from the hotel's warm lobby.

They gave him an "official" version of events leading up to the announcement that he was told to recite to the assembled press, a version few would
question. He hung up and went to the Top of the World. As he briskly walked
alone up Momegana Street, Morris's heart raced with excitement. He was
about to make the most significant announcement of his professional life—
that the United States government had asked the Soviets to assist in the
whale rescue.

Unversed in diplomatic protocol, he did not realize that he was part of
the State Department's scheme to downgrade the whole rescue. He was an
unwitting participant in his own dethronement. Now that the Soviets
were on the way, the U.S. government began a frantic attempt to disengage
itself. The further the government could extricate itself when the Soviet
ships arrived, the less damage to American prestige if the Soviets managed to steal the show. Gorbachev had stung the State Department too

many times in the past. They weren't about to take any chances over three lousy whales.

Morris pushed open the hotel's thick steel door, brandishing a broad, knowing smile. His obsequious friends in the press corps instantly saw that something was up. "What is it?" asked Harry Chittick of ABC. "Have you heard something about the Soviets? We're getting a lot of flak from New York. They need confirmation. The Washington bureau is ready to back me up, but I need something to go on." Morris gave his friend Chittick an exaggerated wink as if to say, "You guessed it."

Morris stood on his tiptoes and shouted, "Everybody listen up. How soon can you all be ready to do an important press conference?" He knew the effect his question would have. The reporters and their cameramen answered with their feet. Everyone within earshot dashed to their edit suites to fetch their equipment and ran outside to claim the best camera positions. As soon as the major networks were set up, Morris would make his announcement.

Because of the time difference, it was too late for the evening news. Morris thought that was a great shame, but in fact it was was exactly what the State Department wanted. It was a widely known secret around media-conscious Washington that Friday nights were the best time to release the worst news. Conventional wisdom dictated that it would be Monday before most people would digest it. In the case of the three whales, it would prove a gross miscalculation. It never occurred to the Foggy Bottom spin doctors that they were using conventional means to deal with an unconventional situation.

Morris carefully positioned himself atop a mound of ice silhouetted against the bleak horizon to read his proclamation. He told the shivering but intent group of two dozen reporters what the Commerce and State Departments told him to say. Namely, that it was they who worked to get the Soviet icebreaker, not Cindy Lowry, Campbell Plowden, or Greenpeace.

Morris's account was accepted at face value. Reporters in Barrow were far enough removed from the story in Washington to have done anything else. Later, when Cindy publicly objected to being totally left out of the official version, several reporters roundly criticized her for trying to "steal" the credit. All she could do was laugh. Greenpeace couldn't win for losing. As the news spread to the handful of reporters watching the infuriatingly nonchalant whales, they hurriedly made their way back to town. By dusk, only a small core remained, just those who opted to stay with the whales rather than chase down a talking head recounting events that were happening thousands of miles away. For the second time in three days, the media missed the news they came for. While they covered Ron Morris's moment of glory in town, they missed the single most dramatic episode of the entire rescue.

Later that afternoon, Cindy had returned to the ice. She stood alone at the edge of the third hole. Several layers of clothing, green down pants, and a heavy white parka provided scant warmth. She marveled at the mastery of her body. It had adjusted to the Arctic long before her mind did. Mysteriously, she had stopped shivering days earlier. Once her body had become acclimated to its new environment, it had begun conserving her precious energy. For the first time since she got the call from Geoff and Craig a week before, Cindy Lowry was at peace, her mind and body as one.

As she looked out toward the white horizon, she wondered what the whales must be thinking. (The rest of us wondered if the whales thought at all.) Did they know how serious their predicament was? She wondered whether they could reach Baja, even if they could be redeemed from their Arctic catacombs. She asked Craig the same questions during a break at the Eskimo shack. His reluctance said it all. His limited expertise told him he could hold out little hope for their survival.

How could Cindy disagree? Until Wednesday night, their condition collectively deteriorated so much they almost died. Then they adopted the attitude that they were on a spa vacation, lounging in the Jacuzzi bubbles as though their troubles had magically disappeared. Did they know they were the darlings of an adoring world? Did they know that close to a billion people, 20 percent of the human species, knew about them? Did they realize they were bringing down a government across the North Pole? Did they know the Russians were on the way to save them?

Suddenly, she had a moment of peace. Knowing her anxiety would return any minute, she relished it. Closing her eyes, Cindy sat down on the ice. She concentrated intently on the silence of the Arctic dusk, broken every few minutes by the reassuringly warm sound of a whale surfacing just a few feet away. Never had she been involved in a more stressful project, but neither had she ever experienced such a moment of total peace. The irony enveloped her.

She had tried meditating before, but it never worked. She wasn't the type. Why, she wondered, was it suddenly working on the frozen surface of the Arctic Ocean, just inches from three gigantic but helpless whales? She imagined her spirit hovering a few feet above her body. Through her closed eyes, she watched the whales perform their ghostly dance. Her fears, like her sensation of cold, vanished. She feared neither for herself nor, oddly, for the whales.

Somehow, they would manage. With this revelation, Cindy's soul reunited with her body. She gradually awoke, refreshed to her Arctic reality. She opened her eyes, radiating a smile lit by an inner tranquillity. The sight of a group of Eskimos laughing heartily in the distance entered her newly recharged consciousness. Cindy slowly walked over to say hi, and to maybe even join in the fun. A block of ice, cut from the edge of the hole, floated on the ocean surface. She saw Malik and Arnold Brower nearly doubled over in laughter. They watched Johnny Brower hamming it up as he balanced himself on the floating slab. The other Eskimos joined him in an Inupiat version of the Beach Boys' song, "Surfin' USA." Johnny Brower was hanging ten in the Arctic Ocean!

It was no small feat. The slab bobbed up and down in the angry current. Staying upright required intricate balance and control. Unlike a tumble from a wave off Malibu, a wipeout here had dire consequences. If he slipped when the ice block was tipped up on its edge, he would fall through and become trapped under the ice. Mercifully, he would have only seconds of consciousness. Half a minute later, Johnny Brower would be dead, his surfing career cut short. Surely, they must know this, Cindy reassured herself. Yet they were products of the Arctic. If they could have such fun watching Johnny Brower doing his best Duke Kahanamoku imitation, she could, too.

When the silliness subsided and Johnny jumped off the slab onto the safety of solid ice, the crew finished cutting the hole. They started dismantling their equipment only to be distracted by the distant sounds of unexplained excitement coming from back near the whales. A look of terror swept across Cindy's face. She appealed to Arnold and Malik for an explanation.

Neither knew any more than she did, but the steady look in their eyes calmed her to the point where she could run with them to investigate the commotion.

Jogging across the flat ice in heavy clothes, Arnold consoled Cindy. "Everything is all right," he assured her.

"God, what's happened?" she cried. "Just let them be all right."

True to his prediction, the two big whales seemed fine. As they approached the darkness of their fourteenth trapped night, the whales suddenly started exhibiting an unusual, robust urgency. The change in their behavior was clear for all to see. It was as if the whales knew something was about to happen. Without warning or explanation, the whales started surfacing more forcefully. Instead of lounging comfortably at the surface, they powerfully cleared their lungs. The mist exhaled from the pair of blowholes on top of each of the whales formed thick V-shaped clouds that hung in the air.

It wasn't panic. It was controlled, determined energy—the building up of momentum, the starting of mighty engines. The whales were about to move.

After a last surging lunge for air, the whales dove deep into the dark, cold water. Instinctively, Cindy and Craig raced to the next hole. They knew the whales would move. Waiting for them to surface, they heard their unmistakable sounds. But the sounds were distant. Excitedly they turned their heads in the noise's direction and found themselves looking toward the lead. The whales had skipped the hole where Craig and Cindy waited, surfacing unexpectedly in the next one. Seconds later they dove again, popping up two holes closer still to the lead. Suddenly, the whales were using the holes with abandon. The Eskimos had been on the right track. The whales understood. For the first time since their stranding, the whales were at last ready to resume their annual journey southward.

Cindy leapt with joy. Her whales wanted to live. She could hardly keep up with them as they hurriedly moved down the Eskimo-carved ice path. At this rate, they would reach the end of the mile-long chain in no time. While Cindy and Craig chased them, Arnold Brower and Rick Skluzacek rushed to move the deicers to each new hole the whales used. They kept one deicer going in the old hole but let the others freeze over. There was no turning back. The whales would have to put aside any second thoughts. If they tried turning around, they would find their old holes sealed within a matter of hours.

It was the high point of the rescue. For the first time since they were discovered exactly two weeks earlier, the whales moved decisively toward the open lead. Cindy could hardly contain her exultation. Tears of joy welled in her eyes, only to freeze before they could make their way down her glowing cheeks. In all her years of rescuing whales, this was the most glorious moment of all. After a week of bitter frustration, acrimony, and resignation, these whales proved to the world that they were determined to survive their brazen tryst with fate.

Fittingly, there were hardly any members of the media on hand for the event. When during the course of the rescue had they covered the truly newsworthy developments? Most were back in Pepe's, recovering from their coverage of Ron Morris announcing the Russians' pending arrival. Cindy hugged nearly everyone she saw. The ice was awash in emotional embraces. Everyone was so caught up in the heady moment, it took several frantic shrieks for attention from a lone Eskimo woman to cut short the euphoric pandemonium.

"The baby, the baby!" she shrieked. "Where's the baby?"

It struck Cindy hard. Where *was* the baby? How could she not have noticed that since they began celebrating she had seen only the two larger whales? She screamed in panic as she sprinted toward Arnold, the whales' protector.

"Bone, Bone," she cried, as if the sea mammal knew its name let alone how to respond. "Has anyone seen Bone?"

Craig George was right. The large whales had been protecting the baby whale. That was why they had only now started to move. When the baby gently slipped beneath the surface, never to be seen again, the survivors readied themselves for freedom. Bone was gone. The problem of how to save three whales had just been simplified by a third.

21

Risking Lives for
a Six-Second Scoop

Arnold Brower was indignant. "Don't scare me like that," he admonished Cindy. "Just watch what you say." He shook his head in aggravated annoyance and insisted that he had just seen the baby whale seconds earlier. Brower retreated into his own well-known dispassion. He focused intently on the hole he was trying to keep clear of ice. Suddenly, he paused before lifting his seal pole out of the water. In a brief moment of uncertainty, he dropped the hollow aluminum shaft and let it float on the water's surface.

Throughout the unbridled emotion of the past several minutes, the seasoned Arctic hunter had remained a pillar of stoicism. He preached to other subsistence hunters the need for practiced discipline in the bitter elements. Now he scolded Cindy, desperately hoping she was wrong. In the Arctic, he lectured her, there was no room for misplaced emotion. Survival depended on the facts, not the unfounded whims of the heart.

"We're out here killing ourselves, and you go and panic over Bone. Just watch," he said, trying to restore their composure. "Just watch."

For the next frightful moments they did. Silently, they stood just inches apart waiting for the baby whale to return. Cindy trusted Arnold. His angry rebuttal reassured her. But this time, Arnold Brower was wrong. Bone was dead. After several moments, acknowledgment of Bone's fate became

inevitable. Cindy broke down, consumed in grief. It was the most irrational week of her life. Her strength was shattered. Bone's death marked the
nadir. The tragic but unavoidable conclusion came just after the elation of
watching the two surviving whales move to the new holes.

Craig and Arnold, in a desperate attempt to calm her down, tried to
coax Cindy off the ice and into a waiting truck to drive her back to town.
The sooner she left, they thought, the sooner she might recover from the
trauma of Bone's death. They were right. She calmed down the minute she
sat down. Her hysteria behind her, Cindy insisted on taking another, last
look for the baby whale and its scraped snout. She closely inspected the first
holes waiting for a sign of Bone. After a moment, she knew it was not to be.
A week of intense proximity enabled Craig and Cindy to grow close enough
for him to clutch her with his down-covered arm.

"You did all you could," Craig comforted her. "Cin, if it weren't for you,
they'd all be dead and you know it."

He was right, but Cindy didn't feel she deserved any special notice.
The whales had needed help and she offered it. There was no artifice to
Cindy. What she felt was what she was. Contrary to Craig's well-meaning
intention, Cindy felt Operation Breakout became what it was not because
of her, but because of the way people responded to her appeals.

Fran Tate, the owner of Pepe's, put up notices in the Top of the World
Hotel to alert all the members of the media and rescuers that her restaurant
was closing early. The past few nights, Tate and her glassy-eyed employees
had been manning the skillets and the deep fryers past midnight only to
open again at seven the next morning. Although she had been threatening
to close at 9 P.M. since the rescue began, this time Craig believed her. Frankly,
he was looking for any excuse to leave. Bone was dead and the melancholy
on the ice was getting him down. Besides, he was hungry, cold, and tired.
The more energy people expended bewailing Bone, the less they would
have for the two living whales, who were still quite desperate themselves.

As soon as Cindy was in the running truck, Craig jammed the transmission into drive, expertly spun his wheels on the ice, turned the vehicle
sharply around, and started the seventeen-mile return trip to Barrow. Round-
ing the northernmost tip of North America, Craig drove around the edge
of the narrow sandspit to the smoother and safer ice of Elson's Lagoon.

Cindy looked out her window and marveled at the totality of Arctic nothingness. She consoled herself by putting things in perspective. The rescue was just a momentary flash. Millions of people from around the globe were following the whales so closely that none of the hundred or so reporters had the time, energy, or inclination to focus on Barrow.

The story would come and go, and the drama would end, but Barrow and its Arctic surrounding would remain. The rescue activity seemed significant when experienced in person or watched on television, but when compared to the vastness surrounding it, it was nothing. Hours after the last rescuer left, the Arctic would envelop the site, leaving no trace of human presence.

While Cindy stared intently into the night, Craig focused on the lone light that shined just over the horizon. It shone distinctly through a thin bank of low-lying fog. *It must be the temporary light put up by the borough to help guide vehicles on and off the ice,* Craig thought. He was startled by its remarkable luminance. Even through the fog, it showed the way for miles. Craig couldn't understand why the light didn't get brighter the closer he got. Perhaps he had lost his way. The very instant Craig contemplated panic, the gravel road that marked the beginning of the continent came into view. He thanked the light that led him there. He thanked the Arctic moon.

When Cindy checked for messages, she hoped to see one from Kevin. Suddenly she missed him terribly. She couldn't bear to be alone in her grief; she wanted to share it. The receptionist could read the disappointment on Cindy's face when she broke the news that no one had called. The first time Cindy wanted messages, there were none. She ran upstairs to phone him. It was just after 8 P.M., Friday night, October 21, two weeks to the day after the whales were discovered and one week since Cindy first started orchestrating their rescue. Until now, she never had the time or reason to miss her boyfriend. Bone's death changed all that. She hurriedly called Kevin's office. As she was about to hang up, she remembered that the election was just two weeks away and that Kevin was probably busy at work. Next to Cindy, elections were the most important thing to Kevin Bruce, Alaska's most successful Democratic political consultant. Surely, he couldn't have gone home yet, she told herself. Maybe he was screening his calls.

"Kevin?" she asked lamely at the sound of the beep. "Are you there?" Before she could finish, Kevin dashed across the room to pick it up.

"Hi," he exclaimed with relief. "I'm really sorry about the baby whale."

"How do you know about that?" Cindy was puzzled. "You're the first person I've talked to since I've been back and I haven't told anybody."

"Oh really?" said Kevin. "It's all over the news. I just saw it on CNN."

Cindy was amazed. It wasn't an hour since Bone was first discovered missing and there were few reporters on the ice to cover it. But in less time than it took Cindy to drive back to Barrow, pick up the phone, and dial Kevin's number, reports of Bone's all-but-certain death were already big news on TV broadcasts, bigger news than the Russians. She marveled at how the revolution in telecommunications had shrunk the world. News, even from one of the most remote regions on Earth, crossed the planet in an instant. Viewers in the Lower 48 learned about Bone's death before most reporters in Barrow.

October 21 was a day of double headlines: Soviet participation and Bone's presumed death by drowning. By emphasizing the bad news, the media might well have sounded the operation's death knell. Unlike most news events that portray negative aspects of the world in which we live, Operation Breakout proved an international sensation because it described humans following a noble impulse to save helpless animals. If the coverage that Friday continued to focus on Bone's death, the story's good feeling might end. News executives didn't want their reports to provoke despair. If it turned as negative as every other story, their audience would lose interest.

Newsmen knew that this was different from almost any other story they had ever covered. It was the ultimate perversion of the cat-up-a-tree story, a redux of the media frenzy surrounding Jessica McClure's 1987 rescue from a well in Midland, Texas. The public's only interest in the whales was to see them saved. People were tired of politics, economics, and war. Aren't we always? They looked to the whales to help them escape, if only for a little while. Notwithstanding the State Department spin doctors, news that the Russians were on the way led Saturday morning papers across the United States and Canada. Many editions carried banner headlines befitting a major story. Weekends are usually slow news periods. But papers need headlines to print on weekends just as on any other day, and TV newscasts still need top stories to broadcast. That weekend of October 22 and 23 belonged almost solely to the whales.

What worked against the State Department worked for Operation

Breakout. Bone's death was not reported in the Lower 48 until after midnight Eastern time, much too late to run in the Saturday papers. By the time Sunday rolled around, Bone's passing was already old news, but Cindy wouldn't have known it by the constant ringing of her phone. Through Friday night, reporters from the Lower 48 and around the world called to verify that Bone had died. Even though it was all but apparent that the baby whale had drowned she didn't want to confirm it until first light Saturday morning. She and the rescuers could search the area once again for the missing whale and then let Ron Morris make whatever pronouncement he saw fit.

Around 10 P.M., Bill Allen and Ben Odom returned to Barrow to help prepare for the arrival of the giant Archimedean Screw Tractor. Allen and Odom's men at Prudhoe Bay were scheduled to work all night breaking down the pontoon ice crusher into sections small enough to fit on board an airplane that would fly it to Barrow, 270 miles away. After a day of round-the-clock maneuverings, Alaska Senator Ted Stevens convinced both the White House and the Pentagon to authorize the U.S. Air Force to deploy the tractor to Barrow. VECO faxed the screw tractor's dimensions from Prudhoe Bay to the Pentagon. The only plane big enough for the massive load was the biggest one in the American fleet, the Lockheed C-5A Galaxy cargo transport aircraft.

Bill Allen was busy until late at night using the phone in Ed Benson's apartment. Benson, who owned the jammed Airport Inn, wanted the big oilman out of his home so his family could get some sleep. Luckily, Benson would win a reprieve after Chuck Baker, another VECO representative, gave up his hotel room for Allen and Leathard in exchange for permission to return to Anchorage. It was a no-lose proposition for Baker. He was the envy of most of us who had to stay in Barrow.

By Saturday morning, Allen and Leathard were famished. They hadn't eaten since leaving Anchorage the day before. The hungry oilmen were first in line at Pepe's on Saturday morning. Cindy Lowry was in the same predicament. While she, too, waited for a table, Cindy immediately recognized Bill Allen's unmistakable Texas drawl. Allen was too busy talking with Pete about details of the screw tractor to notice the tiny woman who orchestrated the massive international rescue. When Craig and Geoff came in, two of Operation Breakout's biggest players were introduced.

Allen politely tipped his ten-gallon Stetson hat as if being introduced to royalty. He broke into a thin sympathetic smile and quietly said, "Ma'am, it's awful damn nice to meetcha. People all over the world owe you a lot of thanks, me included." Cindy warmly accepted his good graces and asked Allen and Leathard to join her for breakfast. They happily obliged.

Before they sat down, Allen whispered in Cindy's ear. "Can I see you over there," he whispered pointing to a quiet corner of the dining room. "I'd like to talk with you in private." Cindy was repulsed at the self-absorbed thought that the gangly oilman might be about to make a pass at her. Allen walked ten paces to the corner while Cindy followed warily behind. When they both stood in front of the kitchen door, Allen leaned against the over-hanging door frame and took on a look of sympathy and understanding.

"Hell, I know how much you wanted to save that baby," he said to Cindy's vanishing smile of curiosity. "I just want you to know that you have done all that you can, and that you have my word that we're going to do our damnedest to save them last two critters. I ain't never seen no whales until I came up here last week, and let me tell ya something, they are incredible animals. We're gonna save 'em, ma'am. I promise you."

Before Operation Breakout, Cindy felt nothing but hostility for oil companies. Come to think of it, she didn't feel much but hostility toward any person or group with whom she disagreed. People who opposed her and her agenda were the bad guys. Ill intent, malice of forethought, or just plain evil were the only possible explanations for opposing anything the environmentalist establishment supported. Oilmen pumped oil. Since oil was bad, those who produced oil were bad.

Now, suddenly, here was the quintessential oilman showing goodness, not evil. Without hesitation, she gave an unprepared Bill Allen an impromptu hug. They laughed, and Cindy walked back to the table sporting her infectious smile that returned for the first time since Bone's death.

In the moment it took Bill Allen to convey his genuine empathy, Cindy realized how muddled her perceptions had become. She was a professional environmentalist whose personal life had been made better by what the oil industry has produced. In fact, were it not for the oil industry there would be no whales left to save. They would have long since been hunted to extinction for their oil. The ultimate irony, of course, was that it was the "evil" oil industry, not purehearted environmentalists, who saved the whales, by providing a better, cheaper, more abundant, and safer source of fuel than whale oil.

While Cindy, Geoff, Craig, and Arnold were getting ready to go back on the ice to continue to search for the missing whale, Ron Morris was trying to find out when the Russian ships would arrive. According to the State Department, the Soviet vessels were due in Barrow the next night, Sunday, October 23, a week to the day after Operation Breakout began, sixteen days after the whales were found. When the two Soviet vessels finished their work on the Northern Pole 31 float station, they faced a three-hundred-mile journey to the southwest.

When the announcement was first made the day before, on Friday, October 21, Captain Sergei Reshetov's best analysis indicated that it would take two days to reach Barrow. However, soon after their departure from the floating ice station, he found conditions much worse than expected. The shifting ice pack made navigation treacherous. His artful dodges and traverses would add hours to the trip. Reshetov was worried. Rarely had he seen such dangerous ice conditions so early in the year. He could only imagine what kind of winter lay in store. He sent a cable to Vladivostok asking officials for aerial ice reconnaissance. Having spent a career in the Soviet Merchant Marine, Reshetov knew not to get his hopes up. U.S. reconnaissance capabilities were light-years ahead of his own country's, and Reshetov knew it. If ever there was time to demand quid pro quo, this was it.

It was the Americans who asked the Soviets for help. Now the Soviets could ask the Americans for help of their own. The Soviet Merchant Marine forwarded their request to the U.S. State Department. Saturday morning, the State Department passed it on to Glenn Rutledge at the Navy/NOAA Joint Ice Center in Suitland, Maryland. Rutledge assembled Arctic ice data compiled daily by the National Ocean Service, an arm of NOAA. He put together large maps detailing ice thickness and openings in the polar pack. The data proved invaluable to Master Reshetov and the Soviet ice-breakers. But as good as the data proved to be, Rutledge knew it could be better. Aside from stranding themselves in the first place, the whales had been carried by an uncanny streak of luck since the very beginning. It was luck that led Roy Ahmaogak to find them in a tiny hole in the ice, and luck that caused the whole world to pull for them and spend millions to free them. Now, as that same luck would have it, American satellite imaging was on the verge of a major leap forward.

On September 24, 1988, just two weeks before the whales were discovered, the U.S. Air Force deployed the most sophisticated weather satellite ever built, launched into orbit aboard an unmanned Atlas rocket. The state-of-the-art $100-million satellite, called NOAA-11, could produce much more sharply defined images than earlier U.S. satellites. But NOAA-11 was not scheduled to start operating until December 1988—too late to help the whales. The media firestorm over the whales proved as much a NOAA emergency as any life-threatening hurricane. The agency had received more publicity in Operation Breakout's first week than it had in the eighteen years of its existence. The previously obscure federal agency, unknown to most Americans, was on the front page of every newspaper in the country. That included the *Washington Post,* the newspaper read by the people who approved NOAA's annual budget. For people inside the Beltway, it was NOAA's coming of age. For the agency, the whole affair was a godsend. NOAA ordered its special satellite turned on immediately.

By Monday, October 24, eight days after Operation Breakout began, the newest and most sophisticated weather satellite ever deployed would have its first assignment. Suddenly, the two whales sputtering in the waters off Barrow had entered the space age. But while a $100-million geosynchronous satellite compiled ice analysis, Eskimo crews under the direction of Arnold Brower continued the task of cutting open holes so the whales could breathe. When Cindy returned to the ice Saturday morning, the whales were energetically popping in and out of the last of the fifty-five holes. They swam under more than a mile of frozen sea in one night. Now, there was no doubt, the whales were on their way. If the Russians could cut through the pressure ridge, they would soon be free.

After a week's practice, the Eskimos were cutting new holes at a furious pace. That Friday night, Ron Morris had pushed them all to work even faster. "The Russians will be here in two days," he told Brower. "They told us they can work only one day. I want the whales as close to that damned ridge as we can get them." Brower took his order and ran. Saturday, Brower's men cut fifteen new holes before noon. The two whales were keeping right up with them. Morris wanted all his guns firing. He pressed Colonel Carroll to get his concrete bullet into the arsenal.

On Saturday morning, the colonel managed to stave off yet another near disaster, potentially the worst one yet. Just hours before, Colonel Carroll's National Guard contingent had completed the last of its redeployment from Prudhoe. All twelve guardsmen landed safely in Barrow aboard two Bell Huey helicopters, the workhorse of the Alaska National Guard. The Guard unit prided itself on its ability to operate in America's most hostile weather.

But that Friday night, Colonel Carroll's unit displayed just the opposite foresight. After shutting down their engines, the guardsmen left the expensive helicopters outside the hangar. Moments later, the helicopters were frozen solid. Discovering the lapse, Colonel Carroll was outraged. He opened the huge bay doors to roll the helicopters inside. Thankfully, Randy Crosby was there to stop him. Crosby was shocked to see the Guard about to break one of the first rules of Arctic aviation: never let frozen equipment thaw too quickly.

"What the hell are you guys doing?" Crosby shouted in disbelief. He explained that if the frozen helicopters were brought inside, vital parts of the aircraft would crack. Crosby told Carroll and his men that his helicopters had to be defrosted slowly. If he wanted the Hueys to fly again, Carroll would have to leave them outside wrapped in nylon parachutes and let the feeble Arctic sun do the rest. Saturday, October 22, was the warmest day yet of the rescue.

While it was still fifteen degrees below zero out on the ice, the temperature in town almost reached the double digits. Scantily clad locals made the conditions seem almost balmy. The heaviest garb to be seen was a light, unbuttoned windbreaker. Even they were scarce. Few wore hats and almost no one wore gloves. Teenagers strutted through the frozen streets in sneakers and T-shirts.

I saw one child dressed in nothing more than a brightly colored bathing suit and T-shirt. He was riding through the icy streets on a bicycle. Reporters stuck out plainly among the locals. To us it was more than cold: it was downright bitter, even in our expensive designer ski clothes. Eskimos never donned hats and gloves in weather warmer than twenty degrees or thirty degrees below, whereas we always wore them.

Later that Saturday morning, the Colonel unveiled the ARCO ice crusher, his latest scheme for Operation Breakout's next media spectacular. For the insatiable press and their whale-crazed audience, the sixth and seventh days of Operation Breakout, Friday and Saturday, October 21 and 22, were a news bonanza. The Russian icebreakers, Bone's death, and now the ice smasher being added to the rescue's climax: this was the Super Bowl of whale-saving.

After traveling to the top of the world to cover what started as a nature story, reporters soon found themselves facing the same inveterate media manipulation they dealt with every day down in the Lower 48. Early Saturday morning, Mike Haller, Tom Carroll's media relations officer, posted a schedule for the day's events at the entrance to Pepe's, in the Top of the World Hotel, and at NARL, where the international and late-arriving press stayed. Activities began at 8 A.M., several hours before daybreak, at the old Navy hangar south of NARL. Colonel Carroll's men hitched ARCO's five-ton concrete block to the CH-54 Skycrane helicopter.

Some reporters faced a dilemma. They could go to the ice with Cindy or watch the bullet. Having each invested up to $10,000 a day in covering the event, the competitive American television networks weren't going to take the chance of being beaten. By Saturday morning, each network had at least two camera crews, enabling them to cover more than one event at a time. While one crew could film ARCO's bullet, the other could be on the ice with Cindy and the two whales.

Amid a modicum of fanfare, half a dozen cameras watched the Skycrane lift the five-ton battering ram off the frozen tarmac. Since the event was designed with the media in mind, Gary Quarles landed the helicopter after a quick circle around the hangar. He took off again to give the cameras a second chance. On the ground, cameramen ran around the helipad to photograph the Skycrane from different angles. The helicopter flew slowly so the camera crews would have plenty of time to board the three SAR helicopters and film the Skycrane while still in flight. Haller knew that the longer the Skycrane flew, the more chance every cameraman would have to take the perfect picture of it.

Carroll agreed with Morris's order not to frighten the whales. He would test the bullet several miles from the Eskimo holes. But by Saturday morning, it seemed that nothing could startle the freedom-starved leviathans. The deafening clatter of the helicopters didn't appear to have any effect. The chances of the five-ton concrete block spooking them seemed remote. While the three press helicopters formed a mile-wide triangle around it, the Skycrane hovered fifty feet above the frozen sea awaiting final orders from Colonel Carroll.

Once again, the colonel was on the line. He was getting used to it. During that time his world underwent a remarkable transformation, from quiet anonymity to the turbulent center of an absurd operation. Whatever Tom Carroll said or did was reported around the world. Tom Carroll was headline news, a key figure in one of the decade's biggest media events. But the height of his great adventure wasn't played out on the ice or in the air; instead, it took place each night on the telephone with a woman 7,000 miles away. Her name was Bonnie Mersinger, and his bond with her was instant. This faceless woman in Washington was suddenly the constant center of his frazzled life. Carroll became convinced that the three whales he was summoned to rescue stranded themselves so that he could meet the woman of his dreams. They spoke every day. Officially, it was a chance for the colonel to brief the White House on the progress of the rescue. But unofficially, it was the chance for Tom and Bonnie to grow closer. With each conversation, their relationship intensified.

After wishing Bonnie the "top of the morning," the colonel gave the order for Quarles to "drop the bomb." Just as it had two days earlier, the free-falling battering ram easily broke through the ice. Quarles punched ten more holes before Arnold Brower and his Eskimo scouts arrived to examine the results. The Eskimos immediately saw a problem. The bullet broke the ice, but it didn't remove it. The heavily broken blocks still floated in place. Brower knew that the only way the gray whales would use a hole was if it had been meticulously combed free of even the smallest pieces of ice.

The bullet was retired after just one run. Operation Breakout had taken yet another of its many ironic twists. The distinguished colonel met with more logistical setbacks in the first week of the whales rescue than he had in twenty years. Yet, Tom Carroll was a national figure. Next to a forty-one-year-old junior senator from Indiana who was about to become vice president, Tom Carroll was the person most Americans associated with the National Guard but for better reasons.

Colonel Carroll learned of the next crisis with the whales when he returned to the Navy hangar. The high-priced NOAA biologists flown in from Seattle were baffled. The two whales had stopped dead in their tracks. They seemed stuck, as if something was preventing them from moving on. The whales' eagerness to forge ahead was as strong as ever. The walkie-talkies crackled with activity. Anybody with suggestions was urged to help.

But the sophisticated technology was of little use. Malik went to the Eskimo warm-up shack without his radio. The rescuers were eager for him to return so Craig raced to fetch him. He waited while Malik finished chewing a piece of smoked walrus meat. On his way out the door, he picked up a chunk of muktuk from the whale he and his crew killed a few weeks earlier and popped it into his mouth. They jumped on the back of Craig's waiting ski machine. The loud roar of the fast machine made conversation en route impossible. Instead, Malik savored the particularly tasty piece of whale blubber. As the crowded holes came into view, Malik wiped his mouth with satisfaction and prepared to get back to the task of saving the dead bowhead's two stranded cousins.

"Little Big Man" jumped off the machine and lifted up his red baseball cap, now a trademark. It was emblazoned with an oval black-and-white patch bearing the name of the trade group to which every subsistence whaler belonged: "Alaska Eskimo Whaling Commission." Malik knew the contours of the frozen ocean he was standing atop better than anyone. Before he even saw them, Malik had a strong suspicion what held the whales back. The instant he peered into the hole they wouldn't enter, his suspicions were confirmed.

Unlike the other seventy holes the whales used in the past twenty-four hours, this one wasn't black. Light reflected from the ocean bottom cast a distinctly gray hue. The whales were stuck at the edge of an underwater sand shoal only twelve feet deep. That was dangerously shallow, even for shore-dwelling grays. The whales had hit a roadblock and, like their rescuers, were unsure how to proceed. Saving whales was new to Malik. Normally, he killed them.

Suddenly, the answer hit him. "A detour," Malik exclaimed. "Would a whale swim if he thought he might get stuck?" he asked no one in particular.

"Let's cut holes around the shoal." During the hour the whales were blocked by the sand bar, Arnold Brower and his Eskimos cut fourteen new holes.

Bill Allen was impressed. "Well, look at that Archie Bowers work," he said, mistakenly referring to Brower. But the holes would never be used. Malik and Arnold Jr. turned their back on the errant path and probed the area for deeper water. As soon as an alternate path was marked and new holes cut, the whales followed. The fourteen misdirected holes froze without a trace.

The rush was on to get the whales through the last four miles of ice and out to the pressure ridge. Supposedly, the Russians were only a day away. The rescuers counted on having but one chance to get the whales through any openings the Russians could cut in the pressure ridge. No one knew what kind of a problem the ridge would present, or if the Soviet ships could even surmount it. Ever since Bone vanished, the whales lived up to their end of the bargain. They burst into the new holes even before they were fully cut. Now more than ever, the rescue's success depended on the Eskimos.

When the Soviets agreed to join the party, the media scrambled for the first pictures of the Russian ships plowing through thick polar ice en route. But NBC was the only network with an independent means to win the race: a helicopter. It was a widely known secret in the prefab corridors of the Top of the World Hotel that NBC would start its chase through the menacing Arctic skies as soon as the Russian ships were within two hundred miles of Barrow.

No one was more aware of the looming scoop than ABC News producer Harry Chittick, who had been griping to Ron Morris for days about NBC's helicopter and the unfair advantage he thought it gave his competition. Jerry Hansen, Chittick's NBC counterpart, reminded Morris that there was no law against renting a helicopter and that, to date, there were no restrictions on flights that prevented the NBC chopper from getting the rescue's best and most reliable aerial video.

Chittick knew NBC had the edge, but he thought there might be a way to steal the scoop right from under Hansen's nose. Chittick spent Saturday morning trying to rent his own aircraft. The airplane he found would enable him to slip right past the slow-flying NBC helicopter and out to the icebreakers. He didn't even need a pilot. He was licensed to fly himself.

Researchers in his Los Angeles office looked up the icebreakers in the maritime bible, *Jane's All the World's Fighting Ships*. Figuring out the icebreakers' speed, the ABC researchers calculated when the vessels would come within range. But by the time Chittick finally rented an airplane, it seemed too late. NBC appeared to have won again.

On Saturday afternoon, NBC's Don Oliver checked in with the international information exchange that connected the Soviet Merchant Marine, the U.S. government, and the Russian ships. Almost everyone knew where the center was located, Randy Crosby's office at the SAR hangar. SAR easily adapted to its new role. It was already headquarters for Tom Carroll's National Guard unit and the transit terminal for the media. SAR was Operation Breakout's official headquarters. The U.S. government reports estimated the Russians to be about 170 miles northeast of Barrow. Then the icebreakers encountered unexpectedly thick ice. The ships reduced their speed to less than three knots, much slower than originally predicted. Moreover, the satellite photographs and computer-enhanced charts transmitted to the bridge of the *Admiral Makarov* revealed that a large ice floe lay directly across their planned route to Barrow. Master Reshetov had no choice but to chart a lengthy detour. The revised schedule estimated the icebreakers would arrive in Barrow between twenty-four to thirty-six hours late.

Though still too far away to help the whales, the icebreakers were within striking distance of making it on the evening news. The NBC helicopter had a standard range of about 350 miles under "favorable conditions," a term which could not be applied to the Arctic. The "no return point" was 175 miles. Flying outbound any further than that meant there would not be enough fuel to make it back. The weather threatened to make the trip even more dangerous.

Dense ice fog hugged the ground, hiding a thick layer of cloud cover just overhead. By the end of October 1988, Barrow was already so cold that even the tiniest particles of water vapor froze into ice crystals so small they escaped even the force of gravity. The ice fog enveloped everything. In settled areas like Barrow, ice fog reduced visibility to absolute zero. By mid-afternoon, Randy Crosby grounded all his helicopters and advised others to do the same. NBC was not about to let the weather get in the way of a good story.

The safety of the freelance crew was a minor impediment to obtaining the first video of the icebreakers, pictures that would run at most for five to eight seconds on the evening news. Viewers would never know the risks taken to get them. The pressure to fly was never explicit. It didn't have to be. News doesn't wait for the timid and it doesn't give second chances. Since NTV, the network my company was hired to represent, was paying for half the helicopter, I insisted we try to get in on the action. Earlier that morning, over Pepe's greasy home fries and soft, butter-soaked Wonder bread, I asked Jerry Hansen, the NBC producer, what he thought about using our chopper to find the approaching ships. Hansen swallowed nervously as if I had spoken a secret too loudly. His eyes looked around to see if anyone had heard, motioning for me to keep quiet. "Everything is being taken care of," he told me. He was right.

My cameraman, Steve Mongeau, and I went to NARL where the helicopter was based. For several hours we waited for the pilots to give the "go." By late afternoon, it was apparent that the ice fog wasn't going to lift. The two pilots showed little enthusiasm for the Saturday-night death run, but they had most demanding clients. They had long since quit reminding us to keep our seatbelts on while hanging out the hovering helicopter's open doors. The weather was as uncertain as the precise position of the Soviet ships. All that was certain was that we were going to look for them. If the icebreakers were 170 miles or closer, they would be five miles inside the "no return point," just ten miles short of the helicopter's maximum range. This was little margin for error. NBC cameraman Bruce Gray remarked that finding the ships in the thick fog with so little room to maneuver would be like finding a needle in a haystack. Long stretches of silence marked the eerie journey out. But as the fuel gauge neared half empty, there was still no sign of the Russians.

Encroaching darkness threatened to spoil more than the photography. As night fell so too did the chances of survival should anything go awry. As No one would have survived of the crew in an emergency landing anyway. We later learned there were no flotation devices aboard the aircraft. As the helicopter came closer to the "no return point," the pilots turned off the inner cabin intercom so they could talk among themselves without us hearing.

If they didn't turn the helicopter around within the next couple of minutes, we would not have enough fuel to get back. There would be no choice but to land on an iceberg and pray to be saved. Because of the safety violations, the pilots didn't want to take the chance of radioing for rescue for fear of losing their licenses. When they turned around to announce the situation, Gray was preparing his camera to shoot. At almost that exact instant, the eerie silhouette of the 496-foot *Admiral Makarov,* the pride of the Soviet icebreaker fleet, loomed menacingly into view. The satellite tracking proved dead on. It was within yards of the pilots' projections. Spinning his finger in the air to signal a flight around the ship, Gray pleaded for the chance to at least get some decent pictures of the immense Soviet icebreakers. He furiously readied his camera for the difficult task of shooting under such rushed conditions. It was now or never.

The chopper dove within just a few hundred feet of the ships towering deck. Curious sailors clambered on deck to inspect the unidentified visitor. Gray told the pilots to slow their air speed so he could make the special adjustments his camera needed to work in the near dark. When the chopper's nose pulled away on its uncertain flight back to Barrow, the only footage of the Soviet icebreakers sat on Gray's lap. He had a marginally important scoop. But as his own life hung perilously in the balance, he wondered whether what he had just done was courageous or stupid.

Flying across the pitch-black Arctic, no one was sure what lay below: water or ice. Either way it was cold and getting colder. Worry intensified. The fuel gauge continued to plummet. With the heat turned off to conserve fuel, the temperature in the cabin dropped below zero. The minutes stretched long and uncertain. Thankfully, a fortuitous shift in the wind cut the helicopter's drag, giving it just enough fuel to allow a safe landing at the NARL helipad. The footage everyone had risked their lives for didn't even air until twenty-four hours later on Sunday's *NBC's Nightly News.* By the time the precious pictures had run, ABC had already aired their own footage shot sixteen hours after NBC's. NBC won the battle but lost the war, a war that, like the rescue itself, was created and fought by and for the media.

22

Sergei Reshetov: "Let's Cut Ice"

L ike the whales they were diverted to save, the Russians were running
very late. By the time the massive ships broke across Barrow's horizon
at around noon on Tuesday, October 25, the two icebreakers were almost
two days behind schedule. The 440-foot *Vladimir Arseniev,* the smaller of
the two ships, led the way. Eighteen days after the stranded whales were
first found, two of the mightiest ships in the Soviet Merchant Navy arrived to complete the trapped animals' improbable route to freedom. The
ships were so large, and the terrain so flat, they were easily visible from
town, some twenty-five miles away. Parked at a safe distance from the pressure ridge, the massive icebreakers were less than ten miles from the whales
they came to redeem.

Crowds of reporters busily jockeyed for position in the line outside the
SAR hangar. They were desperate to see the day's press pool assignment.
Master Reshetov cabled Ron Morris to tell him that the American pool
reporters were welcome on his ship. After all, the Russians had dispatched
the icebreakers with an eye to favorable publicity. Pool coverage rotated
on a daily basis among the four American networks: ABC, CBS, CNN,
and NBC. Because of our own rented helicopter, we rarely had to rely on
the pool. The exception was for access to the Soviet ships.

CNN correspondent Greg Lefevre and his two-man crew were the first non-Soviet television reporters scheduled to board the *Admiral Makarov*. They joined coordinator Ron Morris and his overseer Admiral Sigmund Petersen, the Pacific NOAA fleet commander. Randy Crosby flew them out. We trailed just a few hundred yards behind in our own helicopter. The only difference was that they were allowed to land and we were not. We did the next best thing, augmenting the pool material with our own exclusive aerials. Big deal.

Listening to heavily accented instructions from the *Arseniev,* Crosby eased back the throttle and touched down squarely on the landing pad at the stern of the 496-foot ship. The engine idled while Crosby waited for the signal to power down. His eyes darted about in fascination. As he waited, Crosby couldn't help but think what a far cry this was from a normal day's work.

Ten days before, he was just the director of the North Slope Borough's Search and Rescue department, a peculiar emergency services division established to aid subsistence Eskimos. His primary job was rescuing stranded native hunters stuck on the tundra or a floating block of ice in the middle of the Arctic Ocean. Now he was piloting a U.S. admiral and a CNN television crew, but VIPs were nothing new. Just a year before, Crosby flew novelist James Michener around the Arctic to research his bestselling book, *Alaska.*

But landing on Soviet icebreakers? That was new. The huge hammer and sickle painted on the smokestack dispelled any doubt about where he was. By convention of international maritime law, Randy Crosby, father of four, had just landed in the Union of Soviet Socialist Republics. Crosby saw a heavy metal hatch slowly open at the base of the ship's superstructure. It was the first sign of life. A few seconds later, a small, heavily bundled man tentatively emerged. He walked to the helipad, stopped, and stared. After giving the American visitors the once-over, the unidentified man turned back toward the open door and nodded.

Brandishing warm smiles and effusive greetings, several more of the ship's crew appeared. Ron Morris waved the CNN camera crew out of the chopper first so they could capture every bit of the official welcome on film. A Soviet television crew was already on deck. With both cameras rolling Morris jumped down from behind the helicopter's plastic door to bask in the attention of Master Sergei Reshetov and his next in command,

First Officer Alexander Patsevich. Behind him came NOAA's Admiral Sigmund Petersen.

"Ron Morris, U.S. government," the NOAA coordinator introduced himself to his Soviet counterparts. His rank grew more impressive each time he mentioned it. By week's end, Morris would reportedly tell journalists and rescuers alike that he was the Reagan administration's official representative. The White House was furious. Bonnie Mersinger's line was bombarded by White House and Commerce Department higher-ups demanding that someone "put a muzzle" on the coordinator.

"Who the hell is this guy?" a senior White House official demanded of Mersinger, the administration's whale rescue liaison. It was her job to find out. Just ten days from obscurity, Ron Morris was on record as saying he was an official representative of the president of the United States. Assistant Commerce Secretary William Evans saw the low-level Ron Morris on television speaking to reporters as if he were sent to coordinate the rescue by Ronald Reagan himself. Angry and dismayed, Secretary Evans sent Morris a stern memo of rebuke:

I have been contacted by the White House via the Secretary of Commerce's Chief of Staff with reports that you have represented yourself to the press as an official representative of the President and/or the Administration," the memo began. "This is incorrect behavior and you will cease all contact with the press on the subject of any fisheries program without first clearance from the Assistant Administrator of NOAA for Fisheries. You do not represent the administration. You have either been grossly misquoted or have not made your role clear to the media as a federal employee.

After introductions and a short pose for the rolling cameras, CNN's Greg Lefevre asked the first question. He was surprised to hear the Soviet captain answer him in excellent English. NOAA interpreter Svetlana Andreeva, brought specially from Washington, was delighted to learn she wasn't needed. Maybe now she could go home. Reshetov invited the Americans to his quarters for an obligatory shot of vodka. Even Randy Crosby pounded one back.

When they reached the captain's cabin, Morris opened up a weathered leather satchel and pulled out the most recent satellite image analysis, charts and other data compiled by federal agencies for presentation to the Soviets. Morris and Admiral Petersen briefed Reshetov on Operation Breakout and the last remaining obstacle to the whale's freedom, the massive pressure ridge. After hearing Morris's summation, Master Reshetov opened his arms, clearly relishing the challenge. He turned to the cameras and said, "Let's cut ice."

But before work came a little more pleasure: a second toast of vodka, a tour of the ship, and a chance for the Americans to meet its sea-weary crew. Although anxious to be reunited with family and friends, the Soviet sailors seemed eager to help the trapped whales. Together, the Americans and their Soviet counterparts walked to the dreary officers' mess where a Soviet-style lunch of borscht, potatoes, and a tasteless meat stew awaited them.

Before Crosby boarded the helicopter for the return flight to the United States, a few gregarious Soviet crew members rushed to give him an assortment of pins and buttons. They also gave him a fur hat emblazoned with a gold-rimmed scarlet star of the Soviet Red Army.

"Christ," he chortled as he prepared to lift off from the Russian vessel. "I sure as hell never thought I'd be so damned proud to wear a Commie hat."

Moments later, the American chopper was back in the United States.

Immediately after the Americans departed, Reshetov consulted with his crew to devise a strategy for attacking the pressure ridge. The Americans doubted whether the Soviet ships could break through. Bridling at the implied American insult, Reshetov determined to prove them wrong. He had to decide which of his two ships should attempt the first assault.

The crew combined the remarkably clear American satellite imagery and its own estimations of ocean depth and ice thickness. It recommended that Reshetov deploy the *Vladimir Arseniev* to see if she could find any exploitable weaknesses. Since the smaller ship had a shallower keel, she could more safely break ice over the dangerous shoals and sandbars off Point Barrow.

Because Reshetov was unfamiliar with the American waters, he didn't want to take any chances. If the *Arseniev* wasn't up to the task, he could always call in his big gun, the *Admiral Makarov,* which was anchored just a few hundred meters off the ridge. A trio of pesky helicopters buzzing like mosquitoes swirled overhead as the *Vladimir Arseniev* engaged new powerful engines and belched a huge plume of black smoke. The big ship easily cut a channel to the ice wall, preparing to strike it head on. The *Arseniev* was ready for her first assault on the pinnacled pressure ridge. Just as the American rescuers fit the stereotype of a country excessively reliant on technology, the Soviets were about to epitomize the world's image of their own nation: brute strength and size.

The helmsman threw the powerful engines into reverse. The Finnish-made ship needed room to build up speed before hitting the outer edge of the ridge. The crew braced itself for the first contact. For several minutes, the men waited expectantly, unsure of the impact. The double hull of reinforced steel was designed to withstand tremendous strain, but Reshetov was uncertain whether the grounded ice would give. He expected the worst and ordered the crew to do the same. The *Arseniev*'s bow met the glacial blue wall in a thunderous collision. The deafening sound of 24 million pounds of grinding steel crushing the thick ice was audible for miles.

But the wrenching noise belied the remarkable ease with which the *Arseniev*'s bow parted the ice. As his ship plowed ahead undaunted, Reshetov broke into hearty laughter. The crew joined him, breaking the tense silence. The last remaining obstacle to the whales' freedom was falling beneath the mighty bow of the Soviet icebreaker. For the first time since the whales were discovered eighteen days earlier, Operation Breakout, suddenly renamed Operation Breakthrough by the U.S. government, was on the verge of success.

At sea for the past six months, the crew had no comprehension of the dimensions of the rescue it was instructed to assist. Since they received their orders from the highest levels of Soviet government, the crew naturally assumed it was being asked to perform a daring, critical task, perhaps vital to its nation's security. What the Russians just figured out was that the ice they spent the past four days traversing was much more treacherous than that which they were summoned to cut. The ship's massive bow crushed its way ever closer to the curious crowd of onlookers and the whales they came to liberate.

No one, not even the Eskimos, had any idea the Soviet ships could so effortlessly cut through the ridge of grounded ice. Just minutes before, Gary Hufford, the NOAA ice expert brought specially to Barrow to help in the rescue, told reporters he thought the wall might well be impenetrable. After several hundred yards, the pressure of the ridge ground the icebreaker to a halt, a normal occurrence that Master Reshetov expected to happen much sooner. The helmsman backed ship for another run at the ice wall. A huge cheer erupted as news of the icebreaker's success reached the crowd of rescuers and journalists gathered a few miles away. After ten days of setbacks, something finally worked.

Operation Breakout was reaching its finale. The pressure ridge, thought to be the last great obstacle to the whale's freedom, was no match for the *Vladimir Arseniev*. As soon as the Eskimos could finish their path of ice holes, the whales and the world could get on with their lives.

This would be Bill Allen's last chance to help save the whales. Three days earlier, on Saturday, October 22, a C-5A Galaxy, the free world's largest aircraft, landed at Barrow's Wiley Post–Will Rogers Memorial Airport. Barrow's budget director Dan Fauske, who lived across the street from the runway, was outside shoveling snow from his sidewalk when the huge plane blotted out the sky over the tiny town as it swooped in for a landing. He thought Barrow was being invaded, but he didn't know by whom. The airport had to divert all other traffic while the C-5A straddled the end of the runway. It was too big and too heavy to use the tarmac. In a frenzy of activity involving Colonel Carroll's National Guard unit, the United States Air Force, and MarkAir cargo director Ed Rogers, the unwieldy Archimedean Screw Tractor was extracted from the Galaxy's gaping jaw.

Towed to the old Navy hangar just south of NARL, the screw tractor awaited its chance to show the world that VECO could help the whales after all. On Sunday afternoon, Bill Allen demonstrated it to a skeptical Ron Morris. Just across the road from the hangar, the tractor, spinning its huge screws, made its way awkwardly through the sand and onto the ice. For a few embarrassing moments it slid across the slippery surface without breaking through it. When the screw tractor finally found a weak spot, it left a trail of thick ice in its wake. Like the ill-fated bullet a day earlier, the tractor left too much debris.

But Bill Allen wasn't finished. He hadn't spent more than a quarter million dollars not to get in on the drama's last act. The Russians were making it look too easy. They had thrown down the gauntlet to Bill Allen and his American honor. He wanted that tractor on the ice and he wanted it to work. Over the phone to Marvin King, his man at Prudhoe Bay, Allen designed a sled which the Skycrane could tow behind the tractor to clear the broken ice. Allen drew a sketch of it and faxed it to Prudhoe.

"Put it together as fast as you can," Allen ordered his plant manager. "Carroll says he'll give us a whirl."

King and his men worked through the night Sunday and all day Monday, welding together the makeshift sled. They had to leave it partially disassembled in order to load it aboard the C-130 Hercules cargo plane, which was standing by to airlift it to Barrow. When it arrived, Billy Bob donned a welder's mask and prepared to use the skill he learned so many years before. When he and Pete Leathard found an acetylene torch, they knew they were in business. Ordering in from Pepe's, the two men went to work and didn't emerge until the sled was complete forty-eight hours later. Allen called Colonel Carroll and told him he planned the test run "down to a gnat's ass."

But earlier that day, the jinxed Skycrane, linked to the rescue's most conspicuous failures, was grounded with a fractured blade, damage that would require 100,000 taxpayers' dollars to fix. The hundreds of man hours spent furiously constructing the rush-order sled went for naught. Bill Allen's last dream seemed dashed. By Wednesday afternoon, October 26, less than twenty-four hours after the Soviets first appeared off the Barrow coast, the pressure ridge had been reduced to mounds of ice separating dozens of paths which convincingly disproved its invulnerability to escape paths a quarter mile wide. All that remained between the whales and their freedom was a three-mile stretch of virgin ice.

But ironically, just as the rescuers were bridging the final hurdle, public interest suddenly began to falter. The web of shared concern that had bound together many Americans for two extraordinary weeks started to subside. People were getting bored. The characteristic American demands for immediate results were coming to the fore. When the whales weren't freed right away viewers got cranky, angry, even resentful. Just when the Russian ships gave the rescue its first realistic hope of success, Americans do what they always do—they moved on.

Was the extraordinary expense justified? Was it really worth doing more? How much was too much? When balanced against these questions, the rescue started to seem ludicrous. Sympathy turned to cynicism. Talk radio, then in its infancy, but still the miner's canary of American public opinion, succumbed to the first fumes. Newspapers started printing political cartoons which mocked the lavish attention heaped on the whales. Dan Wasserman, a *Boston Globe* political cartoonist, drew one of Operation Breakout's most memorable satires: Two homeless people sitting on a subway grate donning whale costumes in an inventive attempt to solicit help.

Ben Sargent of the *Austin American Statesman* sketched perhaps the most poignant cartoon: Living skeletons of Sudanese refugees languishing near a bombed-out relief truck. Its radio broadcasting the captioned message, "The world stood transfixed today by the heart rending plight of the California gray whales."

The public's empathy had peaked. The whales didn't have much time and Americans didn't have much patience. Reacting to its audience's changing mood, the press retrenched and subtly began to adopt a more conventional role. By the beginning of Operation Breakout's second week, reporters on the scene started asking the same questions. While not mentioned in any of our reports, the three small children killed in the tragic Barrow house fire served as vivid testimony to our excessive preoccupation with the whales; a watershed of sorts. Just when things looked to be going Ron Morris's way, the first uncomfortable questions were flung at him.

Fortunately for the whales, they were too busy to worry about their growing "image problem." Hoping for a climactic ending to justify their continued presence, most of the media stuck with the whales. By now, there were hundreds of people on the ice: a score of camera crews, dozens of reporters, the Eskimo ice cutters, Ron Morris's cadre of experts, Colonel Carroll and the National Guard, and countless Barrowans. All were urging the whales on. The Eskimos said the Arctic had probably never seen so much activity in its four-billion-year history. Never had the Arctic ice been subjected to so much man-made stress.

But so far the ice was holding up remarkably well. While fifty million pounds of icebreakers pounded away at the ice's outer edges, millions more pounds stressed its surface. Suddenly, this desolate patch of ice was the work place to hundreds of people and all their heavy effects. The ice was the glassy super highway allowing high speed transit for scores of commuters. It was a Southern Californian's dream, a freeway in every sense of the word, a roadway as wide as it was long, with no limits. There were no barriers and virtually no dangers. Vehicles regularly drove at speeds reaching eighty miles an hour, on sheer ice! If we spun out of control, which was not unusual, the only danger was the driver's overreaction. The ice upon which we all depended was also the landing strip and tarmac to a fleet of helicopters and even light fixed-wing aircraft.

The ice we relied on for access to the whales was the very element that imprisoned them. But as they were boldly making clear, it wouldn't imprison them for long. Just a few hours before Arctic darkness would descend upon them on Wednesday, October 25, the two whales seemed to sense that it might be their last day of captivity. The Eskimos were opening holes at breakneck speed just to keep pace with the frenzied whales. Led by Siku, the larger of the two, the leviathans were trying to surface in new holes before they were finished. The whales were so persistent, they were sticking their vulnerable heads within inches of the lethal chain saws.

Malik was forced to take steps to prevent an accidental slashing. Such a catastrophe would have been particularly tragic now that the whales were so close to freedom. He split his twelve-man crew in half. The lead group cut the outline of a hole with their chain saws and moved on to mark off the next one. Meanwhile, the second crew worked on the first hole, pushing the giant blocks of ice under the rim of the hole allowing the anxious whales to surface. Instead of colliding with a deadly chain saw, the worst the whales would bump into was an aluminum seal pole.

It was all they could do to stay in the holes. Geoff and Craig were convinced the whales could see the path to the lead. Hundreds of people piled aboard trucks and snowmobiles. They raced beyond the end of the trail of ice holes to the edge of the Soviet-cut channel. For everyone involved in the nearly two-week-old ordeal, the final hour seemed at hand. Since he was instructed by his assignment desk to "get the whales swimming free," British photographer Charles Laurence humorously described the various possible scenarios. Would the whales pound their flukes with added vigor as their bodies glided across a marked plane separating entrapment from freedom? Or, as a cartoon in the *Richmond Times Dispatch* amusingly suggested, once they were free, would the whales mischievously beach themselves just to drive us all crazy?

On the two previous occasions when actual news did develop—the deicers luring the whales into the first new holes and Bone's death—there were no cameras on hand. But this time was different. The whales were about to swim free, a most difficult moment to capture for sure, but none-theless the reason we were all there. Our job was to record—in words, pictures, and sound—the liberation of the stranded whales as best we could.

But by early Tuesday evening, the ice, which had proved so reliable, was starting to show strain. Large structural cracks were found leading from the breaker channels all the way to the whales. The stress of all the weight the ice was forced to support was proving more than it could safely handle. The ice was starting to break. The risks were presented in no uncertain terms. The more people and equipment that stood atop it, the greater the likelihood the ice would collapse. Those of us who entrusted our lives to the durable ice required no further elaboration. While the ominous news did not keep us away, it tempered almost everyone's enthusiasm.

Everyone, that is, except my cameraman, Steve Mongeau. A few min-utes past midnight on Wednesday morning, long after the rest of us were fast asleep, Mongeau casually told our host, Rod Benson, that he was going to drive out to check on the Russians. Before Rod could warn him about driving out on the fractured ice, Mongeau was gone. Thinking that the special barricades put up to limit access to the ice would be unmanned at such a late hour, Mongeau figured this might be his last chance to take his camera far out on the ice without being hassled.

Driving alone and without a weapon to protect against bears, several more of which were spotted earlier that day, Mongeau headed out past NARL, and around the gravel cul-de-sac. At the roundabout's far end, he plunged over the frozen dirt abutment and onto Elson Lagoon, the most heavily traveled ice road to the whales. Four rescuers tending the whales watched the rapid approach of Mongeau's vehicle with alarm. The closer Mongeau got, the faster he seemed to be going. By design, he was driving straight toward the open water channel, but if he didn't slow down soon, he would fatally plow straight into it.

Cindy looked on in shocked disbelief as Mongeau drove right past her. When the channel finally came into view, he knew that the worst thing he could do was slam on the breaks. If he did, the truck would skid uncontrolla-bly. Instead, he deftly swerved the truck away from Cindy and the open water channel. When the truck spun to a stop and she was satisfied the driver was safe, Cindy's fear turned to fury. She ran over to confront whoever was reck-less enough to nearly kill himself and four innocent bystanders.

"There are no vehicles allowed on the ice," she barked. "What's your name? I'm going to report you."

"To who?" Mongeau answered in jest. "The Russians, or the Americans?"

Mongeau knew he had driven carelessly and wasn't about to deny it. But to get kicked off the ice would spoil his one chance to get night video of the icebreakers. If he picked a fight with Cindy, he knew he would lose. He tried the best tactic he knew: his skillful look of youthful innocence. He tucked his beardless chin into his chest and pretended to reach for words that wouldn't come out.

"Look, I'm reeeelly soooory," he added, intentionally emphasizing his thick Canadian accent. "I'm just out here to take pictures. It's my job. I promise to be more careful." After ten long days of dealing with insatiable egos, Mongeau's apparently genuine contrition reaffirmed her faith in the human species. Her anger quickly turned to solicitude. She wasn't a policeman, she confided, so she couldn't stop him, but she warned him not to go any further out.

"It's for your own safety," she added for emphasis. With that, Mongeau drove away. But to Cindy's astonishment, he was heading straight for the dangerous ice she had just warned him to avoid.

"This guy's out of his mind," she said to Craig. "He's trying to kill himself." Far from it. He was just a gutsy twenty-year-old kid out to prove himself. He was determined to show that he had the right stuff to make it as a network cameraman. That required the willingness to take risks that could cost him his life. This assignment was his first big chance. It was an opportunity other young cameramen could only dream of. This was the fish he wouldn't let get away. Since arriving in Barrow, Mongeau had already risked his life hanging out of helicopters and chasing polar bears. So far it had paid off handsomely. Lots of his video had already aired in Japan and on several NBC News broadcasts. But the coup he would savor most lay just moments ahead.

Before retiring for the night, Sergei Reshetov agreed to keep his icebreaker away from the whales. Moscow promised he would only have to work one day for the Americans. One had already stretched into three. Reshetov and his tired crew were desperate to get home. So far, only the *Arseniev* had been cutting ice. The water was thought too shallow and dangerous for the larger icebreaker, which sat anchored and unused in the waters off the pressure ridge. But Master Reshetov was growing impatient.

When the *Arseniev* first sliced through the outside of the ridge, Reshetov asked the Americans for permission to bring his ship all the way to the holes. He was confident enough in his ships' sonar depth readings to risk traversing the shallow waters. The *Arseniev* could crush in an hour what would take the Eskimos another two days to cut through. But the Americans said no. Not so much for the shallow waters, but for the safety of the whales. Cindy and Arnold worried that the whales would be too frightened to enter the breaker channels and perhaps even retreat into older breathing holes.

Reshetov was tired of relying on the Americans. While he wanted the whales freed, he also wanted to go home. He waited until he thought everyone had cleared the ice. At just past 3 A.M., Wednesday, October 26, nineteen days after the whales were first discovered, Master Sergei Reshetov ordered the *Vladimir Arseniev*'s helmsman to propel the massive ship forward in a bold, headlong dash toward the whales.

But before issuing the controversial command, Reshetov weighed the risks. He knew he was about to violate standing orders from the Americans not to come too close to the whales. He also knew that the closer his ship could get, the less distance the Eskimos would need to cover with their chain saws. If he got too close to the whales, he ran the risk of running them over. He also realized he was giving the Americans no warning of his daring plan.

What the Soviet captain did not know was that a young Canadian cameraman was alone on the ice that cold dark night on an intuitive hunch that something newsworthy might happen. The Canuck photographer's hunch paid off. His was the only camera to capture Reshetov's intrepid adventure. Ignoring rumbling warnings from the shaking frozen floor beneath him, Mongeau got out and walked to within yards of the ship's massive hull. He captured from remarkably close range the powerful sights and grinding sounds of the icebreaker's overwhelming force as it crushed its way toward the stranded whales.

His next shots were among the best of the entire rescue. Lying prone with his camera right down on the ice, Mongeau framed a shot of the two gray whales surfacing frantically in the foreground while the daunting bow of the massive icebreaker loomed dramatically in the background. For the first time since the American public became obsessed with them almost two weeks earlier, the trapped mammals looked tiny. Compared to the monstrous vessel towering right over them, they were. Slipping perilously down a rocking ice floe knee deep into the frigid water, Mongeau was shaken enough not to further press his luck.

23

Free at Last

First light Wednesday morning revealed icebreaker channels just 400 yards from the two surviving whales. If anybody had questions as to how it happened, they could ask Steve Mongeau. He had the only footage. With cunning, poise, and talent, the twenty-year-old Canadian had more than proved he belonged in this business. He had the stuff. Morris never mentioned the violation to Reshetov. The Russian captain's aggressive ice-breaking brought the whales closer than ever to freedom and with no apparent damage.

The excitement sparked by the pre-dawn developments was palpable all over town. Barrow took on a festive air. The whales would soon be free, and Operation Breakout over. But before it ended, Barrowans wanted to savor their glory. Residents no longer seemed frightened or unsure of all the visitors. They became more friendly, grateful their forced hospitality was only a temporary condition. Businesses closed down. The North Slope Borough Government office, the biggest business of them all, took the after-noon off. For the first time since the rescue began, classes were dismissed early. Word spread that the whales would be free by nightfall.

Local teachers acquiesced when the students clambered for one last chance to see the creatures that helped put their tiny village on the map. By the hundreds, Barrowans, young and old, went to bid the whales farewell. But once they got there, they seemed more fascinated by the media than by the cetacean duo. After all, whales were much more common. They saw them all the time and ate their meat at every meal. By mid-afternoon, the line of parked vehicles along the ice looked like a misplaced crowd awaiting a space shuttle launch off Cape Canaveral. Dozens of pickup trucks, vans and cars sat with engines idling, Eskimos chattering animatedly in their native Inupiat. Suddenly and without warning, Siku, the larger of the two surviving whales, vanished.

Poutu, the other whale continued to surface normally in the last hole. Malik and Arnold were stumped. Unlike Bone, who vanished under the ice five days earlier, Siku was the strongest and most vibrant of the three whales. The instant Siku was discovered missing, Malik knew something significant was about to happen. Without explanation to others around him, his dark Eskimo face beamed with a new revelation. He dropped his seal pole and lumbered to the icebreaker's channel just a few hundred yards away. Craig looked at Arnold as if pleading for an explanation. At the same instant, they dropped their poles and raced to Malik. They simultaneously figured out what he was doing. He was waiting for Siku to pop his head through the ice-littered channel.

If Siku did appear in the channel, he might not be so easy to see. The channel was six miles long and up to a quarter mile wide. But of one thing Malik was almost certain. Siku must be somewhere in the channel. Malik yanked down on the bill of his bright red baseball cap in a nervous habit acquired over five decades of whaling. As he scanned the water for a sign of the missing whale, he held up a thickly calloused hand to further shield his eyes against the blinding glare of the daylight bouncing off the Arctic ice. Through the sharp ice shards floating in the man-made channel, Siku's head appeared.

Surfacing in the water's wide expanse, the huge whale seemed suddenly small and frightened. Its vulnerability underscored the many traumas it had endured. Defying human logic, Siku reached the channel by swimming under nearly a quarter mile of ice. For the first time since it was found nineteen days earlier, the whale was swimming in broken ice. Despite Siku's battered condition, the newly gathered crowd was elated. The whale was in the channel, the home stretch.

The Eskimos let out the cheer reserved for the most joyous of all occasions: the catching of a bowhead whale. Arnold embraced Malik as if he just returned from a successful whaling mission. Eleven days earlier, at the specially-convened whalers' meeting, Malik convinced Arnold and other young whalers that the whole exercise might well be a mission for Inupiat survival. If the Eskimos could convince the world that they really did depend on an animal they revered for tens of thousands of years, then maybe the world might start to understand. As the whales were about to be freed, Malik's theory could begin the test of time.

Locals, rescuers, and reporters frantically tried to reach the suddenly distant whale. While still within the purview of Operation Breakout, Siku, the lead whale, was finally alone, far from the gentle hand of a well-wisher and no longer dependent upon a tiny machine flown in from Minnesota. The lead whale experienced its first moments of liberation, trying to navigate its way through the dangers of the icy sharp waters, removed from its human protectors. Siku's reunification with its natural environment must have been a difficult adjustment.

Poutu, the lone whale remaining in the hand-cut opening, bobbed frantically up and down. Maybe Poutu was reacting to Siku's underwater moans and squeaks. Perhaps through the gray whale's highly sophisticated and poorly understood method of communication, Poutu knew where Siku was. Poutu took one last long breath and vanished deep beneath the water. Moments later, the smaller whale surfaced within yards of its leader. It, too, had swum under the quarter mile of ice and emerged in the icebreaker channel. At the rate the two whales were swimming, they would be gone by morning. If all went well, the two whales would arrive in California at the end of January 1989, just about the same time as the man who gave the rescue his official blessing: President Ronald Reagan.

Bonnie Mersinger insisted that Colonel Carroll contact her the moment it looked like the whales were free. The White House was anxious to make the announcement that the operation was finally over. The whales had become the comic obsession of the humor-starved White House press corps. Each morning at the daily briefing, the customarily stuffy and self-absorbed White House correspondents bombarded spokesman Marlin Fitzwater with tongue-in-cheek questions about the geopolitical implications of the latest earth-stopping developments emanating from the Barrow

ice pack. Fitzwater reveled in the levity and promised to have the last
laugh.

Late Wednesday morning, Alaska time, Carroll called Bonnie to relay
the rescue's latest intelligence. The whales were almost free. Bonnie ran
excitedly through the corridors of the West Wing to tell Fitzwater the good
news. The whales were free. So certain did the news seem, Fitzwater thought
the time arrived to cash in on his promise. The amiable press secretary
grinned mischievously. "The whales are free," he exulted with outstretched
arms.

The gathered press burst into spontaneous applause. Who says the cynical press are heartless? To those reporters assigned to cover the West Wing,
Operation Breakout seemed over. The misconception was short lived. Colonel Carroll called Bonnie a few minutes later to tell her the bad news: The
whales were not yet free. Close, but not yet.

"I don't know if you're religious," he asked her, "but if you are, I suggest
you pray to whichever god you believe in." The next day, Fitzwater commented that humble pie was always his favorite.

Ever since the Russians announced they were on the way, the rescue
command discussed what to do if it appeared the whales would survive.
Should they tag or follow them, and if so, how? Now that the whales were
in the channel, the rescuers had both their first and last opportunity to tag
them to monitor their progress. Aside from the staggering problems of
electronic tagging, which made tracking all but impossible, Ron Morris
and the other rescuers faced an ethical problem even larger.

Was it "right" to tag the whales after all they had gone through just to
satisfy the curiosity of an obsessed world? Ron Morris wanted to keep his
options open. The two biologists he flew in from Seattle were experts at
tagging marine mammals and always carried the tags with them in the
event the decision was made to use them. After all that man had done for
the whales, it was the least the whales could do in return, wasn't it?

Tagging a marine mammal, particularly one that weighed 50,000 pounds,
was no easy task. For the electronic device to work properly it had to be
shot deep into the small of the whale's back with a crossbow by an expert
archer. But that opportunity never presented itself when the whales were in
the holes. When confined to the small holes, the whales had only enough
room to expose their heads. But even in the channel, where the whales

started to surface normally, the chances were slim that the cumbersome devices could be properly implanted. It was also likely that the procedure could further stress the whales. Unlike radio transmitters attached to land animals, tagging marine mammals was extremely expensive and very unreliable. It was a new, unrefined technology. The waterproof radio transmitters only worked for about a month and required aircraft with special detection equipment to track them. In the ice-choked waters of the Arctic, tags probably wouldn't have stayed on the whales for more than a few days.

But beneath all the rationalizations lay an unspoken explanation for not tagging the whales. The whales' long-term prospects for survival were limited. It was very late in the season to be starting the migratory swim south. The whales were weakened by their ordeal. Ron Morris had to ask how the public would respond if the transmitters were found a week later in the belly of a polar bear? More importantly, what would that mean to NOAA, the agency that stood to gain so much from one of its greatest public achievements? What would happen to that fattened budget allocation about which NOAA bureaucrats were already licking their chops?

If the whales weren't tagged, the world would never know what really happened to them. Since a long and arduous journey lay ahead, maybe it was a good thing no one would find out; just the stuff of which legends are made. It worked. What we didn't know and would never learn didn't spoil a great story.

Together again, the two whales swam toward the open lead some three miles through the channel. As quickly as the whales dashed through the ice littered water, news of the great escape engulfed the press corps. It sounded like the last chance to see the whales before they pounded unencumbered flukes in the open lead en route to California. The whales stopped dead in their tracks as the commotion on the ice mounted. It was as if they suddenly became aware that once they crossed into the open lead, they would leave the blanket which draped them with protection for nearly three weeks.

Ron Morris's concern grew with the number of well-wishers who crowded the ice for their last glimpse of the whales. His first step was the most drastic. Over his walkie-talkie, he instructed everyone to immediately evacuate the area. He ordered all air traffic to stay at least four miles away from the channel and to fly above one thousand feet. As darkness fell, a wave of anticipation swept across Barrow, catching up residents, reporters and rescuers alike. They all might well have seen the last of the whales. Nevertheless, Morris wanted Reshetov to stay overnight just in case.

After almost two sleepless weeks, the anxiety and irritability showed in the glassy eyes of almost everyone. The pressure fell hardest on Ron Morris, the coordinator and the man ultimately responsible for the rescue. When his order to evacuate the ice was openly flaunted, Morris lost his temper. In its final hour, he could do nothing but watch as his authority was yanked from under him. Ron Morris wasn't the only one whose neck was on the chopping block. The same was true for us. Reporters came to Barrow to record the rescue. As it reached its climax, so too did our coverage. The United States Secret Service could not have kept us off the ice, let alone Ron Morris. Nevertheless, he fruitlessly sought to rein us in. He was at the end of his rope, his exasperation apparent to everyone.

Morris called for reinforcements. Mayor George Ahmaogak, back in town for Operation Breakout's conclusion, agreed to a special deployment of the North Slope borough policemen to help National Guard units guard the common ice entry points. But it would take two divisions to properly patrol fifty miles of frozen coastline and interdict the dozens of ski machines and automobiles intent on running the blockade.

Morris's edict extended to the rescuers themselves. But even his own underlings ignored him. Cindy, Geoff, and Craig had not worked so hard for so long to leave the whales at the rescue's critical last juncture. For two weeks they had risked their lives to help the stranded creatures, and they certainly weren't about to stop now. They were not out to humiliate Morris. All they cared about was the whales. The trapped animals would never have made it this far without their help. Greg and Rick with their deicers, Arnold Brower Jr. and a skeleton crew of Eskimos, joined them to keep the last few holes ice-free in case the whales were forced back by a frozen channel.

That night, around 10 P.M., Ron Morris was socializing at Media Central, the lobby of the Top of the World Hotel, when he learned the extent of his own emasculation. He overheard someone mention that Cindy and "the others" were still out with the whales. The lateness of the hour combined with exhaustion and one too many highballs triggered the penultimate tantrum. He stormed out of the Top of the World and into his running truck, crimson with fury. Gunning the sensitive engine, he drove to his nearest check point. En route, he shouted invectives over his radio to everyone assigned to listen.

Top members of the command monitored Operation Breakout's frequency on a twenty-four-hour basis, but anyone working was supposed to have their radios turned on. Geoff, Craig, Arnold, and Cindy were no exception. Their radios were in perfect working order. They worked, perhaps too well.

"Get those damned Eskimos off the ice," Morris shouted as he raced onto the darkened ice. Everyone heard it. Everywhere, the reaction was the same. The SAR hangar command center fell dead silent. Randy Crosby searched for a face that could tell him he didn't hear what he knew he had. Instead, his eyes met Tom Carroll's. The colonel shrugged his shoulders, and lowered his head in embarrassed disbelief. It was the Eskimos for whom these two white men felt the deepest regret.

There were only about twenty people authorized to use the frequencies assigned to Operation Breakout. But almost everyone listened. Curious locals and news hungry reporters tuned in around the clock to follow the latest developments. To both rescuers and reporters, the two-way radio was an indispensable tool. For many of the Operation's key personnel, it was a lifeline. Malik, for instance, didn't have a telephone. The radio was the only way for the command to reach him. He was sitting alone after another long day quietly drinking a cup of green tea at Sam & Lee's Chinese restaurant on Nachick Street. He nearly choked when he heard the defamation blurted out over his radio.

Malik was stunned. He had argued for cooperating with the charade. He convinced others to approve rescuing the whales rather than harvesting them. He argued that Barrow stood to gain by helping free the whales. Morris's eight unforgettable words ran the risk of undoing everything Malik had worked for. Malik didn't know how to express his frustration, but he was hardly so fragile as to be undone by intemperate words. Malik took a deep drag from his stale cigarette and turned his radio off.

On the ice, it was Arnold Brower Jr., the probable target of the unfortunate slur, who took to calming Geoff, Craig, and Cindy. His reaction was the same as Malik's. Did non-Inuit's really think that Eskimo's were so brittle as to be broken by some stupid sentence? The anger was less toward Morris than the condescending and patronizing reaction of the self designated sensitive types.

Just how weak did the white man think Inupiats were, Brower wondered. He calmly walked over to Geoff and Craig and turned off their radios. Then he pulled his own walkie-talkie out of his parka pocket, depressed the transmit button to respond to Morris: "It's out of your hands now." Without waiting for a response, he clicked off the radio. Getting back to work, Arnold wouldn't let the others even discuss the thoughtless remark.

They had a job to do, he reminded them. If he could hum along to the tune of the indignity, then so could they. The three worked silently on, none discussing what they all were thinking. A faint beam of light caught their attention. The closer it got, the angrier they became. They were watching the headlights of a vehicle driven by the man who had just offended them so deeply, a man who at that moment had no idea of the extent of damage he inflicted upon himself. The beam caught the four transfixed figures standing against a backdrop of the brightly lit deck of *Vladimir Arseniev*. Morris jumped out and slammed the door behind him. As he walked toward the defiant rescuers he could make out their expressions of feigned disinterest.

"What the hell do you think you're doing?" he shouted. "I said no one is to be on this ice." He ducked his head slightly before realizing his vulnerability.

"You just don't get it, do you?" Arnold asked Morris, in an earnest attempt to embarrass him. Craig and Geoff pretended to ignore the presence of the man who was clouding them in such shame. Cindy fought to contain her tears. By betraying the others, Morris had betrayed her. Knowing he had lost Brower, Morris turned to Craig to see if the biologist would still obey him. Nothing aggravated his insecurity more than being ignored. It wasn't revenge that dictated Craig's reaction. It was fear, fear that he couldn't control his anger, that he would lash out with his fists at his small, rakishly bearded adversary. His emotion would have propelled a blow with potentially dangerous force. He had to restrain himself, but it wasn't easy. Morris kept pushing, looking for the reaction that would vindicate his own outburst.

"It's them, isn't it," Morris asked, pointing an accusing finger at the stoic figure of Arnold Brower. "That's all you care about." Morris had stumbled upon a theme he was determined to pound home as best he could.

"That's the only reason you're here. It's all this 'Inupiat power' crap, isn't it? 'Hooray for the Eskimo' You can admit it. All you care about is making sure they look good," he shouted, his finger still pointing at Brower. "You've been on their side since the beginning."

"Shut up," Cindy shrieked. Cindy thought of Geoff, Craig, and Arnold as the indispensable triad that kept the whales alive. More than that, what she refrained from saying, she didn't refrain from thinking. They were heroes and she loved them. Cindy was appalled by Morris's attacks.

Even after all the anger Morris aroused in him, Craig put aside his anger when he saw Cindy in tears. First it was Arnold calming Craig and Geoff who were furious at the slight of their Eskimo friend. Now Craig did the same for Cindy who was devastated by Morris's confrontation. Using an English translation of an Eskimo expression Cindy didn't understand at first, Arnold instructed the two of them to "feel light." He wanted them to release a mystical weight that held down the human spirit. Cindy's empathy released an energy of warmth connecting the four together as one. Their unity had been immeasurably enhanced by the adversity thrust upon them. In the minds of those he thought he ruled, Ron Morris no longer existed.

Did they sense the human drama unfolding around them? The whales pushed on. Suddenly, they no longer seemed subject to the limitations of their own species. The whales followed the powerful beam of light from the deck of the Soviet icebreaker. To the astonishment of the whale biologists, the animals swam through water littered with jagged chunks of ice. Remaining doubts about the whales' willingness to take risks to achieve their freedom were shattered.

On Thursday morning, the whales were paying the price for their unexpected boldness. Arnold Brower was the first to discover them gasping for breath in a small hole kept open by butting their heads through the ice debris. They were bleeding. The ocean water steamed from the pools of warm blood gushing in it. They could barely manage to push their red, battered snouts through the ice that had formed overnight. The skin around their sensitive breathing holes was tender and sore. The whales seemed so close to freedom just hours before. Now they listed on the verge of death.

Before he could radio the news back to SAR headquarters, Brower noticed that a small piece of ice was stuck in Siku's blowhole. The more deeply the whale breathed, the wider the blowhole opened. But that only made the problem worse. The wider the blowhole opened, the more firmly lodged the piece of ice became.

Arnold jumped off his parked ski machine and ran out toward the edge of the ice. Looking across the wide channel, he knew the whale would die if it wasn't helped. He immediately probed the ice covering the newly refrozen channel. It was already thick enough to support not only him but his snowmobile. He turned off his radio the instant he heard the voice of Ron Morris exhorting him to get off the ice. Neither Morris nor anyone else had the slightest idea what was going on out on the ice and Arnold didn't have the time to explain it.

When he reached the struggling whales, Arnold scrambled on his belly to the edge of the hole, pulled off his gloves, and extended his outstretched hand toward the whale's obstructed blowholes.

He gently stroked the tender area to reassure the whale that he meant no harm. Apparently reassured by the Eskimo hunter's touch, the whale remained long enough for Brower to dislodge the ice. He reached his bare hand into the tender cavity and grabbed the chunk of ice. The whale writhed in pain as he pulled it out of its raw, bleeding orifice. In the intensity of his efforts to aid the choking whale, Brower didn't even notice that Malik was right beside him, caught up in a breathless race to enlarge the small hole. Malik fished chunks of floating ice from the frigid water with his gloveless hands and pitched them over his head. Malik skated across the refrozen channel to retrieve a shovel and seal pole from the back of his ski machine. The two Eskimo whalers expanded the hole until both animals could breathe safely again.

Less than a mile from the open lead and freedom, the whales were once again confined to a tiny, frightful hole. Nonetheless, the two whales made remarkable progress through the lead before they got stuck in the frozen water. Overnight, the whales swam through almost two miles of the channel. Arnold and Malik knew that if new holes weren't opened soon, the crisis their bare hands just alleviated would soon recur. Arnold switched on his walkie-talkie and radioed an urgent appeal for five chain saw crews to get on the ice as soon as possible. He and Malik decided to fall back on the only tactic that worked. Now that the pressure ridge was sliced away, the native crews could easily cut holes parallel to the channel, protecting the whales from its brutal conditions. If everyone were mobilized for a total and final push, the holes could be dug in a few hours.

Brower went right over Ron Morris's head to summon his own crews. He made his own decision without bothering to consult the man who was ostensibly his boss. Morris didn't overlook the insubordination. By early that morning, everyone had heard the horrible tale of the previous night's debacle. But that event appeared to have little effect. Morris lost his temper. He was willing to admit that much. But that changed nothing. He was still coordinator, and in his mind, his word was law. He reached for his radio and repeated his unenforceable declaration that no one was allowed on the ice. Only when his orders were flagrantly countermanded by his own subordinates did the nightmare sink in. His authority had been completely emasculated in the eyes of those he commanded.

Just minutes after their arrival, the first crew sawed open a new hole. Brower wasted no time waiting for the whales to make the discovery on their own. He flipped around the ends of his seal pole and shoved the blunt end in the water. He gently poked the whales so as to annoy them enough to leave the hole. After a few less than comfortable jolts to the mid-section, the whales got the message and headed toward the only haven they saw: the new Eskimo hole. For the time being at least, the whales were safe.

Morris raced out to the whales yet again in another mistaken attempt to confront Brower. When he arrived, he found the Eskimo and his crew working frantically to open new holes for the whales. No matter how he ranted and raved, Morris couldn't seem to get Brower's attention. Brower just kept digging while trying to ignore the sounds as though they came from an errant pest.

Finally, as if to swat it away, he lifted his eyes from the holes on which they were focused. He glared piercingly into Morris's eyes before he quietly uttered the same words he used only hours before. "It's out of your hands." He withdrew his gaze and returned to his task. The message was clear. If he knew what was good for him, Morris would not challenge Brower or his men again. Morris got the message and withdrew to safer terrain, the SAR hangar.

From there he contacted Sergei Reshetov aboard the *Vladimir Arseniev*. The Russian captain didn't need to remind Morris how anxious the Soviets were to get home. Reshetov also did not have to be told about what was happening on the ice. All he had to do was peer down from his perch eight stories above it. Surprising even to him, the channels his ship plowed through just twelve hours before had frozen over solid. He knew his ship's job wasn't done. There were more passes to be made before he could get home.

By noon, the *Arseniev* wasn't alone. Bill Allen had climbed in the cockpit of his oddly named screw tractor and planted a huge American flag atop the cab. Amid cheers, Allen's versatile tractor plowed through the Soviet paths, spitting out smaller chunks of ice. Wrapped in the mantle of Old Glory, Allen was determined to prove his country was still the key force in the rescue. Billy Bob Allen was stealing the show.

"Oh, me," he exulted as he spun his way through the channels. A camera crew captured radiant shots of Billy Bob Allen driving the tractor like a child in his first bumper car at an amusement park.

Finally, after almost two weeks, Bill Allen himself was out. He was so excited as he twisted and turned he forgot to check his fuel gauge. When he did, it was too late. The screw tractor had run out of gas. By late afternoon, standing atop his idled tractor, Allen exulted ebulliently as he watched the whales swimming freely in the channel he helped cut.

"Just get a load of that Archie Bowers," he said to Pete Leathard. "Mercy, that son of a bitch sure can work, can't he?" It was the highest compliment Allen could bestow on the Eskimo leader. Now, there was no turning back. The whales were only a few hundred yards from the lead.

Operation Breakout, cum Operation Breakthrough was a success. More than two weeks and $5.5 million later, there was nothing more to do. Eskimos, their Caucasian countrymen, and Russians had cut a ten-mile path through thick Arctic ice. All they could do was wait for the whales to do the rest. As the sun set on Thursday, October 27—twenty days after the whales were first found off Point Barrow—a wave of relief swept over everyone. Rescuers were delighted that the whales could now swim free. Billy Bob was delighted at the prospect of finally closing his hemorrhaging checkbook, and reporters were anxious to go home.

Thursday night, Morris gave what he promised would be his final press conference. While not absolutely sure, Geoff, Craig, and the other biologists were reasonably certain that shortly after dark, the whales would slip through the last vestiges of the channel and enter the unfettered waters of the open lead. Their Barrow misadventure behind them, the whales were almost surely free. At first light, Friday morning, Randy Crosby flew the final mission. Flying twenty miles up and down the lead, he saw not a trace. The whales were gone.

Fittingly, Malik was the last American to see the two whales before darkness. Petting Siku good-bye, he wished the two creatures the luck he knew they would need to survive on their long voyage. Ordinary gray whales would be hard pressed to make it through the multiple dangers that lay ahead. Treacherous ice floes extended for several hundred miles along Alaska's northern and western rims. Next, there were pods of killer whales waiting for weak and wounded prey. And finally, if they made it that far, the whales would have to dance through minefields of great white sharks lurking off the coast of the Pacific Northwest in search of weakened prey.

But these whales had proven themselves anything but ordinary. These whales touched hundreds of millions of hearts and captivated the fickle attention of a self-obsessed world. They brought together people, industries, and nations in a way man himself never could. If only for a fortnight, the three whales were at the center of the world. They were history's most fortunate creatures.

Lucky whales.

24

Consequences

Success or not, the media dubbed Friday, October 28, Operation Break-out's final day. If, at first light, the whales still hadn't left the ice pack, we defiantly resolved that we would. We phoned our loved ones, told them the story was over, and booked flights home.

Everyone agreed. There was nothing more to be done. Now that the pressure ridge no longer barred the whales from entering the open channel of water, the whales remained the only obstacle to their own freedom. We desperately tried to convince our assignment editors that the rescue's human aspect had concluded. From every indication, the American people were tiring of the story. They, too, had seen enough. If ever Operation Breakout gave the media and the world a chance to cut and run, this seemed the moment.

But when Malik discovered the lead whale Siku nearly frozen in the icebreaker's paths on Thursday morning, Barrow was overwhelmed by feelings of frustration. On Wednesday night, October 26, the whales seemed free. But the next morning, they once again demonstrated their penchant for getting stuck. The same faulty genes that trapped them the first time did it again. The whales could not find their way out of the icebreaker channel before it froze solid overnight. Instead of finally beginning their migration, they became stranded in yet another tiny hole. It seemed like the whole mess was starting all over again. Fortunately for the whales and the weary media, the Russians remained one final night. The whales at last slipped through the channels to open water sometime early Friday morning when the icebreakers returned to clear new pathways through the ice.

After almost two weeks at twenty degrees below zero, there was just no more left to give. From its outset, Operation Breakout was nothing more than an artificial enterprise, created not for the whales or their species, but for the media. Like any other news story, Operation Breakout needed a beginning, a middle, and, most important, an end. If it appeared that the rescue would continue indefinitely, that most critical criterion would be violated. But of course, the very notion of the rescue operating in a vacuum was absurd. The media was the rescue.

The contrast to Operation Breakout's final hours could not have been more striking. Barrow was the Arctic equivalent to Saigon right before the fall. People were desperate to get out.

It wasn't the NVA we feared, but Barrow itself. Don Oliver, a veteran of that frantic Indochina exodus, worked just as busily to get out of Barrow. He was helping his video editor, Steve Shim, pack all of NBC's equipment when the phone rang. It was NBC's Los Angeles bureau. Immediately, Oliver knew he wasn't going to like what he was about to hear. Oliver rejoiced in his industry nickname, El Diablo. Remarkably, Barrow and its endless privations had yet to ignite the temper for which he was legendary.

"We want you to stay on a couple of days," came the unsteady voice from Los Angeles. "You know, just in case the whales come back." It was so cold in Oliver's Top of the World Hotel room, you could almost see steam pour out of his ears. The thought of still another day in Barrow made Oliver long for Saigon, April 1975. Watching his colleagues head for warmer climes pushed Oliver over the edge. El Diablo was about to erupt.

"In case they come back?" he shrieked incredulously, his face crimson. "We're booked on the 12:30 flight and we're not going to miss it. The whales are gone, gone, gone. They aren't coming back, and if they do, that will be their problem, not mine! You got that?"

The hotel's entire first floor fell silent. This was an impressive display of rage, even for the master himself. Maybe he was out for a personal best, his producer Jerry Hansen joked. We could all sympathize. Oliver, like the rest of us, had served his time. Why was his sentence extended when all other prisoners at Barrow Correctional were being paroled?

Harry Chittick, the ABC producer, walked toward us from the far end of the hall seemingly unfazed by Don Oliver's deafening outburst. Like the rest of us, he had a plane to catch. As he passed Oliver's open door, none of us spoke. We wondered how Chittick would handle the delicate situation. Would he slip quietly past, pretending to ignore the erupting red-caped devil, or would he peak in to catch the master of rage in action.

Getting to the door, Chittick stopped, turned to Oliver and waved good-bye. Pausing in midtirade, Oliver turned to Chittick, flashed him a brief but warm smile, winked, stretched out his hand in a gesture of farewell, and picked up his tantrum right where he left off. Chittick laughed, hoping Oliver's latest explosion would produce the desired results. Oliver flashed Chittick a jubilant thumbs-up sign.

For Oran Caudle, it was like waking from a dream. Just hours before, he had worked frantically to keep the North Slope Borough television studio from collapsing under the strain of twenty-six demanding broadcasters barking orders in half a dozen languages. Suddenly, life hurtled back to pre-Breakout normality. There were no more network feeds, no more pushing, no more shoving and, thank God, no more shouting. For the first time in more than two weeks, Caudle turned off the North Slope Borough television transmitter. As the light on the console faded, Caudle knew another decade might pass before it was ever used again.

But Oran's work remained incomplete. He had only a few hours to convert his global communications center into a stage ready fit to host a hundred Eskimo students from Ipalook Elementary dressed as goblins and ghosts for "Fright Night 1989." The local Halloween pageant was a major annual event on Channel 20. For Barrow's youngest residents, the whales swam free in the nick of time. The whale rescue helped fulfill the electronic media's technological promise of a global village. The world had been bound together in a common, seemingly noble aim. But the minute that aim was achieved, the world went home. For all the time the media spent in Barrow, few of us stayed to reflect on our impact on that remarkable hamlet we so briefly called home.

Like life itself, Operation Breakout was born, matured and, finally, died. Its death came swiftly. The story that led newscasts from Minneapolis to Moscow and Boston to Bombay one night was not so much as mentioned the next. It was time for the world to move on. With a few hours left to kill before our flight back to the world we so desperately missed, Masu Kawamura, the Japanese correspondent, cameraman Steve Mongeau and I all drove out to Point Barrow for one last look at the site where the world had focused its attention for the last two weeks. I wondered what the endless expanse of icy terrain really looked like. Now that everyone else had left, maybe we could find out.

The only Arctic we knew was lined with cables, cords and wires. The sheet of ice we stood on for so many long hours had reverberated with the sounds of man: the buzzing of helicopters, the whine of chain saws, the hum of idle engines, the chatter of human voices.

Even the throaty "FFWWWSSSSHH" of a whale exhaling depended on man. Without him, the whales would long since have died. Except for the howl of the Arctic wind, the ice would have remained utterly still, a seemingly lifeless, frozen desert.

We crossed over the sandy hump that separated North America's most extreme tip from the stark white horizon of frozen sea for perhaps the 50th time. Yet in a remarkable way, it seemed like the first. The dense early-morning fog burned off to reveal a distant Arctic sun that shone brighter and stronger than on any of our previous trips. It cast a deceptive light of warmth where none existed.

For the first time since our arrival, the three of us felt alone. Not only was man gone, so was his every trace. His hand-cut holes were solidly refrozen. The windswept snow and thick blue ice were virtually all that colored the lifeless landscape. The only evidence of one of the most colossal events the Arctic had ever seen harkened back to the rescue's earliest days: a few rectangular blocks of ice pulled out of the water by the Eskimos before they learned to shove them under the ice shelf. There the blocks would remain until the brief Arctic summer would thaw them some months later.

As I surveyed the endless expanse of frozen void, I couldn't imagine this was the same place hundreds of people stood just hours before. It was a completely different world, a world whose reality was emphasized by the scathing bitterness and eerie howl of its biting wind. This was the world that existed before the Whales of October. This was the world that would endure.

Encumbered by thick, heavy gear, I gazed across the Arctic emptiness realizing this was as close as I would probably ever get to fulfilling my childhood dream of walking on the moon. I patiently waited for Masu and Steve to finish taking their last pictures. When they started back toward the truck, I urged them to keep going. Telling them I would be but a minute only piqued their curiosity.

At that moment, I got my reward. Once confident no one would ever see or know, I crunched the wide bottom of my boot against the dry snow and lumbered about on the Arctic Ocean's flat, frozen surface pretending I was Neil Armstrong walking on the moon.

In an odd, almost indefinable way, it seemed as though everyone involved in the rescue was bequeathed a uniquely meaningful reward. Odder still, these rewards seemed commensurate with the recipient's contribution to helping the whales. Take me, for example. I did nothing to directly help the whales. All I did was report the efforts others made to help them.

By Friday morning, October 28, 1988, one hundred and fifty journalists from four continents, the American and Soviet governments, ARCO, VECO and Greenpeace, together with two brothers-in-law from Minnesota, had spent more than $5,795,000 to see to it that two whales stranded at the top of the world could swim safely into the Arctic Ocean's last swath of ice-free water. Their efforts dwarfed not only most human rescues, but all sense of proportion.

Most biologists agreed there were likely more gray whales in October 1988 than ever before; around 22,000.

Yet all the heroics and expense served only to return two whales back to sea. If marine biologists, who guessed these particular whales may have been genetically flawed, were right, the whale rescue might have done more harm than good. There must be a reason nature wanted to be rid of these whales, they argued. Allowing them to pass their defects on to future generations might weaken the species, perhaps leading to still more whale strandings and maybe even more Operation Breakouts. The Eskimos could only hope.

In fifteen days, the three major American television network newscasts ran more than forty stories about those amazing whales, devoting nearly 10 percent of their programs' air time to coverage of the world's greatest nonevent. Even more incredibly, coverage of the rescue supplanted coverage of the climax of the 1988 presidential campaign.

The revolution in television technology allowed hundreds of millions of people to watch the rescue—more than watched Neil Armstrong walk on the moon. In the all-important television ratings book, more people than watched the single greatest achievement in the history of man watched the rescue of three trapped whales.

Even Arab terrorists were affected by the world's whale obsession. Sheik Sayyed Hussein Fadlallah, the founder of the Shiite Lebanese terror group Hezbollah complained that the West was losing its interest in ransoming his Western hostages. He was right, but, unfortunately not for long. At least Fadlallah knew he could get back on the front page whenever he wanted. All he had to do was order his Jihadi henchman to snatch or murder another innocent American, emboldened by the fact that he could carry out his latest outrage with impunity. Fadlallah knew that his latest victim's government would respond the same way it had with every other terrorist act. Call it an outrage, promise retribution, and in the end, do nothing at all.

Before the whales, television's immediacy was more likely to be associated with Lebanon's venomous snake pit than with Alaska's North Slope. A cheaply shot video of another hapless American hostage pleading his kidnappers' demands or, in the grizzly case of executed American hostage Colonel Rich Higgins, dangling from the end of a rope, seemed to be the American dinner hour's constant companion. That America would commit such tremendous resources to save three whales while doing precious little to protect its own citizens in enemy captivity could only delight Sheik Fadlallah. It certainly empowered him and the group he founded. As of this 2011 writing, Hezbollah is the defacto ruling party of Lebanon and one of the most potent terror forces in the world.

America's once legendary resolve had been reduced to saving three whales. But we couldn't even do that without asking our number one enemy to finish the job for us, a fact the United States Coast Guard used to lobby Congress to fund the construction of a third American icebreaker.

The same phenomenon that catapulted little Jessica McClure into the national spotlight two years earlier when she tumbled into a well in

Midland, Texas, propelled the whales into the national spotlight. The story was simple: either Jessica and the whales would be saved or they wouldn't. The then relevant MacNeil-Lehrer *PBS Newshour* didn't have to cross-examine a panel of experts to dissect the issue. At least not at first. Operation Breakout started because it was easy. A wind of simplicity blowing across a world made dizzy by its own complexity.

In the beginning, nothing seemed to interfere with the story, neither the facts nor the relevance. Television producers knew everybody loved whales. Greenpeace spent the past fifteen years teaching us that whales had to be saved, wherever and however they were threatened. Combine that with its slick Madison Avenue sales job, and there were the makings of a media "made-to-order-event."

Desperate Americans who clung to the premise that "whales are people too" made the rescue possible, only to learn they were much, much more. Up-close pictures of them struggling for survival transmitted instantly anywhere on earth, was dream television. Nothing sold like whales. The larger and longer the rescue became, the more millions of viewers glued themselves to their sets, sending ratings into the stratosphere.

News coverage of the whales earned the networks cheap, easy money without the inconvenience of soul-searching. Nobody liked constant bombardments of bad news. Give the people what they want. "Don't worry," went the year's Number One hit song, "be happy." It seemed too good to be true, and in the end it was.

By the time the Russians did show up, Operation Breakout had transformed itself into exactly what it was supposed not to be. America sought out the whales to escape its own reality, when in fact the whales forced America to confront it. The country's mindless lovefest turned into a healthy self-examination. We got the opposite of what we bargained for and exactly what we needed.

Washington Post columnist William Raspberry summed up the mood of the positivists when he called the three dramatic weeks a time when "the world was able to rise above its divisions of culture, competition, political ideology, and even the pursuit of money to join in a common, noble cause." Raspberry was right (maybe for the last time). But so was Sayyed Fadlallah.

Anticipating the crush of reporters anxious to get home, MarkAir scheduled a last-minute third flight out of Barrow for Friday, October 28. Euphoric Outsiders rejoicing in their Arctic liberation packed all three planes. The Eskimos' fortnight on the cusp of national recognition was sealed behind the pressurized door of that day's last flight. When the maroon and white airliner's wheels lifted off Wiley Post's snow-covered runway, Barrow was once again alone at the top of the world. The only difference to this hardy Eskimo village was that its few weeks in the limelight had put a couple of million dollars in its pocket.

The whale rescue gave the Eskimos of Barrow the chance of a lifetime, the opportunity to introduce themselves and their way of life to people around the world. For two weeks in October 1988, Barrow became the center of a world that all but ignored it. For these two weeks, the tiny Eskimo hamlet seemed transplanted to some other more accessible latitude, its eternal isolation somehow suspended, its bitter elements miraculously mitigated. This illusory transformation ended with the abruptness of an Arctic wind. Barrow picked up its timeless pace just where it left off.

Winter was fast on its way. While the October rescue turned out to be the coldest experience most Outsiders would ever live through, to the Eskimos it was nothing but a late autumn nip. To them, their winter didn't officially start until November 17, the day the sun slipped below the horizon, not to rise again for two and a half months. November 17 was the first of a sixty-seven daylong night.

The year 1988–89 brought more than the customary darkness and bitter cold. It also brought the coldest and longest winter ever recorded in North America.

I went back to Barrow in January 1989, along with my colleague Michael Richardson to take a second look at the place. As I stepped off the plane that dangerously cold January noon, I felt as if I had never been there before. Pitch-dark at high noon.

January in Barrow made me yearn for the halcyon days of October. An ambient temperature of minus fifty-eight degrees was Barrow's way of saying Welcome Back. Nostrils and eyelids froze on contact with the cold. So too did just about everything else. Spit froze in mid-air, clattering when it hit the ground. But Barrow was lucky. It was on the coast. Just a few miles inland, temperatures dropped to eighty degrees below zero. Dick Mackey, two-time Iditarod Trail Sled Dog Race champion, logged the coldest temperature ever recorded in North America at his truck stop in Cold Foot, Alaska, 250 miles south of Prudhoe Bay on January 21, 1989: minus eighty-two degrees. It sure didn't feel like a record, Mackey said. It was just the first time the U.S. Weather Service gave his official station a thermometer that went below minus eighty degrees.

Isolation and depression hung over Barrow like the permanent bank of ice fog which blanketed that forlorn outpost nine months of the year. The days of Barrow's prominence seemed as remote as an ancient whaling epic. Did Barrow always seem hopeless and remote? I asked. "Nope," Barrowans demurred, as if astonished anyone could reach my conclusion. "This is normal."

The press's relentless coverage of the nonevent touched people all over the world. No matter where in the world I traveled in the next few months, almost every person I met was well versed in the plight of the whales. The whales had become celebrities.

Cindy Lowry's reward was obvious. The whales were free. Single-handedly, she catapulted the whales from Arctic isolation to global stardom. Because of her, the California grays turned into the luckiest whales that ever lived. History's most massive animal rescue was waged on their behalf.

Greenpeace turned whale-saving into a cash cow. Their dynamo Alaska field coordinator started not just a mammoth rescue, but the biggest source of new money and members in the organization's history. Operation Breakout was an unexpected cash cow. Memberships and contributions shot up 400 percent in the rescue's aftermath, the greatest single increase up to its time.

Biologists and naturalists far removed from the scene at first claimed there was no way the whales could be spared from a fate they deemed inextricable. As progress pushed the leviathans closer to that very possibility, the distant, dispassionate scientists discarded their mistaken theories. The scientists were wrong and the whole world knew it. In an attempt to salvage their credibility, they "refined" their views.

Even if the whales could get past the pressure ridge, naturalist Roger Caras tried convincing Ted Koppel on ABC's *Nightline*, they could never surmount the myriad obstacles that separated them from their breeding grounds off Mexico's Pacific coastline. Since the whales weren't tagged for monitoring, no one could ever prove Caras wrong.

And that was just what NOAA wanted. Shortly after the rescue, the National Oceanographic and Atmospheric Administration printed up colorful brochures and passed them out to whale boat tour operators on the Pacific Coast helping sightseers identify Siku and Poutu. No damage could come its way. If the whales were found, NOAA would be vindicated, if they weren't, there would still be no proof the animals weren't enjoying their anonymity in the wet beyond.

To those who spent time with the whales, even people like me who knew little about them, it was clear this trio possessed something special. Of the untold thousands of gray whales who have died in ice strandings throughout history, these were the ones that united the world. That alone made them unique.

But there was more. After twenty-one days of frozen confinement, the two surviving whales conquered more than ice-covered seas. They transcended the perceived bounds of their own species. Before the rescue, scientists believed that gray whales would not be able to swim through icy waters, even to save their lives. After two weeks of proving the scientists right, the whales in the end proved them wrong. Changing our perceptions of them forever, the two whales battered and bloodied themselves in the ice-thick water, knowing it was life's only route.

Before the rescue, science could offer no evidence that gray whales' behavior could be modified. Unlike the killer whale, the gray whales could not be trained. There would never be any gray Shamus. But from the moment the deicers were dropped to do their Minnesota magic in the new Eskimo holes, the whales were active participants in their own rescue. If any two whales on earth could overcome the obstacles encountered clearing Barrow's ice pressure ridge, these were the whales to do it, Roger Caras and his predictions of doom notwithstanding. Science was rewarded with evidence that gray whales were even more intelligent than previously thought.

The millions of people who watched the whale saga got one of two rewards. They were either overjoyed at the whales' freedom because they genuinely wished them well, or they were just so sick of hearing about them that they were relieved it was finally over.

The whales gave Vice President Bush a chance to jab Michael Dukakis: "I just hope they don't end up in Boston Harbor," the nation's most polluted big city waterway, in Dukakis' state. For Michael Dukakis, the whales' freedom presented his self- destructing campaign with a Catch-22. At first, the Massachusetts governor's staff must have welcomed all the attention focused on the whales' crisis instead of their own. But when the story never ended, there was less time until the election, time they desperately needed to make up for blowing the huge lead they had as recently as Labor Day. The inept Dukakis campaign had to get back in the headlines. When it finally did, it was more bad news. Dukakis' dirty tricks manager John Sasso, fired then rehired for the same reason—his mastery of political dirty tricks—probably wished for the biggest trick of all: re-stranding the whales.

For Ben Odom, the senior vice-president of ARCO Alaska and one of the rescue's two biggest financiers, the rescue proved fortuitous. Soon after the whales swam free, the thirty-five-year ARCO veteran retired, just in time to leave on one of the industry's rarest and highest notes. His oil company had helped save two whales and softened the hearts of environmentalists everywhere.

Just six months after the rescue's final news story, Alaska, once America's most isolated state, was back in the news again. This time, the story was only too real.

At 9 P.M., March 24, 1989, the *Exxon Valdez*, a 987-foot supertanker, left the port whose name she bore en route to Long Beach, California. On board were more than fourteen million gallons of grade A North Slope crude oil pumped down from Prudhoe Bay through the billion-dollar 825-mile-long Trans-Alaskan pipelne.

After changing to an inbound shipping lane to avoid a glacial ice floe, Captain Joe Hazelwood turned over command of his vessel to Third Mate Gregory Cousins. It was 11:50 P.M. Eighteen minutes later, Captain Hazelwood and the rest of the sleeping crew were jolted awake by a terrific screech which rang through the giant vessel as it struck a shoal just a few hundred yards west of Bligh Island.

The oil industry had spent the past twenty-one years warning Alaskans that supertankers were much more dangerous than pipelines. However, that lesson has not been needed, neither with the *Exxon Valdez* nor, apparently, any of the literally hundreds of tanker spills since.

In a calculated attempt to escape liability, Exxon blamed it all on Captain Hazelwood. For months, the company succeeded in convincing nearly everyone that Hazelwood was drunk at the time of the accident. In fact, there was no evidence to support the Exxon charge, an allegation every crew member denied. Ten hours after the accident, Hazelwood's blood alcohol level was higher than the Coast Guard legal limit but below the Alaska driving limit. Toxicologists said it was likely that Hazelwood reached his test levels by alcohol ingested after the accident, not before.

Just six months after glowing from their greatest public high, the oil industry was reeling from its deepest low. The good will they worked so hard to generate in October drowned in eleven million gallons of solidifying oil that oozed its way down Alaska's coast.

The extent of the environmental damage predicted by the experts was thankfully highly exaggerated. While much sea life died, how much was never known. What was known was that the sound and its rich commercial fisheries recovered far faster and more completely than anyone expected.

Among the potential victims were the very whales Alaskan oil titans ARCO and VECO expended themselves to save. More ominously, Exxon also endangered more than two-thirds of the entire gray whale species that swam through the Sound to and from Mexico. With the food chain poisoned, biologists could only hope that genetic mutations caused by the toxins would not be passed on as permanent species changes. The biggest company in the industry that worked so hard to save three whales was now accused of endangering the entire species. Exxon got its due, with costs run into the billions, but unfortunately at the whales' expense.

The oilman's nightmare became the newsman's dream. Lambasted by a late-waking American public, the press returned to Alaska in a big way. Coverage of the disaster dwarfed that of the whale rescue, as it should have. Many of the same reporters assigned to Barrow in October packed their bags in a similar rush to head to another Alaskan port of call, Valdez, a thousand miles south of Barrow. That was the reporters' reward.

Sitting in VECO's Anchorage headquarters on Sunday, October 30, all Billy Bob Allen could do was stare at his desk calculator. Tallying up what his company just spent to save the whales, the liquid crystal displayed an astonishing figure: $350,000. How on earth had he let himself go through that much money? Shortly after the Exxon catastrophe, Allen got his reward. VECO won the prime contract to clean up the mess. The contract would soon mushroom to hundreds of millions of dollars. VECO's new image of whale-saver helped Pete Leathard, Allen's chief executive, land one of the biggest contracts in state history. If whales ever get stuck again, Leathard won't waste a minute to rustle ol' Billy Bob from his Colorado ranch.

The first environmental job Bill Allen took brought him fame, the second brought him fortune. Billy Bob Allen's environmental conversion paid off. Greenpeace whale coordinator Campbell Plowden waited nine months for his reward. On August 2, 1989, the Republic of Iceland announced a two-year moratorium on all commercial whaling. The crisis that brought Prime Minister Steingrimur Hermannsson's government to its knees half a year earlier finally became too much. Iceland could no longer fight the economic clout of an increasingly united world. Iceland had no choice but to get out of its seven-million-dollar whaling business.

No country on earth seemed more remote from Barrow, Alaska, than Iceland. It seemed the most unlikely place to become embroiled in the affairs of a place like Barrow. Yet the tiny seafaring nation perched halfway between the Old World and the New was turned on its ear by the whales of October.

While Iceland killed seventy-five whales in 1988, it also fell prey to a crippling economic boycott costing it more than $50 million, nearly four percent of the tiny nation's gross national product, the Soviets, who slaughtered more than twice as many gray whales that same year, sent two ice-breakers on a three-day diversion. The Soviets reaped praise, Iceland scorn. While serenading Moscow with cheers of "Hail the Whale Savers," the world taunted Reykjavik with jeers of "Boycott the Whale Killers."

The Soviets masterfully buried a hundred years of plunder beneath the bow of the Finnish-made *Vladimir Arseniev* while Iceland lost thousands of jobs. The Soviet Union was the hero, Iceland, the goat.

Japan, the foreign country most interested in the whale rescue, was the world's single largest whaling nation before Operation Breakout, and was the single largest whaling nation more than a year later, killing 1,200 whales in 1988 alone, almost ten times as many whales as the rest of the world combined. The rescue that captivated so many viewers from Hokaido to Honshu did nothing to stop Japan's relentless pursuit of endangered whales. Not only did Iceland quit whaling while the Russians continued, but the Soviets were rewarded just a few weeks later. The United States, still smarting from the Soviet whale rescue, rushed tens of millions of dollars worth of emergency supplies to Yerevan, the capital of Soviet Armenia, following its devastating earthquake. Channels opened just weeks before between the United States Coast Guard, the U.S. National Guard, and the Soviet Merchant Marine were used again to get as much assistance to the Soviets as quickly as possible.

But the rescue's greatest reward went to Colonel Tom Carroll and White House aide Bonnie Mersinger. After weeks of increasingly intense telephone conversations, Carroll finally went to Washington to meet the woman who had captured his heart. Passing through the tunnel separating the two United Airlines concourses en route to his connecting flight in Chicago's O'Hare Airport, the colonel found his once sturdy stomach quivering to the hypnotizing allure of the new-age music and neon light show swirling above the long moving walkway.

What was he doing, he asked himself. He called Bonnie, who managed to maintain remarkable composure when in fact she was just as anxious as he.

"Aren't you even a little nervous?" he asked her, desperately hoping she shared his angst.

"Nope," she said confidently. "I'll see you in two hours."

The nervousness she had confidently denied just a few hours before suddenly gripped her as she watched the plane carrying her beloved colonel taxi toward the gate. Maybe she had gone too far too fast. How would the seemingly staid colonel react to her welcome present: a stretch limousine waiting outside the terminal to whisk the new couple on their first steamy, skylit tour of the nation's capital. Her fears quickly vanished after a long, passionate embrace.

Tom Carroll and Bonnie Mersinger were married on August 12, 1989. They live in Anchorage where they can be seen driving a silver Maserati sporting a license plate emblazoned with dark blue letters that read: GR WHALE.

Thomas Carroll was quickly promoted to Brigadier General and realized his life's career ambition when he was named Adjutant General of the Alaska National Guard. Tragically, General Carroll was killed in a plane crash on approach to Juneau International Airport in 1992.

Two years later his widow, Bonnie, founded the Tragedy Assistance Program for Survivors, designed to help loved ones of fallen servicemen. In the intervening years, TAPS has created a national network of more than 25,000 grieving families it tries to link up with one another and with mental-health and military professionals to learn to cope with sudden death. Its work assumed national importance on September 11, 2001.

Acknowledgments

That I had the odd thought of writing a book about such a seemingly odd event wasn't odd in and of itself. What was odd was that it actually happened.

The idea first struck me on my way home from Alaska. I didn't have the first clue about where to go or how to get there. I called Rich Bock, publicity director for N.Y. News Corp. at G. S. Schwartz & Company in New York.

Not only did he call back less than two hours later with the name of an agent, but had already scheduled a dinner meeting with her that very night. "Anything else?" he asked before jumping on the crosstown bus for the Knicks game.

Margaret McBride, the perfect agent, found the perfect publisher, Hillel Black.

His most indebted nephew learned long ago, Nobody Argues with Uncle Bob, particularly when he's right.

Thanks to Suzy Tucker at Klineman, Rose and Wolf in Indianapolis for transcribing long hours of audio tape interviews.

Graciousness is a Richardson family gene. Take Michael's cousin, Nancy Bigelow. A long-lost penniless cousin shows up with an equally destitute stranger on the step of her one-room log cabin outside Fairbanks, asking just to stay one night. "No problem," Nancy offered. "Just as long as you know it's twenty miles to the nearest indoor plumbing." Almost a week later, we were still there—stranded, smelly victims of the coldest week in the history of North America.

It took nearly eight months to write this book. Eight months in which special thanks are due to my friend and associate Mike Kelly.

He and his Hamilton Communications staff, Dawn Harris, Ted Grybowski, George Corby, Mary Pat and Jim Kelly, John Laidlaw, and Pete Zangeri, kept the doors to NY News Corp. open. Mike Kelly's cooperation and patience will be long appreciated.

So, too, will the friendship and dedication of NY News Corp. Marketing Director Ed Heifer. Thanks to Jack Malick who had the sense to stay away from Barrow.

Thanks to MarkAir Cargo Director Ed Rogers, who arranged Barrow transportation, and thanks, too, to Joe Schrier for his work in adapting this story to the visual medium.

Michael Richardson and I mixed the mortar and laid the bricks, but Hillel Black was the project foreman. He took a chance on a then-untested author. His vision gave the book meaning, purpose, and direction. He knew precisely where he wanted it to go and how to get it there.

Margaret McBride, my expert liaison, told me how unheard it was for a first-time author to receive so much attention from anyone, let alone a man as respected as Hillel Black. Only now, when I face the prospect of getting along without him, do I begin to realize how much I appreciate, admire, and respect my new friend, Hillel Black.

Finally, to Mom and Dad, nothing could begin to describe my deep appreciation and love for you both. All I can say is, "Thanks."

TRIBUTE

What kind of a person would put up with me day and night for eight straight months, never issue a complaint—well, hardly ever issue a complaint—and be even more a joy to work with at the project's end than he was at the beginning? Michael Richardson, that's who.

Fortunately, I never understood how much work was involved in writing a book. If I did, it would never have happened.

To Michael Richardson, a man of high honor, integrity, and decency, if not ribald humor, you have my deepest thanks, and heartfelt best wishes.

Index